THE ASTR
COMP

Provides an introduction to astrological studies, a comprehensive but readable reference work which is of value to both the newcomer and the practising astrologer.

Also in this series

ASTROLOGICAL COUNSELLING
Christina Rose

ASTRONOMY FOR ASTROLOGERS
John and Peter Filbey

CHART SYNTHESIS
Roy Alexander

FORECASTING BY ASTROLOGY
Martin Freeman

HORARY ASTROLOGY
Derek Appleby

HOW TO INTERPRET A BIRTH CHART
Martin Freeman

MUNDANE ASTROLOGY
Michael Baigent, Nicholas Campion and Charles Harvey

NATAL CHARTING
John Filbey

SYNASTRY
Penny Thornton

THE TWELVE HOUSES
Howard Sasportas

THE ASTROLOGER'S COMPANION

by

John and Peter Filbey

THE AQUARIAN PRESS
Wellingborough, Northamptonshire

First published 1986

British Library Cataloguing in Publication Data

Filbey, John
The astrologer's companion.
1. Astrology
I. Title II. Filbey, Peter
133.5 BF1708.1

ISBN 0-85030-452-0

The Aquarian Press is part of the Thorsons Publishing Group

Printed and bound in Great Britain

CONTENTS

'Not in the clamour of the crowded street,
Not in the shouts and plaudits of the throng,
But in ourselves, are triumph and defeat.'

Longfellow

INTRODUCTION

The purpose of this work is to provide an introduction to various astrological studies which, it is hoped, will be helpful particularly for those new to astrology. The language of astrology can, at times, be abstruse and we have therefore endeavoured to clarify technical terms and expressions whenever possible. It is not intended that the book should be treated as a textbook but as a 'companion' to whom one can turn for information and assistance as and when the need arises.

Although the scope of the book ranges from basic astronomy to modern developments in astrology, several interesting aspects of astrology have been omitted due principally to the limitations of space. Some of the topics have been dealt with briefly, others in much greater detail because it was thought that they required an expanded description to be fully appreciated.

Astrological thinking is undergoing a transitional stage and although conflicts of opinion exist concerning astrological concepts, many of the controversial issues act as a stimulus in the search for fundamental truths.

Throughout this book, we have tried to maintain an unbiased approach, particularly in relation to those aspects of astrology upon which there is no general agreement — for example house division. Also, although the use of logarithms is laborious and outdated, their inclusion may, initially, prove helpful for beginners. Once a confident approach to calculations has been achieved and the basic 'arithmetic' of astrology understood, then the use of a calculator is the quickest and easiest method available. The micro-computer is, of course, even better and will perform a whole variety of functions applicable to astrology.

In the preparation of this book, we have been greatly assisted by the wide variety of astrological literature, both ancient and modern, and this has proved both interesting and informative. The British astrological journals *Astrologer's Quarterly* and *Astrological Journal* contain a wealth of valuable articles, opinions and data, as also does *Spica*, a journal of sidereal astrology now unfortunately defunct. To all these, we acknowledge our debt of gratitude and thanks.

1.
BASIC ASTRONOMY

Earth and Sky

Modern astronomy has revealed the magnitude and grandeur of the universe, and the Earth, once considered the all-important centre, is now shown to be an insignificant speck in the scheme of the material universe. For the astrologer, the Earth is, however, all-important because it is the correspondence between heaven and earth which denotes the basic concepts of astrology.

Astronomical knowledge has many divisions, and although the study of the stellar universe (all that is beyond the solar system), with its teeming millions of stars and nebulae, enables us to appreciate the scale and immensity of space, it is the solar system and our place in it which command the attention of astrologers.

The Earth, once thought to be flat and situated at the centre of the universe, is now known to be a spherical body revolving in an elliptical orbit around the Sun. It is the fifth largest planet, with a rotational motion which results in every place on Earth experiencing day and night, and its revolution around the Sun determines our year. The motions of the Earth are complex and all observations relating to them need to be corrected as they involve a combination of several factors such as rotation, revolution, precession and the whole movement of the solar system in space.

Although we know that the Earth is not at the centre of the universe, we use geocentric charts because we are dealing with the angular relationships between the planets with respect to Earth for a given location on the Earth's surface (latitude and longitude). Our view of the heavens is governed by our place of observation, hence the importance of knowing the time and place in order to calculate an accurate astrological chart.

The relationship between heaven and earth is firmly established by the Earth's orbital revolution around the Sun and the Sun's apparent movement along the Ecliptic. In addition, the Earth's rotation on its axis — its daily cycle — defines the Ascendant through the intersection of the local horizon with the Ecliptic. Thus we have two major correspondences: (a) the Earth's yearly revolution around the Sun (Ecliptic and zodiac); and (b) the Earth's daily rotation on its axis with the emphasis on local time and place.

The Celestial Sphere

In order to determine the location of heavenly bodies, frames of reference are required, and the hypothetical concept of a celestial sphere supplies this requirement.

If we imagine the sky as a vast inverted bowl, the stars and other heavenly bodies will seem to be on the inside of a large sphere with the Earth at the centre. Within this imaginary hollow sphere, half visible, half unseen, the Earth rotates upon its axis, and as a result of this rotation, the observer's view of the celestial sphere appears exactly the same as if the Earth were stationary and the celestial sphere rotated around the same axis at the same speed or velocity but in an east to west direction. This apparent westward movement of the

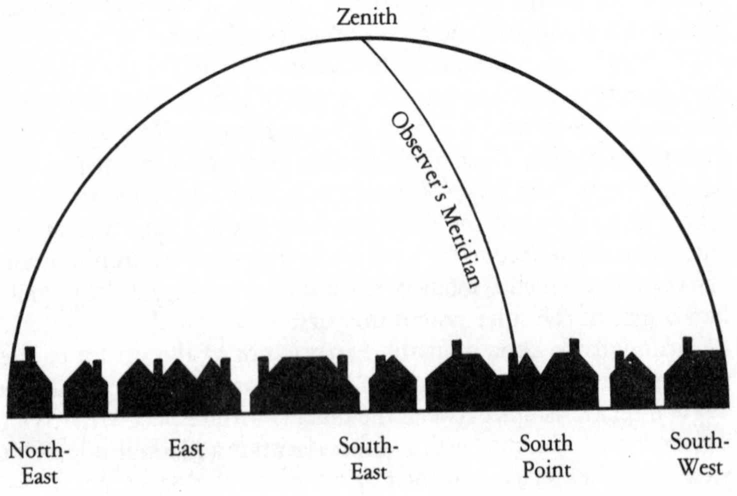

Figure 1 The Observer's Meridian.

celestial sphere causes the Sun and the other bodies to appear to rise east of, and set west of, the observer's meridian.

One prominent star remains nearly still; we always find it in practically the same direction and altitude (height above the horizon) in the sky, so it must be very near the end of the axis. This star is the Pole Star (Polaris). By observation, the unchanging point or pole can be fixed accurately among the stars, and the position of Polaris determined to within a degree or so of the Pole. The opposite Pole in the other hemisphere is not marked by any bright star but is equally locatable. Midway between the poles is the great circle of the Celestial Equator. On the celestial sphere, we can also determine the point vertically overhead (zenith — see Fig. 1) and its opposite point (nadir) and the great circle midway between them — the horizon.

The three great circles of reference for locating an object (celestial body) relative to any place on Earth are: the *Horizon;* the *Equator*; and the *Ecliptic.* If we project the Earth's equator onto the celestial sphere, we have the *Celestial Equator*, (immediately over the Earth's Equator), and this imaginary circle extending round the heavens divides it into two apparent hemispheres, the northern and southern; in the middle of each are the imaginary points known as the *Celestial Poles,* immediately over, and corresponding to, the North and South Poles of the Earth.

The *Ecliptic*, another imaginary circle, forms an acute angle with the Celestial Equator or Equinoctial (as it is sometimes called). The Ecliptic represents the apparent annual path of the Sun in the heavens, or the actual path of the Earth as viewed from the Sun, and it may be considered as dividing the heavens into two hemispheres, the central points of which are called the Poles of the Ecliptic. The circles of the Ecliptic and the Equator intersect in opposite points of the heavens: at the commencement of the signs Aries and Libra; the First Point of Aries (Vernal Equinox) and the First Point of Libra (Autumnal Equinox). When the Sun in its annual journey reaches these two points, it is spring (Aries) and autumn (Libra) in the northern hemisphere. The reverse applies in southern latitudes — northern spring is southern autumn and northern autumn is southern spring. At this time of the year when the Sun is at the Equinoxes, there is equal duration of day and night all over the Earth, hence the term Equinox. The highest points of the Ecliptic, that is, those farthest from the Equator, are called the *Solstices* and are the points which the Sun reaches when it enters the signs Cancer and Capricorn (Summer and Winter Solstices in June and

December). When the Sun reaches either of these two points, it appears to 'stand still' — hence the term Solstice — and has acquired its greatest declination (height or distance from the Equator), before it returns again towards the opposite Solstice.

At the time of the June Solstice in the northern hemisphere, the vertical Sun traces out the imaginary circle known as the 'Tropic of Cancer', and at the time of the December Solstice, the imaginary circle known as the 'Tropic of Capricorn'. These tropic lines have no reference to the heavens but merely indicate the latitude (23° 27′) where the Sun is directly overhead at maximum declination 23° 27′, either at the June Solstice when it enters the sign of Cancer, or at the December Solstice when it enters the sign of Capricorn.

The Ecliptic is divided into twelve equal signs, each sign containing 30°. The Equator or Equinoctial is divided into twenty-four parts (hours), each hour corresponding to 15°, which is the extent or arc of the heavens which apparently passes over us in that space of time. The circles of the Ecliptic and the Equator with their appropriate divisions and graduations are, for the purpose of locating the precise position of any celestial body, either in Right Ascension (R.A.) and Declination (Dec.) using the Equator, or in latitude and longitude, using the Ecliptic.

The Horizon circle which divides the celestial sphere into two hemispheres — upper and lower — is the *Rational or Celestial Horizon*, every point of which is 90° from the observer's *Zenith* (the point directly overhead). The apparent (visible) horizon is an imaginary plane extending all round an observer situated upon any part of the surface of the Earth, at the utmost limits of which plane the concave hemisphere of the heavens appears to meet the Earth's surface. The *Rational Horizon* is a plane parallel to the visible horizon, passing through the centre of the Earth and extending to the heavens, which it divides into two hemispheres, the central point of the heavens immediately overhead being the zenith and that of the lower hemisphere being the nadir. These two points are the Poles of the Horizon. The vertical circle passing through the zenith and nadir of the observer and the north and south points of the horizon is the *Meridian* of the observer. Another vertical circle, passing through the zenith and nadir of the observer and the east and west points of the horizon, is called the *Prime Vertical* (the plane of which corresponds to the points of intersection of the horizon and the Equator). All great circles passing through the observer's zenith are perpendicular to the Celestial Horizon and are termed vertical circles.

Astronomical Co-ordinates

The co-ordinate systems are usually classified as: the *Horizon system*; the *Equator system;* and the *Ecliptic system.* (See Fig. 2-4.) Of these, the astrologer is principally concerned with either the Ecliptic system or the Equator system. The Horizon system uses the co-ordinates of *Altitude* (the angular distance of an object above the horizon) and *Azimuth* (the angle between the vertical plane through the object and the observer's meridian plane).

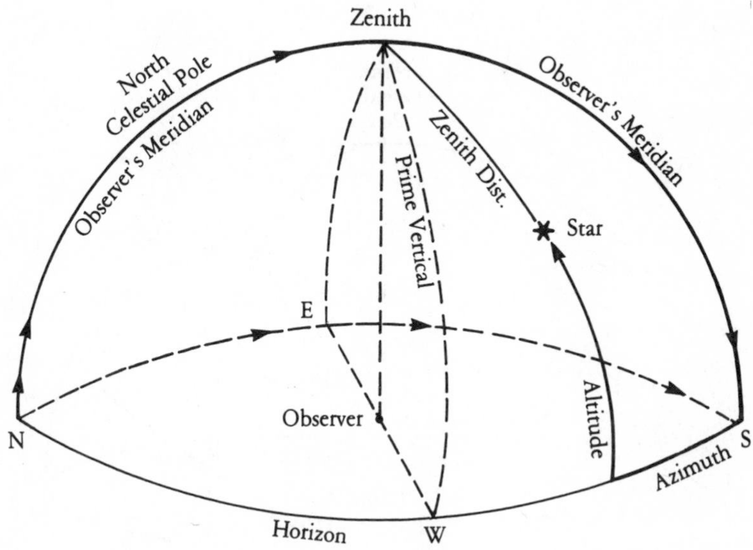

Figure 2 Horizon System Co-ordinates.

The Equator System

As the name suggests, uses the great circle of the Equator as its principal frame of reference. The Celestial Equator is a projection of the Earth's Equator onto the celestial sphere and the Celestial Poles are the poles of rotation of the celestial sphere which are directly overhead at the terrestrial poles. The zero point of the Celestial Equator is the First Point of Aries (Vernal Equinox) and this point, which is like a 'celestial Greenwich', is the point of intersection at any moment of the Celestial Equator and the Ecliptic. Whereas the Horizon system uses altitude and azimuth, the Equator system uses *Right Ascension* and *Declination*. Right Ascension is the angle between the *Hour Circle* (a great circle passing through a celestial body and the celestial poles), through the object and the First Point of Aries. The measurement of Right Ascension is made eastward along the Celestial Equator from the Equinox (First Point of Aries), sometimes in arc (0°-360°), but more usually in sidereal time, one hour being equivalent to 15°. Right Ascension is, in effect, the interval in sidereal time between the transit of the Equinox and that of the object concerned. The angle between the hour circle through the object and the observer's meridian is sometimes used as an alternative

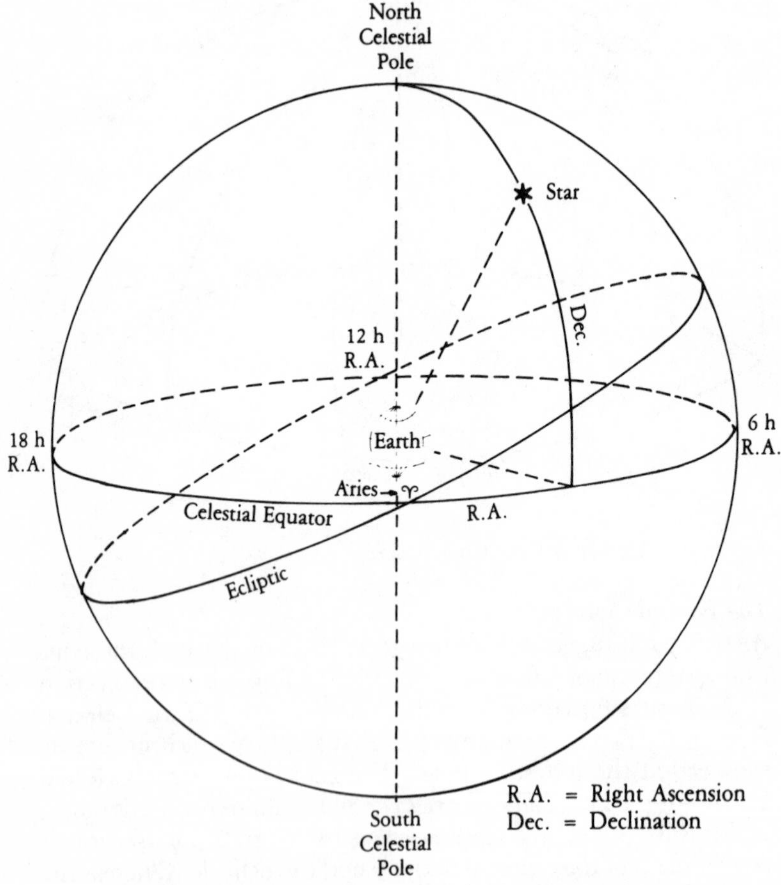

Figure 3 Equator System: Right Ascension and Declination.

and termed the *Hour Angle* (the difference between the Right Ascension of the object and the Right Ascension circle on the meridian at the time of observation), and measured westward from the meridian.

Declination

The other co-ordinate of the Equator system, is the angular distance of an object or body either north or south of the Celestial Equator. It corresponds to latitude on Earth and is measured from 0° to 90°. Some reference works indicate north declination by the symbol + (positive) and south declination by – (negative). Normally, the astrologer is not concerned with measurements in Right Ascension, except for specialized work, such as certain types of directions and progressions. However, a knowledge of the system is useful, since from these co-ordinates, the positions of the Sun, Moon and planets are converted into celestial longitude, which is the co-ordinate listed in most ephemerides.

The Ecliptic System

The intersection of the great circles of the Ecliptic and the Equator marks the zero point (First Point of Aries) for measurement of *Celestial Longitude*. The Ecliptic Poles — points on the celestial sphere — are 90° from the Ecliptic (about 23½° from the terrestrial poles), and for all practical purposes the Ecliptic and its poles can be considered as fixed on the celestial sphere. The plane of the Ecliptic is not coincident with that of the celestial Equator, and the angle between the two planes is 23½° and known as the *Obliquity of the Ecliptic.* This represents the maximum angular distance of the Sun north or south of the Celestial Equator at the Solstices.

Celestial Longitude is the angular distance along the Ecliptic between the plane through the object and the First Point of Aries. This co-ordinate is measured in degrees and minutes of arc eastward from the First Point of Aries, and is used to determine the position of a planet or body. If, for example, the Sun or a planet has an absolute longitude of 210°, we know that it is in 0° Scorpio, (210 over 30 = 7 complete signs) measured from 0° Aries.

Celestial Latitude, the other co-ordinate of the Ecliptic system, is the perpendicular distance of an object from the Ecliptic in angular measure, or in other words, the angular distance between the Ecliptic and a celestial body measured in degrees and minutes, either north

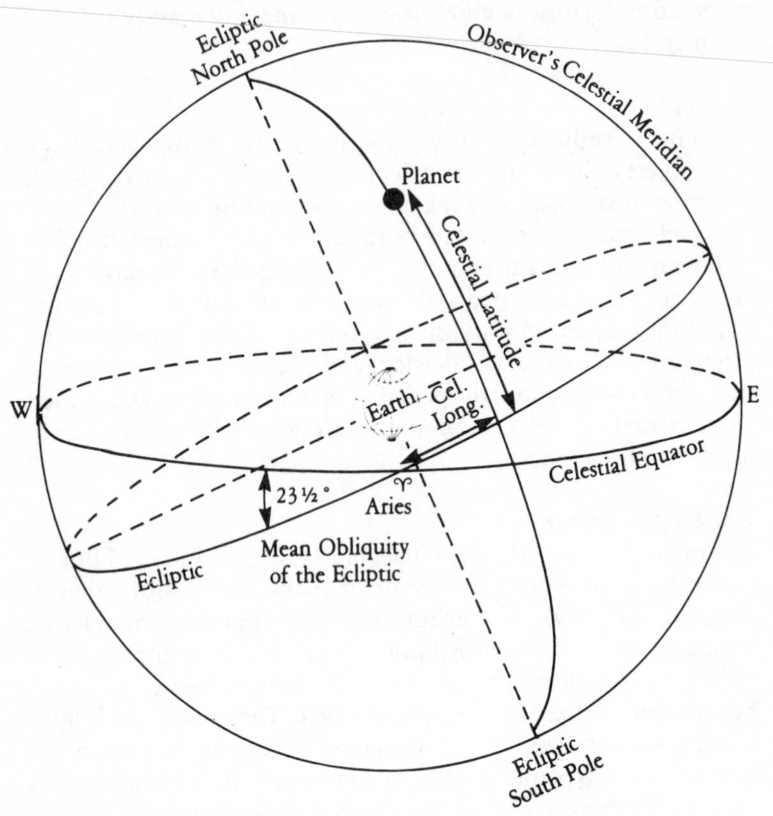

Figure 4 Ecliptic System Co-ordinates

or south of the Ecliptic. It should not be confused with terrestrial latitude, which is, of course, measured from the Earth's Equator. A planet is exactly on the Ecliptic when its latitude is zero.

For the astrologer, a knowledge of the basic fundamentals of astronomy is useful, because it enables one to appreciate the remarkable parallelism between celestial phenomena and human experiences. An understanding of astronomical technicalities is not essential for the practice of astrology, but the student should, at least, be familiar with the various lines, circles and projections which are important in technical astrology.

The Celestial Sphere

We will now consider an observer at three different positions on earth: the North Pole, the Equator and at an intermediate latitude (Figs. 5-7).

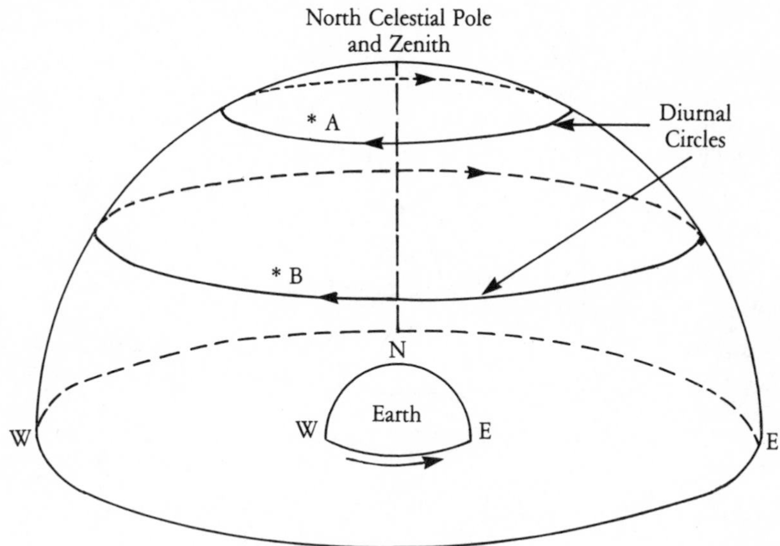

Figure 5 The Celestial Sphere: North Pole.

Fig. 5: North Pole

At the pole, the observer's zenith and the North Pole will coincide as do the Celestial Equator and the Celestial Horizon. If we consider A and B to be fixed stars and their declinations practically constant, each remains at the same angular distance from the Celestial Equator and therefore from the horizon as, in this case, the horizon and the Celestial Equator coincide. Thus, the diurnal circle coincides with the declination circle and altitude circle. The rotation of the Earth causes the stars to appear to move westward in diurnal circles which are parallel to the Equator and to the horizon. Therefore, the stars (A and B) remain continuously above the observer's horizon — i.e. they are circumpolar.

Fig. 6: Equator

At the Earth's Equator, the zenith lies in the Celestial Equator which

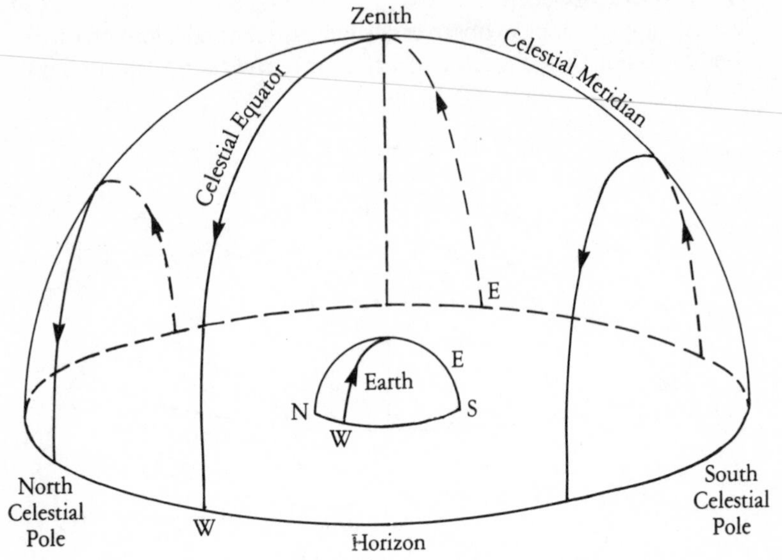

Figure 6 The Celestial Sphere: Equator

coincides with the Prime Vertical, and the Celestial Poles lie in the horizon. The diurnal circles of stars A and B are now perpendicular to the horizon and are half above and half below the horizon, so that the stars A and B will only be visible half of the time. At the Equator, all stars rise vertically, and no stars are circumpolar since they all rise and set.

Fig. 7: Intermediate Latitudes
In the intermediate latitudes (between the Earth's Equator and the Poles), the Celestial Pole appears at the same altitude in the sky as the observer's latitude, and the plane of the horizon is oblique to the plane of the Celestial Equator and the diurnal circles. For an observer in northern latitudes, any celestial body which is north of the Celestial Equator will be above the observer's horizon for more than twelve hours, while any body which is south will be above the horizon for less than twelve hours. Bodies whose declination places them within, or north of, the circumpolar circle (Circle of Perpetual Apparition) will not set. Similarly, bodies within or south of the Circle of Perpetual Occultation are invisible.

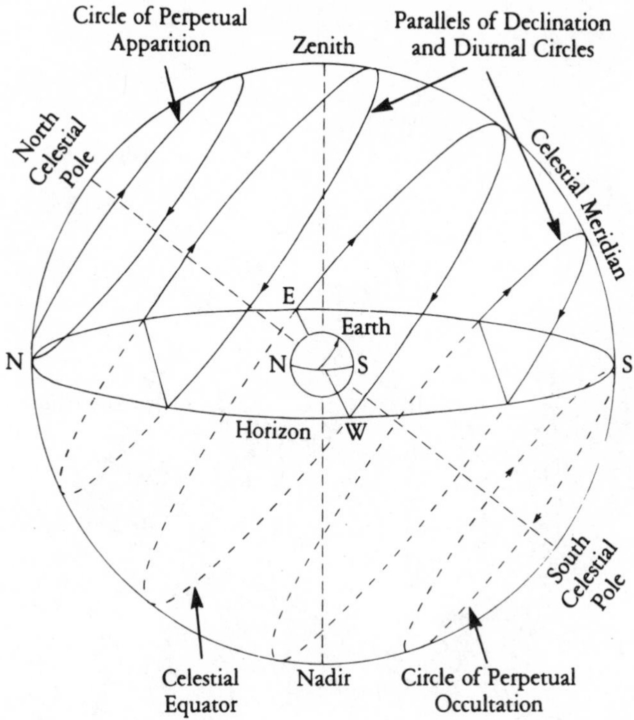

Figure 7 The Celestial Sphere: Intermediate Latitudes

The Solar System — Sun, Moon and Planets

To the solar system belong the Sun, Moon, Earth and planets with their satellites. Those planets which are visible to the naked eye do not twinkle like stars, and unlike stars, they move or 'wander' at varying distances and speeds. All the planets, with the exception of Pluto, move around the Sun in orbits which are in almost the same plane as the Ecliptic, keeping to the narrow band called the *zodiac,* which extends about eight degrees either side of the Ecliptic. The angles at which the planets' orbits are inclined to the Ecliptic, (their orbital inclinations), vary from 46′ (Uranus) to 7° (Mercury), while Pluto's is about 17°. Most planets have orbital inclinations of between 1° and 4°. The two points where a planetary orbit intersects the Ecliptic are called the *ascending node* and the *descending node*, the former where the orbit is moving from south of the Ecliptic to

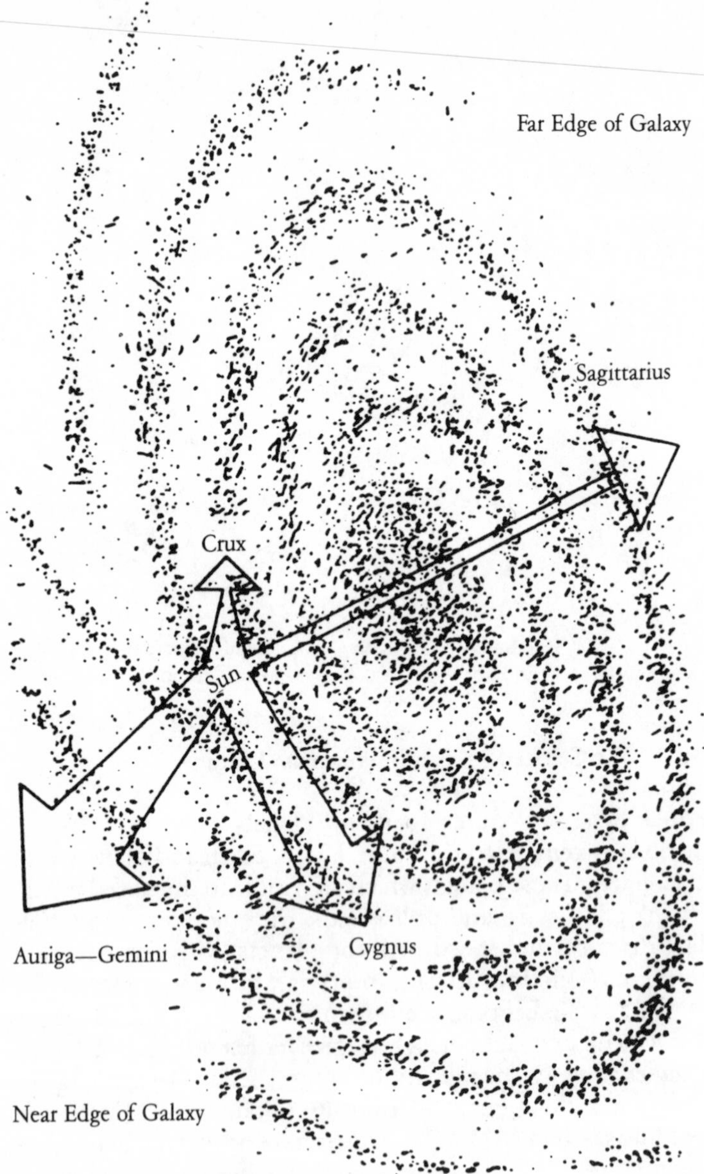

Figure 8 Our Galaxy.

Planet	*Mercury*	*Venus*	*Earth*	*Mars*	*Jupiter*	*Saturn*	*Uranus*	*Neptune*	*Pluto*
Distance (mean) from Sun (millions of miles)	36	67.2	93	141.6	484.3	886.1	1783	2793	3660
Period of revolution about Sun (sidereal)	87.9 days	224.7 days	365.25 days	686.98 days	11.86 years	29.46 years	84.01 years	164.79 years	247.70 years
Diameter (miles)	3000	7700	7927	4219	88700	75100	29300	31200	3700
Period of rotation about axis (sidereal)	58.5 days	243 days	23 Hrs 56 Min	24 Hrs 37 Min	9 Hrs 51 Min	10 Hrs 14 Min	10 Hrs 48 Min	14 Hrs	6 days 9 Hrs
Inclination of orbit to Ecliptic	7° 0′	3° 24′	0° 0′	1° 51′	1° 18′	2° 29′	0° 46′	1° 46′	17° 10′
Eccentricity of orbit	0.206	0.007	0.017	0.093	0.048	0.056	0.047	0.009	0.246
Mass (Earth = 1)	0.05	0.81	1.00	0.11	318	95	15	17	?
Density (Water = 1)	5.4	4.99	5.52	4.12	1.3	0.7	1.65	2.0	?

Figure 9 The Solar System: Planetary Data

north of it, and the latter where the orbit is moving from north to south. The orbits of planets are not circular. They are slightly elliptical, the degree of ellipticity being called the *orbit's eccentricity* which varies between O (for a circle) to 1, and eccentricities of planetary orbits vary from 0.007 (Venus) to 0.246 (Pluto). When a planet is at its nearest approach to the Sun, it is said to be at *perihelion*; when it is at its furthest point from the Sun, it is at *aphelion*.

The Sun is the largest and most massive body in the solar system, and it occupies a central position with the planets revolving around it. (See Figs. 8 and 9.) In increasing distance from the Sun, these planets are Mercury, Venus, Earth, Mars, Jupiter, Saturn, Uranus, Neptune and Pluto. The orbits of Mercury and Venus lie inside the Earth's, so these two planets are called *inferior* and never appear far from the Sun. The other planets, from Mars outward, have orbits which lie outside the Earth's, so they can be seen at any time of night. These are known as the *superior* planets.

The Sun

Dimensions and data:

Radius	696,000 km.
Mass	328,000 Earth-Moon masses
Mean density	1.41 tonnes per cubic metre (1.41 × that of water)
Distance from Earth	149,600,000 km.
Angular diameter	32′
Apparent magnitude	−27
Absolute magnitude	+4.8
Surface temperature	5,500°C
Spectral type	G 2
Luminosity (power output)	3.9×10^{26} watts

The luminosity of the Sun gives us an idea of just how colossal its power output is, and this output has been maintained at an almost steady rate since the Sun's formation approximately 5,000 million years ago. All life on Earth depends for its light and heat upon the Sun which is an enormous sphere of intensely hot, incandescent gas, principally hydrogen and helium, and so great is its volume that more than one million Earths could be packed inside it. The surface of the Sun is called the photosphere, above which is the chromosphere, a layer of thin gas about 6,000 miles deep, and higher up still is the solar atmosphere (the corona) which is made up of very thin but very hot gas, at a temperature of over one million degrees Centigrade and extending for several hundred thousand miles out into space. The corona is visible only during a total solar eclipse or by means of a device called a coronagraph.

Dark markings known as sunspots sometimes appear on the Sun's surface. A sunspot is made up of two parts, the dark region in the centre (umbra) surrounded by a lighter area, grey in colour (penumbra). Sunspots are either isolated or occur in groups, often overlapping and of irregular shape. They persist for periods ranging from a few hours to several weeks, and they range in size from a few hundred miles across to much larger than the Earth. First discovered in 1611, sunspots are associated with local and powerful magnetic fields although the Sun itself has a general magnetic field which is much weaker. Appearing dark only in contrast with the brilliance of the photosphere surrounding them, they would actually outshine an illuminatd electric light-bulb if they could be seen on their own, being about 2,000°C cooler than the rest of the surface. It is possible to observe sunspots, but only by the safe method of projecting the Sun's image through a telescope onto a white surface, taking care to avoid looking through the eyepiece directly at the Sun as this could cause blindness. It is dangerous to look directly at the Sun. All observations of the Sun should be made by projecting its image. As the Sun rotates so the sunspots will appear to drift slowly across its face from day to day. This rotation takes 26 days near the equator but 37 days near the poles, because the Sun, as a non-solid body, rotates differentially. The number of sunspots which are visible at any one time does not stay constant but undergoes a variation, over a period of eleven years, the number rising to a maximum in the years 1947, 1958, 1969 and 1981. This periodic variation, known as the sunspot cycle, was first discovered by the astronomer Schwabe in 1852. Near times of spot minima, weeks may go by without any sunspots appearing at all.

The elements of which the Sun is composed are: hydrogen (75 per cent); helium (23 per cent); and about sixty other substances forming the remaining 2 per cent, such as oxygen, carbon, sodium, magnesium, iron and calcium, all reduced to the state of a gas in the intense heat. The existence of these elements was established by means of the spectroscope, since each substance emits light of specific wavelengths and can be identified by their dark Fraunhofer lines in the solar spectrum. Towards the Sun's centre the pressure, temperature and density of the gas all increase dramatically, reaching values of 15 million degrees Centigrade with a density twelve times that of lead (around 160,000 kg per cubic metre). In all parts of the Sun, the tremendous pressures pushing outwards are exactly balanced by the weight of the overlying gas layers pushing down, so these equal and opposing forces maintain the Sun as a stable star. In the core, these pressures and temperatures cause such violent collisions between the atoms that the forces which hold them together are overpowered, resulting in a plasma of sub-atomic particles, hydrogen nuclei (protons), helium nuclei (alpha particles) and electrons. In the vast thermonuclear furnace that is the Sun's core, nuclear reactions take place in which four protons are fused into one alpha particle, and in this process a small amount of matter is transformed into a very large amount of energy. Billions of such fusions occurring in this way convert 4 million tons of matter every second into a tremendous quantity of energy, which is then transported to the Sun's surface mainly by radiation and by convection currents near the surface. When it reaches the photosphere, this energy pours out into space at the rate of some 300,000 million watts through every acre of solar surface, in the form of visible light, infra-red (heat) and radio-waves, while in the shorter-wavelength region of the electromagnetic spectrum, energy is in the form of ultra-violet light, X-rays, gamma rays and charged particles. Only about one two-thousand millionth of this energy is intercepted by the Earth and certain wavelengths are largely blocked out by the Earth's atmosphere and do not reach the surface, only light, heat and some radio-waves being able to penetrate in any great quantity.

Apart from sunspots, there are several other manifestations of solar activity, such as prominences, plages, faculae and flares. Prominences, visible only at the time of a total solar eclipse or with a coronagraph, are surging clouds of hot gas which burst up out of the Sun's surface into the corona, occasionally reaching heights of several thousand miles. They are red in colour and resemble flames. Plages and faculae are active regions in the chromosphere and photosphere. Flares are explosions of energy in the Sun's atmosphere, lasting only a few minutes, triggered by localized powerful and unstable magnetic fields. Shock waves, travelling at over 1,000 miles per second, are sent through the solar surface by flares, and vast quantities of energy are released, particularly in the form of X-rays. Radio waves are emitted continuously by the Sun, but there are occasional intense bursts (also called 'noise storms'). It is possible to receive radio waves from the Sun, but only on specially constructed equipment.

The Sun affects the Earth and its surroundings in various other ways apart from sending us light and heat, and such phenomena are generally referred to as 'solar-terrestrial effects'. Included among these are the temporary disruption of short-wave radio communications, when X-rays from a solar flare interfere with layers in the Earth's ionosphere from which radio waves are bounced, and also the aurorae. Electrons stream in from the Sun, ionize the gas in the Earth's upper atmosphere and cause the fluorescent glows in the night sky known as Aurora Borealis (northern dawn) or Aurora Australis in the southern hemisphere. The Earth's magnetic field guides the electrons towards the magnetic poles and, for this reason, aurorae are generally visible only in high latitudes. The aurorae appear in the form of rays, arcs and luminous curtains, often of many different and changing colours and brightnesses. A stream of very thin gas is continuously being pushed out from the Sun in all directions into space. Consisting of ionized sub-atomic particles and known as the solar wind, it also affects the Earth and other planets by bending their magnetic fields round to form 'magnetospheres' for each planet.

The Moon

Dimensions and data:

Mean distance from the Earth	238,840 miles
Diameter	2,158 miles
Mass	$^1/_{81}$ that of Earth
Mean density	3.3 tonnes/cubic metre (3.3× that of water)
Orbital revolution period (sidereal)	27 days 7 hours 43 mins. 11 secs.
Orbital revolution period (synodic)	29.53 days
Orbital inclination to Ecliptic	5° 08′
Orbital eccentricity	0.055

The Moon is the Earth's nearest neighbour in space and its only natural satellite.

The phases of the Moon (see Fig. 10), occurring in a cycle every 29½ days, are caused by the Moon's orbital revolution around the Earth resulting in a constantly changing angle between the Sun, Earth and Moon. As the diagram shows, the Moon passes in succession from New through the crescent phase to First Quarter, then through the gibbous phase to Full, then gibbous, Last Quarter, crescent and New again. The direction of the Moon along its orbit is eastward, at a rate of 13° 12′ per day or about ½° per hour, which means that it will rise later than it did the previous night. A waxing Moon (increasing in light from New to Full) is east of the Sun, so it is prominent in the sky during the afternoon, evening or early part of the night. When it is Full, the Moon must be opposite to the Sun, so it rises at sunset, sets at sunrise and shines all night. A waning Moon (decreasing from Full to New) being to the west of the Sun is likely to be seen later in the night or in the early morning. The line which separates the illuminated and dark sides of the Moon is called the terminator.

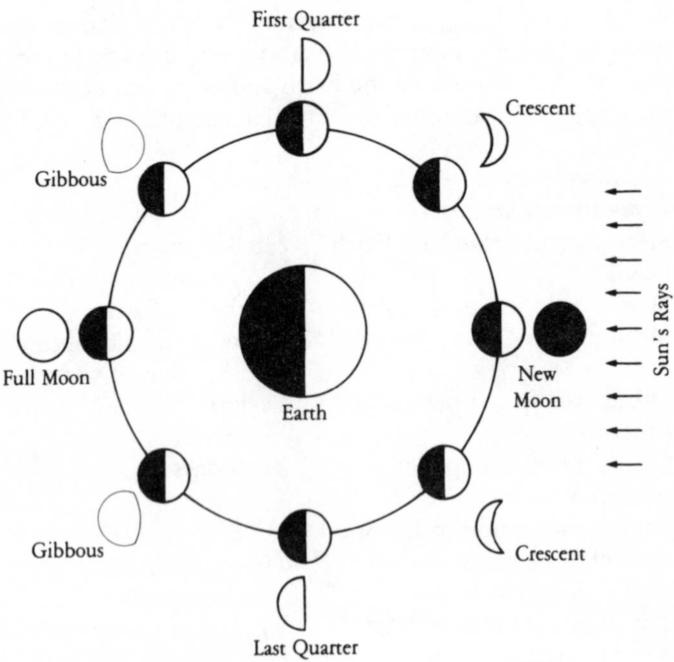

Figure 10 The Phases of the Moon.

The altitude of the Moon, when it is crossing the meridian due south, depends on its phase and on the time of year. During the winter, for instance, the Full Moon appears high up because it is in the same part of the sky that the Sun is in during the summer; conversely, the Full Moon in summer appears low down in the sky like the Sun in winter (a Full Moon is always opposite to the Sun). The Moon's altitude at culmination, for the various seasons, is given below:

Season	*Moon High up*	*Moon Low down*
Spring	First Quarter	Last Quarter
Summer	New Moon	Full Moon
Autumn	Last Quarter	First Quarter
Winter	Full Moon	New Moon

When the Moon is near the Celestial Equator it will cross the meridian at an intermediate altitude.

The time delay in the Moon's rising from night to night is called the retardation, but this is variable and depends upon the angle at which the lunar orbit intersects the eastern horizon. If this angle is sharp, then the retardation is low, sometimes only fifteen minutes, explaining the phenomenon known as Harvest and Hunter's Moons of early autumn when, for several nights in succession just after Full, the Moon rises less than one hour after sunset. Conversely, in spring the Moon rises more than one hour later each night near Full, because of the steep angle then between the lunar orbit and the eastern horizon. Retardation is on average 50 minutes.

Relative to the star background, the Moon takes 27⅓ days to complete one orbit of the Earth (the sidereal period), but because of the Sun's apparent eastward movement along the Ecliptic at 30° per month, the Moon must 'catch up' with the Sun and, since it takes about two days to cover this extra distance, the period between one New Moon and the next (the synodic period) is 29½ days.

The true motion of the Moon through space is a path that causes it to weave in and out of the Earth's orbit, alternately lagging behind and racing ahead of the Earth throughout each month, this motion being caused by the gravitational control exerted on the Moon by both the Earth and the Sun. (See Fig. 11.) So the Moon does not actually orbit the Earth in a series of loops but in fact travels with the Earth on its journey around the Sun each year. If we assume the Earth to be stationary, however, then the Moon's motion is an apparent orbit of the Earth, and this orbit is an elliptical one with an inclination to the Ecliptic of 5° 08′ and an eccentricity of 0.055. This eccentricity causes a variation in the Moon's distance from the Earth during each month, from 221,000 miles at minimum (perigee) to 253,000 miles

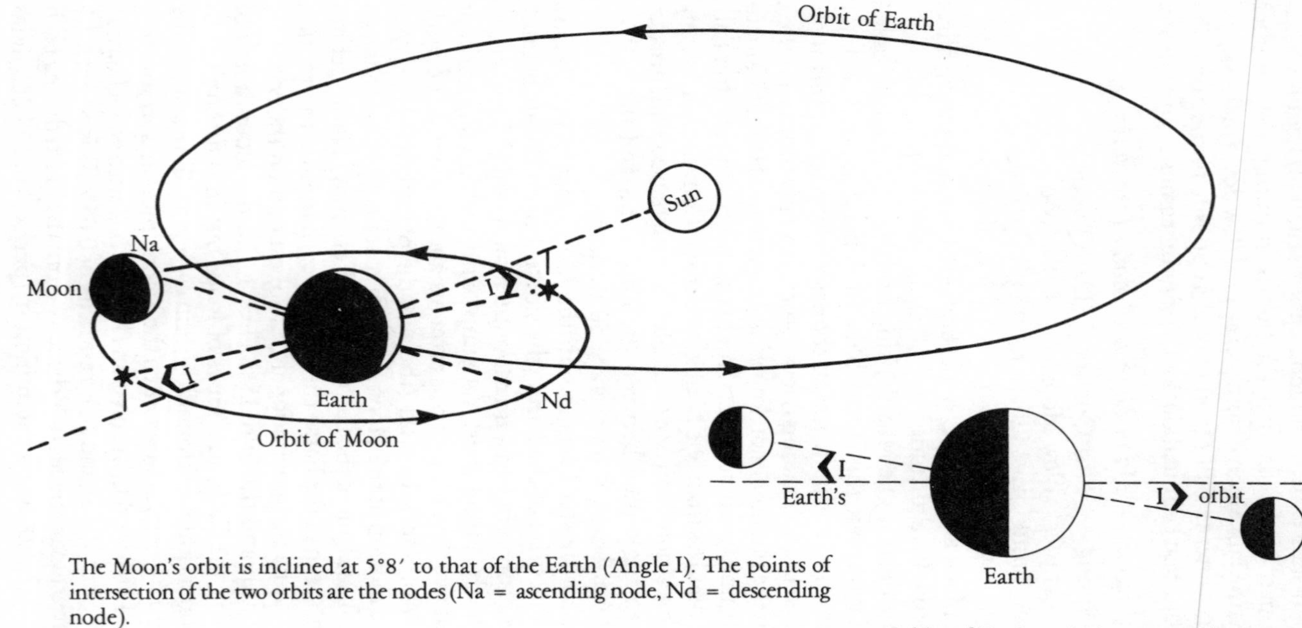

The Moon's orbit is inclined at 5°8′ to that of the Earth (Angle I). The points of intersection of the two orbits are the nodes (Na = ascending node, Nd = descending node).

Figure 11 Orbits of the Moon and Earth.

at maximum (apogee), and a corresponding variation in the Moon's apparent angular diameter from a maximum of 33′ 31″ to a minimum of 29′ 22″. Because the lunar orbit is elliptical, the Moon's speed constantly changes throughout the month, and hence the interval between any two successive quarter phases (normally about 7½ days) can be as short as six days or as long as nine days. The two points where the lunar orbit intersects the Ecliptic are called the ascending node and the descending node, the former where the orbit is crossing the Ecliptic from south to north, the latter where it is crossing from north to south. These two nodes are 180° apart and circle around the Ecliptic once every 18½ years (the Saros cycle), and when a New or Full Moon falls near one of the nodes, there is a solar or lunar eclipse. Eclipses take place at six-monthly intervals, the months in which they occur depending on the position of the nodes in their 18½ year cycle.

From the ascending node, the Moon's ecliptic longitude is measured, and its latitude (distance from the Ecliptic) varies between ± 5° 08′. The latitude of the Moon affects its declination, which determines the altitude at which it will cross the southern meridian at any given place. At the latitude of London, the maximum altitude at which the Moon can appear is 67°. Various factors cause slight variations in the Moon's longitude, these factors being known as Equation of the centre, Evection, Variation, and Annual Equation. Equation of the centre is caused by the eccentricity of the lunar orbit and can cause a longitude displacement of the Moon of as much as 6.3 degrees from its mean position. Evection is caused by variations in the orbital eccentricity and the longitude displacement can be up to 1.3 degrees. Variation is caused by the Moon experiencing a variable gravitational pull from the Sun, as its distance from the Sun changes throughout the month from a minimum at New Moon to a maximum at Full; the longitude displacement is 0.6 degrees maximum. Annual Equation, causing a longitude displacement of 0.2 degrees at maximum, is a consequence of the variable gravitational pull of the Sun on the Earth and Moon, because of the changing distance between the Sun and Earth — Moon throughout the year owing to the Earth's orbit being elliptical; this variation of distance is 3 million miles. If these above corrections are not applied, and the Moon is assumed to follow a circular orbit around the Earth at uniform speed, then the mean position of the Moon can be up to 8½° different from its actual measured position.

Over a period of several thousand million years, tidal forces have gradually slowed the Moon's axial rotation, until it is at present equal to its period of revolution around the Earth. This type of rotation is called 'synchronous' or 'captured', where a satellite's rotation and revolution periods are exactly equal to one another. As a result of this, we see the same side of the Moon always turned towards us, but slight variations, called librations, do occur. Libration in longitude arises from the fact that the Moon's speed along its elliptical orbit is not constant, and hence the rotation and revolution constantly become out of step, causing the Moon to rock slightly from side to side. Libration in latitude results from the 1½ degree tilt of the Moon's axis to the perpendicular of the orbital plane, so that it is possible to see the same distance around the polar regions of the Moon. Diurnal libration is seen when the Moon is either rising or setting and is caused by the fact that the Earth's radius is an appreciable fraction ($^1/_{60}$th) of the Earth — Moon distance, and it is possible to observe about one degree around the Moon's upper edge. From Earth, up to 59 per cent of the lunar surface may therefore be seen as a result of the librations, the remaining 41 per cent being permanently invisible.

Occasionally, the Moon passes in front of a star or planet and covers it for a short period. Such an occurrence is called an occultation and, although the Moon's edge can take several minutes to cross a planet, it crosses a star instantaneously. For this reason occultations of stars, when they take place, can be used to establish the Moon's exact position on the celestial sphere.

It is possible to see some features on the Moon's surface even without a telescope. A pair of binoculars or a small telescope, with a magnification of only 10-30 times, can reveal much more detail such as craters, mountain ranges and the dark regions called 'seas' (maria). These features are best seen near half-moon when the low angle of the Sun causes long shadows. The surface of the Moon (the regolith) consists of rocks covered by a thin layer of powder and dust, and most of the Moon's visible face is covered by rugged uplands which are white or pale yellow in colour. Most of the craters, which are named after famous scientists and astronomers of the past, are concentrated in these parts with relatively few on the dark plains. Lunar craters are usually circular in form, with the floor lying below the level of the surrounding terrain and a rim lying above it. However, there are considerable variations in the size, shape and appearance of the craters, since the diameters range from less than one mile to 180 miles, and the shape can vary from circular to uneven with fractured walls, and some craters have flat, dark floors while others have central mountain peaks. Craters are not nearly so deep as they look. Mountain ranges on the Moon often stretch for hundreds of miles, with peaks rising to as much as 30,000 feet, and are named after mountain ranges of Earth. The dark plains were imagined by the early astronomers to be liquid seas, but they are in fact regions of solidified lava and they occupy basins, some of which are roughly circular in form while others are irregular. They are usually a few hundred miles wide and are bluish-grey in colour. Also present on the Moon's surface are minor features like rilles or clefts, ridges, geological faults, and ray-systems.

Gravity on the Moon is only one-sixth that of Earth, so the Moon has lost practically all of any atmosphere it once had. Water cannot therefore exist in the liquid form on its surface and neither can life. Temperature variations are extreme because of the lack of an atmosphere, the surface rocks heating up to as much as 100°C during the long lunar day (fifteen Earth-days), while during the equally long nights the surface cools to as low as −200°C, and this surface is also exposed to various dangerous radiations from space. Other consequences of the absence of an atmosphere are the jet-black shadows, and the Sun and stars appearing in a black sky at the same time.

The Moon's interior is similar to the Earth's, both worlds having hot interiors, dense cores surrounded by mantles of heavy rocks, and a surface crust. The old idea that the Moon once broke away from the Earth is no longer held to be valid, and astronomers now consider that the Moon formed independently of the Earth. The upland regions formed first about 4,500 million years ago when the lunar crust cooled and solidified, and later lava flooded up from the interior, likewise cooling and solidifying to form the dark plains. Some of the lunar craters are volcanic in origin while others were caused by falling meteorites.

In 1959, the far side of the Moon, which is never seen from the Earth, was photographed by the Russian spacecraft Lunik III. Much additional knowledge about our satellite has been gained from the Ranger and Surveyor spacecraft of the 1960s and the manned Apollo flights of 1969-72.

The Planets

Mercury

Mercury is the nearest planet to the Sun, in orbit at an average distance of 36 million miles and completing one revolution every 88 days. Because of the high eccentricity, however, this distance can vary considerably, and consequently, the maximum elongation east or west of the Sun can alter between 18° and 28°. This planet is not visible in a dark sky from Britain and is best seen on Spring evenings or Autumn mornings, when the Ecliptic makes a steep angle with the horizon. On Spring evenings, it can be seen just after sunset low down in the west or south-west, when it is close to eastern elongation; while on Autumn mornings, it is visible just before sunrise low down in the east or south-east, when close to western elongation. It is unlikely to be seen at more than ten degrees or so above the horizon, and care must be taken to avoid looking at the Sun.

Mercury is the smallest planet, with a diameter of 3,000 miles, an orbital revolution period of 88 days (its year) and a rotation period of 59 days (its day). There is no appreciable atmosphere and certainly no life, since the planet's proximity to the Sun produces temperatures in excess of 400° Centigrade during the long days. Telescopes show only a few markings on the planet's surface, but spacecraft flying past have shown a world very similar to the Moon, with craters and smooth plains of which the largest, called Caloris Basin, is 800 miles across. Mercury is the second hottest planet and the smallest in size and mass; it has the shortest sidereal period and has been known from remote antiquity.

Venus

This is the next planet out from the Sun, at 67 million miles, completing an orbit once every 225 days. This planet has an orbit which is closer to being circular than that of any other planet and an axial rotation period of 243 days. Its diameter is 7,700 miles. Venus is the brightest of the planets and often appears really brilliant, because it is covered in thick white clouds which are an excellent reflector of sunlight. Unlike Mercury, Venus may be seen in a dark sky in Britain, because its maximum angular distance or elongation from the Sun is 48°. Also, it is visible for weeks or months at a time, whereas Mercury's visibility is confined to a few days either side of its elongation. Venus is visible in the west or south-west after sunset (evening star) or in the east or south-east before sunrise (morning star), often at a considerable altitude above the horizon.

Venus and Mercury are known as inferior planets, because their orbits lie inside that of the Earth, and as they orbit the Sun, they pass successively through inferior conjunction, western (morning) elongation, superior conjunction, eastern (evening) elongation, finally returning to inferior conjunction. Mercury passes through inferior conjunction once every 116 days, and Venus does so once every 586 days on average, these intervals of time being known as the 'synodic period' of the two planets. Through a small telescope, Venus shows phases like those of the Moon, and so does Mercury although, appearing much smaller than Venus, its phases are much more difficult to observe. Due to the inclination of these planets' orbits to the Ecliptic, transits of Mercury and Venus across the Sun's disc occur only rarely (Mercury: 1960, 1970, 1973, 1986, 1993; Venus: 1761, 1769, 1874, 1882, 2004, 2012).

The surface temperature of Venus is exceedingly hot (nearly 500° Centigrade), and the atmospheric pressure is ninety times greater than the Earth's. The surface is invisible from Earth owing to the dense cloud cover, but in recent years it has been possible to map the surface by means of radar and spacecraft. The results have shown Venus to be a hostile, lifeless place with a dull, gloomy landscape strewn with loose rocks and dust and, in places, craters and mountains.

Mars

Mars is the fourth planet in the Solar system, being positioned next after the Earth. Its average distance from the Sun is 142 million miles but, owing to the high orbital eccentricity (0.09), this distance may vary between 129 and 154 million miles. It orbits the Sun once every 687 days, and comes to opposition once every 26 months on average, but the high orbital eccentricity causes its distance from Earth to vary from one opposition to the next. When Mars is at perihelion and in opposition to the Sun at the same time, it is said to be 'at perihelic opposition', and its distance from the Earth is then only 35 million miles. This happens once every fifteen or seventeen years (1909, 1924, 1939, 1956, 1971 and 1988) and the planet is then, for a few weeks, very favourably placed for observation. If Mars is near aphelion at its opposition, however, it is 60 million miles from us and has an angular diameter of only 14 seconds; at perihelion and in opposition to the Sun at the same time, the angular diameter is 25 seconds. After each opposition, the planet recedes rapidly from the Earth to reach superior conjunction with the Sun about one year later, when its distance from us has increased to 235 million miles, while its angular diameter has shrunk to less than 4 seconds.

Being a superior planet (outside the Earth's orbit), Mars may be seen at any time of the night and at its brightest, it outshines every other planet, except Venus. Mars is a small world, with a diameter of 4,200 miles, and an axial rotation period of 24 hours 37 minutes, and its colour is orange-red, with some darker markings visible which have been carefully mapped. These darker regions were once considered to be areas of vegetation, but in the 1960s this idea was disproved, when the surface conditions were found to be hostile to life, particularly with its thin carbon dioxide atmosphere. The dark regions are known to be craters, mountains, extinct volcanoes and sinuous channels. The channels are up to 1,000 miles in length and 100 miles wide, and bear a striking resemblance to dried-up river beds, which they probably are, since there may well have been a time when the planet's climate and atmosphere were fundamentally different to what they are today, and water was able to flow. The surface of this planet is covered with loose rocks and dust, and large areas are subject to severe dust storms which are whipped up by high winds, particularly when the planet is near perihelion. After the storms, the appearance of the darker regions is often changed considerably, and dust suspended in the Martian atmosphere gives a pink sky.

Mars has two satellites or moons named Deimos and Phobos (Terror and Fear). Deimos orbits Mars once in 30 hours and Phobos in just 7½ hours. Each moon is less than 15 miles across. Phobos presents an interesting phenomenon in that, to an observer on Mars, it would rise in the west and set in the east three times a day.

Prior to the space age, much of the information concerning Mars was obtained using telescopes, but various space probes, such as the Mariner and Viking, have greatly contributed to our knowledge of the 'mysterious red planet'. Mercury, Venus, the Earth and Mars are all predominantly solid and rocky, with relatively small volumes and high densities and, as such, are called the 'terrestrial planets'. The next four planets, Jupiter, Saturn, Uranus and Neptune, on the other hand, have large volumes and low densities, and because of their compositions, they are known as the 'gas giants'.

Jupiter

Jupiter is the largest planet in the solar system, with an equatorial diameter of 89,000 miles, and it completes one orbit of the Sun every

11.86 years at a mean distance of 484 million miles. Markings can be seen on Jupiter's disk through a telescope, and these features take the form of alternating light and dark bands which are parallel to the planet's equator, with finer detail such as spots, wisps and arches, the colours ranging from white through yellow to grey or brown with reddish or bluish tinges. Dark caps cover the polar regions. These features appear to drift quickly across the disc since the planet spins very rapidly on its axis, once round every 9 hours 55 minutes, which accounts for its slightly spheroidal or flattened form. The visible markings are only the upper part of a cloud blanket which completely covers the planet and which consists of crystals of ammonia, ammonia hydrosulphide, water ice and water droplets, all floating in a deep atmosphere of hydrogen and helium. The exact structure and composition of Jupiter's interior remains unknown, but there is likely to be liquid hydrogen below the atmosphere, with solid metallic hydrogen lower down, all surrounding a core of iron and rocks. Although the atmosphere is very cold (between −120°C and −170°C), the extreme pressures in the interior generate heat which drives the storms in the planet's atmosphere, and there are frequent lightning discharges. These storms are visible as the constantly changing markings on the disk. A distinctive feature of this planet is the Giant Red Spot, 20,000 miles in length, and which has been seen for over 300 years.

Jupiter has a very powerful magnetic field (20,000 times stronger than the Earth's) and in 1955, the planet was found to be a source of radio waves. Of the fifteen satellites which circle this planet, four (called Ganymede, Callisto, Io and Europa) are visible through a small telescope, these four being known as the 'Galilean' moons after their discovery by Galileo in 1610. These moons are icy worlds comparable in size to, or somewhat larger than, our Moon and one of them, Io, has active volcanoes on its surface. The remaining satellites are much smaller.

Saturn

Saturn is the second largest planet in the solar system, with an equatorial diameter of 75,000 miles. It orbits the Sun at a mean distance of 886 million miles, once in every 29.46 years. Like Jupiter, this planet is considerably flattened at the poles because of its rapid rotation (once in every 10 hours 14 minutes). Saturn appears, through a telescope, as a yellowish-white disk crossed by darker brownish-grey bands, and occasionally spots are visible, although the detail is much less than on Jupiter. These bands are the upper parts of clouds of frozen ammonia crystals, floating in a deep atmosphere of hydrogen and helium which become metallic lower down under great pressure, while lower down still there is probably ice surrounding a rocky core. Although the great pressures generate some heat, the atmosphere is very cold (around −180°C), and the very low density of the planet as a whole means that it could float on water, were there an ocean large enough to contain it.

Saturn is unique among the planets in that it is surrounded by a system of rings. Three of these are visible from the Earth. The outermost is dull white (10,000 miles in width), then a gap of 3,000 miles (called Cassini's Division) separates it from the central ring, which is the brightest and widest (16,000 miles), and finally, there is a dull grey, semi-transparent ring of 10,000 miles width. These rings, of a white or yellowish-white colour, are composed of millions of lumps of ice and rock, whirling round the planet at speeds of tens of thousands of miles per hour in a great swarm, but although this ring-system is so wide (170,000 miles), it is extremely thin (10 miles). Because Saturn and its ring-system are inclined at 26½° to the orbital plane's perpendicular, the rings appear at different angles as the planet travels round the Sun. At two points in its orbit — at the planet's equinoxes which occur every 14 or 15 years — the rings appear edge-on to the Earth, and their thinness causes them to disappear for a while. A few other, much fainter, rings exist outside of the main system, but these are not normally visible from the Earth.

Saturn is now known to have twelve moons in orbit outside the ring system, of which the largest (Titan) is as big as Mercury and is covered in an orange fog. Our knowledge of Saturn, as with Jupiter, has greatly increased during the last few years due to the observations and measurements taken by the Pioneer and Voyager spacecraft. In particular, a great deal has been learnt about Jupiter's satellites and Saturn's rings.

Uranus

Beyond Saturn lies Uranus, which was unknown to the ancient astronomers, although it is occasionally visible to the naked eye. Observations and studies of Uranus played an important part in determining the chemical constitution of the atmospheres of the giant planets. Uranus was discovered telescopically on 13 March 1781 by William Herschel while he was carrying out surveys of the sky. At first thought to be a comet, it was eventually found to be a new planet.

Moving far beyond the orbit of Saturn, Uranus completes its circuit of the Sun once every 84 years at an average distance of 1,783 million miles. Its diameter is 29,000 miles and, through a telescope, appears as a greenish-white disk crossed by a few darker bands (although no detail is visible through small telescopes). The atmosphere is a deep one of hydrogen and helium with methane and ammonia, surrounding a core of ice and rock, and temperatures are very low (−200°C). The planet rotates quickly (10 hours 48 minutes) and the axial inclination is unusually high (98°) so that each pole points alternately towards the Sun. It has five satellites, all less than 1,000 miles across, and in 1977, a faint ring-system, similar to Saturn's, was found. When Uranus was found, there was a plan to name it Georgium Sidus — George's star — after the reigning monarch (George III), but eventually it was given its present name, although in older ephemerides the name Herschel is listed for this planet.

Neptune

Neptune was discovered in 1846 independently by the two mathematicians John Adams and Urbain LeVerrier. After Uranus had been observed for a few decades, it became clear that it was not moving in its predicted path, but was acting as if another, yet undiscovered, planet was affecting it gravitationally (perturbation). The calculations of Adams and LeVerrier were sent to the Berlin Observatory in September 1846, where on the 23rd of that month, astronomers d'Arrest and Galle found the new planet, less than one degree away from its predicted position.

Neptune's orbital revolution period is 165 years, and its distance from the Sun is 2,793 million miles. Its diameter, based on recent measurements (1969) is 31,000 miles, which is slightly larger than Uranus.

Through a telescope, the planet appears as a very small bluish-white disk, and detail on its surface is very difficult to establish. Its exact constitution is unknown, but it probably has a solid core, and is known to have an atmosphere of hydrogen, helium and methane. Temperatures in the atmosphere are around −220°C. Although the structure and composition of Neptune are uncertain, it is thought that this planet is similar to Uranus. It has a rotation period of about 15 hours. Neptune and Uranus, together with Jupiter and Saturn, make up the four 'gas giants' — large planets of relatively low density with an appreciable proportion of their masses contained in their atmosphere.

Neptune has two satellites, Triton and Nereid. Triton is one of the largest moons in the Solar system and was discovered by Lassell in 1846, a few weeks after the discovery of Neptune. Nereid is much smaller (200 miles) and was found by Kuiper in 1949; it orbits Neptune once in 362 days, while Triton goes round once in 6 days. The discovery of Neptune by mathematical analysis was a brilliant confirmation of Newton's laws concerning the mass and motion of bodies.

Pluto

Irregularities in the orbit of Neptune led astronomers to postulate the existence of a ninth planet, and in 1930 their claims were confirmed. The existence of Pluto was established mathematically by Percival Lowell, and it was discovered observationally by Clyde Tombaugh in January 1930, fourteen years after Lowell's death. The astronomer Lowell (who also observed 'canals' on Mars), carried out computations, in order to determine the mass and position of an unknown planet which was thought to be responsible for the irregularities in the orbits of Uranus and Neptune. An extensive photographic programme by Tombaugh of Lowell's Observatory in Flagstaff, Arizona, led to the discovery of Pluto, which was first sighted on 21 January 1930.

Pluto is a highly eccentric planet which moves in an orbit greatly inclined to the Ecliptic (about 17°), with a mean distance from the Sun of 3,666 million miles and an orbital revolution period of 248 years. Owing to its highly eccentric orbit (greater than that of any other planet), Pluto at perihelion is within the orbit of Neptune, and perihelion will occur in 1989. This planet is visible only in fairly large telescopes, and no markings can be seen on its surface. It has a diameter of about 3,700 miles and rotates once every six days. Unlike the four previous planets, Pluto is solid throughout. The surface of Pluto is extremely cold — around −230°C (or only about 40-50° above absolute zero). It is unlikely that Pluto has an atmosphere, because its low surface gravity is unable to hold onto any gaseous hydrogen or helium, and the extremely low temperatures mean that compounds such as water, carbon dioxide, ammonia and even methane are all in the frozen state upon its surface.

Various estimates have been made concerning Pluto's size, and these vary from between a diameter of 2,000 miles to one of 6,000 miles, with a mass of about one-tenth that of the Earth. In 1978, it was found that Pluto possesses a small moon provisionally named

Charon. This satellite revolves in a period of just over 6 days. The brightness of most planets changes, generally because their distances from the Earth constantly alter. Pluto, in contrast, has an intrinsic fluctuation, first noted in 1955 by R. H. Hardie, of approximately 20 per cent over a period of 6.39 days. This light variation, which has been increasing since first detected, is attributed to a gradually changing aspect of the planet as it revolves around the Sun. The satellite period (6.39 days) is identical to the light period, but Charon is much too faint to account for the light variation. Therefore, we have satellite revolution and planet rotation of exactly the same period, with Pluto and its moon appearing to have complete synchronism.

Other Bodies of the Solar System

In addition to the nine planets, there are many planetlike objects in the Solar system which, although not classified as planets have, in some cases, diameters greater than Mercury. Apart from the planetary satellites such as the moons of Jupiter, Saturn and some of the other planets, there are in addition lesser bodies, some of which are of considerable size, with well-known orbits.

In the last few decades, principally due to space research programmes, interest in the lesser bodies has increased, and intensive studies have been undertaken with a view to establishing connections between the mechanics of planetary motion and astrophysics.

The solar system has one principal body, the Sun, around which circle its satellites: the inner terrestrial planets, the outer Jovian planets (Jupiter, Saturn, Uranus and Neptune), and the swarm of minor bodies such as asteroids and comets.

Asteroids

Asteroids or minor planets lie between the orbits of Mars and Jupiter and number over 40,000. The origin of these minor planets is not known with certainty, but it has been suggested that they are the debris left after the formation of the principal planets, or they may be the remnants of former planets which for one reason or another disintegrated. Asteroids look exactly like stars, and can only be identified by their positions and movements from night to night. Most of these asteroids are small; the largest of them, Ceres, is only 430 miles in diameter and was found by Piazzi in 1801. Of the others, only Vesta and Pallas exceed 250 miles. Some attention, astrologically, has been given to Ceres, Vesta, Pallas and Eros, but much more study and research is needed concerning their significance before any firm conclusions can be drawn.

Comets

Comets are large objects consisting principally of gas, dust and small particles. There are normally three parts to a comet, the coma (head), the nucleus, and the tail. The coma forms the bulk of a comet's volume, and it is that part of it which gives it its distinctive fuzzy appearance. The chemical elements and molecules which make up the gas of the coma are carbon, carbon monoxide, oxygen, amine, cyanogen, water, cyanide and carbon sulphide, and there are also ions (electrically charged particles) of nitrogen, carbon monoxide, water, hydroxyl and carbon dioxide. The typical nucleus consists of water ice, within which are trapped various other substances, and when the comet approaches the Sun, the heat from the latter causes the ice to sublimate, that is, to change directly into water vapour. As the comet draws near to the Sun, it encounters a constant stream of electrically charged particles continuously moving away from the Sun, called the solar wind. This solar wind impinges upon the coma and forces some of its material to move directly away from the Sun, and the comet therefore develops a tail, which always points away from the Sun. So, when a comet is receding from the Sun's vicinity, it will move tail first and not head first, leaving a trail of dust behind it along most parts of its orbit. Cometary orbits are not only often highly elongated; they are also sometimes highly inclined to the plane of the Ecliptic. This means that, unlike the planets, which keep to a narrow band in the sky (the zodiac), comets can appear in any part of the sky, although as a general rule, they are most conspicuous when they are near to the Sun. Although there are possibly millions of comets, within and without the Solar system, the orbits of only about 600 have been determined. Of these, about a hundred are referred to as 'short period', orbiting the Sun once every 200 years or less. These comets keep within the confines of the Solar system and move in orbits which do not incline steeply to the Ecliptic. 'Long period' comets, of which about 500 are known to exist, appear to belong to a different class, since their orbits are highly inclined to the Ecliptic and are often retrograde. They originate from well outside the solar system, possibly from as much as two light-years away (12 million, million miles) or half-way to the nearest star.

One of the most notable comets is Halley's Comet, which has been observed and recorded for centuries. This comet returns every seventy-six years and its last return was in 1985/86. It was Edmond Halley (1656-1742) who first showed that comets move in a very elongated elliptical orbit round the Sun. The return of this comet has generated great interest and, doubtlessly, space-age technology will enable further discoveries to be made concerning cometary action. Comets have always had an astrological significance; often regarded with awe and foreboding. These 'hairy stars' may be the indicators of death and calamities but, as with so much of astrological tradition, only detailed research will confirm whether comets are associated with the 'shape of things to come'.

Meteors and Meteorites

Comets leave behind them in their wake a trail of debris, in the form of dust, small particles and occasional larger chunks. When the Earth passes through such a trail, the particles rush into the atmosphere and burn up in streaks of light, called meteors. These streaks normally last for only a second or so because the particles, about the size of sand grains, burn up quickly in the friction generated by their passage through the atmosphere. At certain times of the year, showers of meteors occur (one every few minutes, originating from a point in the sky known as the radiant). Some meteors are large enough to survive the descent to the ground, and occasionally these *meteorites* may weigh several pounds or, in extreme cases, many tons. Meteors, or 'shooting stars' exist either as showers or in isolation (sporadic). Meteorites like comets and meteors are really space debris. The rapid advance of observing techniques means that a vast amount of information concerning interplanetary material will be obtained and this will add greatly to our knowledge of the solar system. A study of 'space debris' can show not only interplanetary relationships, but also (from an analysis of the material), the conditions and influences existing when the solar system first evolved.

Celestial Mechanics: Laws of Planetary Motion

The solar system consists of the Sun; the planets and their satellites; and comets and meteorites, along with dust and debris. All the bodies in the system obey well-defined laws and observe great regularity in their motions. The most important of the several laws relating to planetary motion are the three laws discovered by Johannes Kepler between the years 1609 and 1618. (See Fig. 12.) These laws, deduced from the observations of Tycho Brahe, enabled Isaac Newton to formulate his law of universal gravitation, and which eventually led

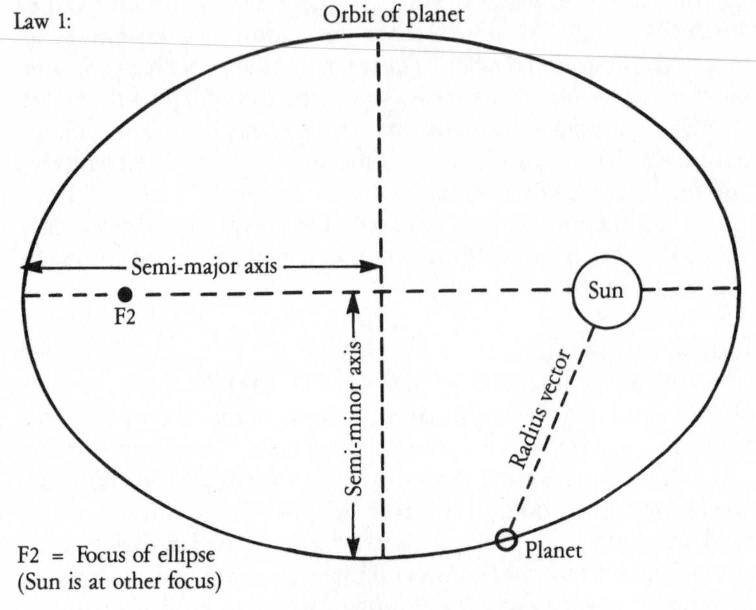

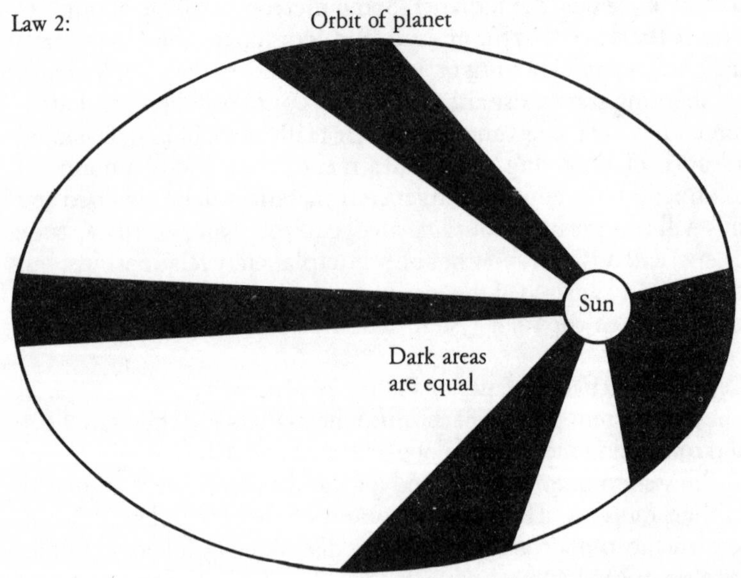

Figure 12 Kepler's Laws of Planetary Motion.

to Einstein's theories of relativity. These three laws are:

1 *The planets move in ellipses with the Sun at one focus of the ellipse.* This law indicates the shapes of the orbits and the path which the planet will always follow.
2 *The radius vector (the imaginary straight line joining each planet to the Sun) sweeps out equal areas in equal times.* This second law involves a continually varying rate of motion. The speed is not constant, the planets moving faster the closer they are to the Sun. The maximum speed of any planet is attained when it is closest to the Sun, the minimum when it is farthest. These two points on the orbit being perihelion (closest) and aphelion (farthest). Although the speeds of the planets in their orbits are not constant, the radius vector of each planet passes over equal areas in equal times.
3. *The squares of the planets' revolution periods are directly proportional to the cubes of their distances from the Sun.* This law known as the 'harmonic law' defines the relationship between the planet's orbital motion and its distance from the Sun. The period is the time that it takes the planet to complete one revolution around the Sun. For example, the Earth takes 365 ¼ days approximately, Mercury 88 days and Pluto about 248 years. By knowing the mean distance of a planet from the Sun, we can obtain the exact period of a planet's orbit.

The laws of planetary motion as defined by Kepler were a brilliant discovery and, although the third law was not complete, they enabled Newton to show that planets behave as they do because of the universal law of gravitational attraction.

Retrograde Motion

The true motion of the planets cannot be observed from the Earth, because the Earth itself is in constant motion. As viewed from Earth, it is only the motion of the planets relative to that of Earth which can be observed. During a certain period before, around and after opposition, a planet will *appear* to change its normal eastward motion and go into reverse, moving westward against the stars. A planet which does this is said to be moving *retrograde*, and this phenomenon is caused by the Earth overtaking the outer planet. (See Fig. 13.)

At two points, usually a few weeks either side of opposition, the Earth is moving directly towards or directly away from the planet,

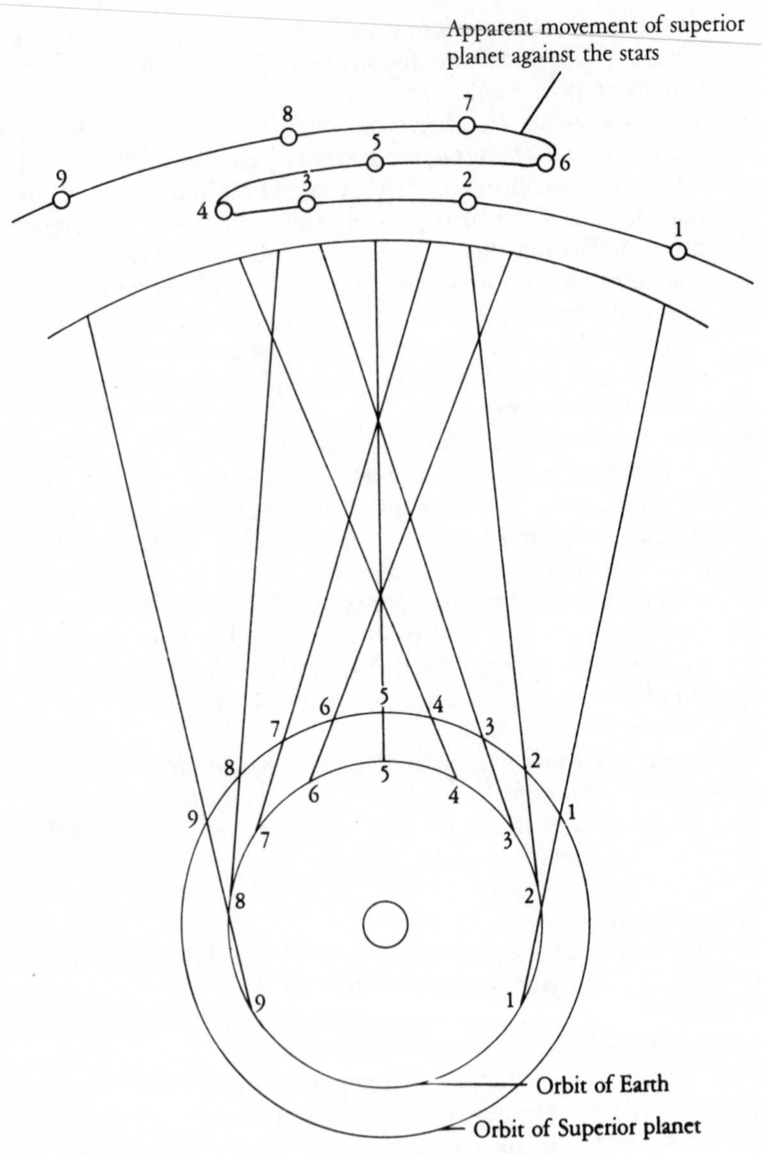

Figure 13 Retrogradation.

which then appears stationary. At the planet's stationary points, its motion changes from direct to retrograde or vice-versa. Retrograde motion is a perfectly natural occurrence, and depends upon the geocentric view and distance, and the period of retrogradation is greater, the more remote the planet happens to be. Each planet is retrograde for varying periods of time.

Precession of the Equinoxes

The phenomenon of precession was discovered by the Greek astronomer Hipparchus in the 2nd century BC. Briefly stated, Precession of the Equinoxes is the annual occurrence of the Vernal Equinox at about 21 March, nearly 20½ minutes before the Earth has made a complete orbital revolution around the Sun, so that each year at that instant, the Sun crosses the celestial Equator at a slightly different point. (See Fig. 14.) As a result of precession, every star — except those less than 23½° from the Ecliptic Poles — passes through every hour of Right Ascension from 0-24 hours, once every 25,800 years; also the declinations, every 12,900 years swing to and fro 47° (23½ × 2) greatly changing the stars visible at a given place and season.

The Vernal Equinox is used to define the Tropical Year, which is the period of time elapsed between two successive passages of the Sun through the Vernal Equinox. As the Equator is always at right angles to its own pole, the movement of the Celestial Pole around the Pole of the Ecliptic will cause the vernal-equinoctial point to slip backwards along the Ecliptic at the rate of 1° in 71½ years. Precession is therefore a purely terrestrial effect related to the Earth itself. If the Earth were not an oblate spheroid, but a perfect sphere, there would be no precession and the tropical zodiac would be fixed.

The continuous minute tilting of the Earth's axis by the Sun and Moon causes the Celestial Poles and Equator to change their places continuously among the stars in harmony, so that at each successive moment, the Celestial Equator intersects the Ecliptic at a slightly different point — in the opposite direction of the Earth's orbital motion — to the one it would occupy if left undisturbed. The gravitational forces of the Sun and Moon pull on the Earth's equatorial bulge, as though trying to bring the Earth into an upright position. However, the spinning Earth acts like a gyrostat causing the Earth's axis (which would otherwise always point to the same position on the star sphere) and the celestial Poles to rotate round the poles of her orbit (those of the Ecliptic) in circles 23½° distant from them

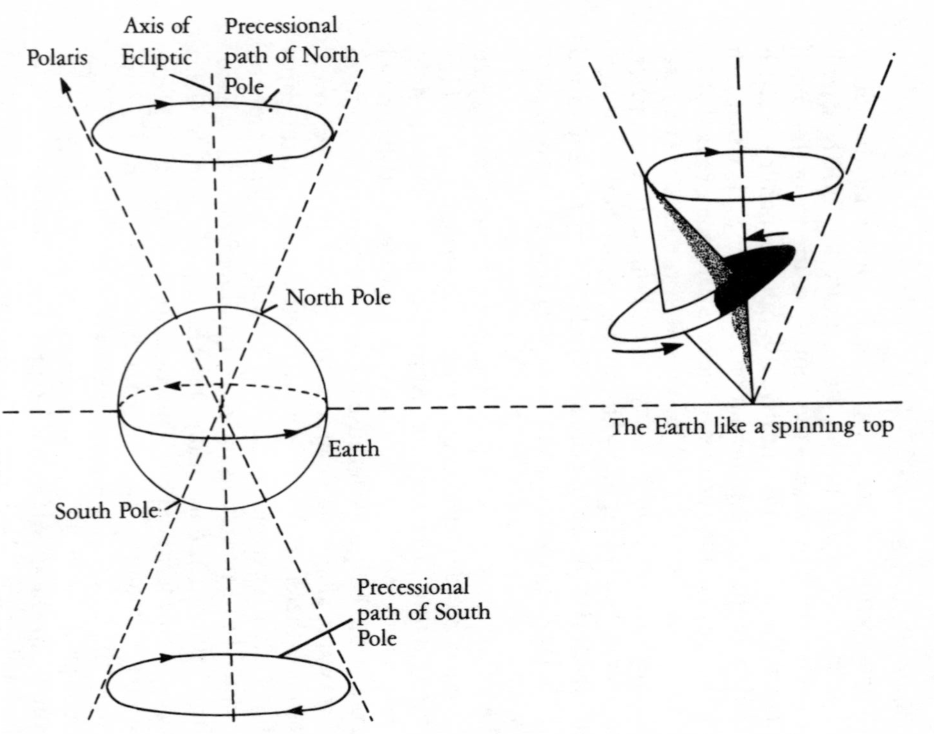

Figure 14 Precession of the Equinoxes

in a period of 25,800 years, displacing the Vernal Equinox in the opposite direction to her orbital motion.

As precession is continuous, the Celestial Equator intersects the Ecliptic at a point about one-seventh of a second of arc west of the position the day before at the same hour, so that right ascension is measured from a slightly different point on the star sphere each day. About 21 March each year, the Vernal Point is approximately

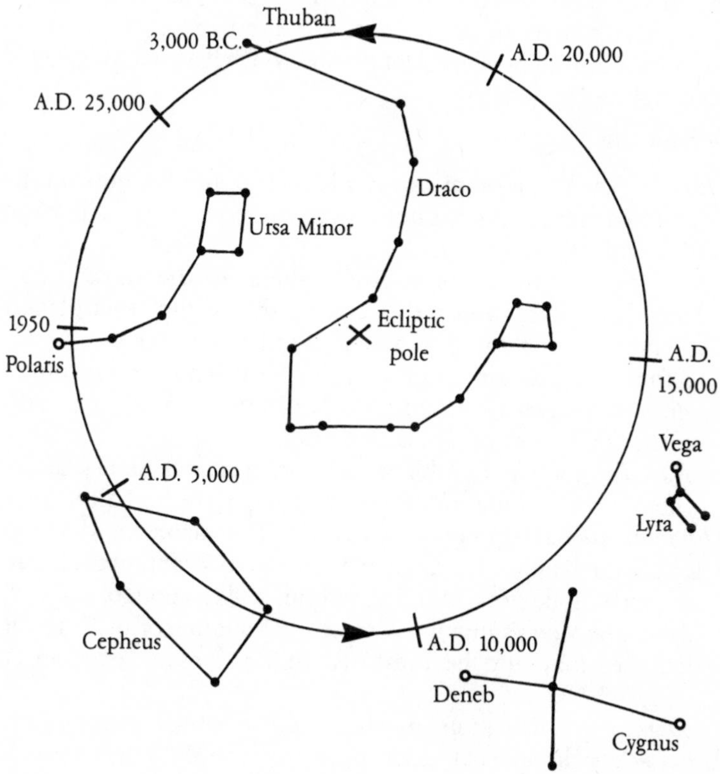

Figure 15 Path of the North Celestial Pole

50 seconds west of its position a year before, or about 3 seconds of right ascension (1° in 71½ years). As celestial longitude is measured along the Ecliptic from the Vernal Equinox, it changes with

precession, but latitude which is measured north or south of the Ecliptic does not change. At the present time, the North Celestial Pole is near the star Ursae Minoris (Pole Star) and its nearest approach — less than half a degree — will be in the year 2100 AD. (See Fig. 15.)

The position of stars is listed for a definite epoch, e.g. 1 January 1950. This is done because it is not possible to produce maps and catalogues to keep abreast with precession. In plotting positions of celestial objects observed before or after the epoch date, astronomers must calculate the amount of precessional change in right ascension and declination for the appropriate interval of time. In the ephemerides used by astrologers, the tabulations of planetary positions are given in celestial longitudes which have been converted from right ascensions.

Definitions

Altitude: The elevation of a heavenly body above the horizon. Its vertical distance from the horizon, measured in degrees (horizon 0°, zenith 90°).

Apex: The region on the celestial sphere, in the constellation Hercules, towards which the Sun, Earth and the other planets are moving, at a speed of about 12 miles per second.

Aphelion: The point in the orbit of the Earth, a planet or a comet, where it reaches maximum distance from the Sun. The Earth reaches this point on or about 1 July.

Apogee: The point in the orbit of the Moon or of an artificial satellite, where it reaches the maximum distance from the Earth.

Apparent diameter (angular diameter): The diameter which an astronomical object appears to have when it is seen from the Earth, measured in degrees, minutes, seconds and fractions of a second of arc. The Moon's angular diameter is 31 minutes of arc. Angular diameter may also be measured in fractions of a radian (1 radian = 57°).

Apparent noon: The moment when the Sun crosses the meridian.

Appulse: The distance of nearest approach of the Moon or of a planet to a star.

Apse: The points in an orbit, where the orbiting body is at its nearest or furthest from its primary. For the Earth, these points are respectively perihelion (q.v.) and aphelion (q.v.).

Arc: The curved line on the circumference of a circle, that lies between the intersections of two lines from the circle's centre with the circumference. On the celestial sphere (q.v.), an arc is the shortest distance between two stars.

Arctic; Antarctic: The Arctic is the polar area north of latitude 66°33′ north. Antarctic is the opposite region, the polar region south of latitude 66°33′ south.

Armillary sphere: A device consisting of metal rings representing the astronomical projections (Celestial Equator, Ecliptic, meridians and lines of right ascension and declination). Chiefly used during the eighteenth century and earlier.

Aspect: The angle between two planets, or between the Sun or Moon and a planet at any particular time, as seen from the Earth. (See also page 131.)

Asteroid: Minor planet, normally found in orbits between those of Mars and Jupiter.

Astrolabe: A device, used chiefly up to the seventeenth century, to measure star positions, consisting of three rotatable plates. One of these plates shows a star-map, another shows the observer's horizon.

Astronomical co-ordinates: Values in a reference system used to define a position of a body on the celestial sphere (q.v.). The three principal systems are: 1. Horizon system (q.v.; see Fig. 2); 2. Equatorial system (q.v.; see Fig. 3); 3. Ecliptic system (q.v.; see fig. 4).

Astronomical Unit: One of the standard measurements of astronomical distance. Equal to the mean distance between the Earth and the Sun, or 93 million miles.

Atmosphere: A layer of gas surrounding a planet, at its greatest density nearest the surface. The atmosphere is maintained by the gravitational attraction of the planet. The gases contained in an atmosphere depend upon the planet's escape velocity, which in turn depends upon the planet's mass. Thus Jupiter's atmosphere consists principally of hydrogen, because Jupiter is a massive planet with a high escape velocity which has been able to 'hold on to' the fast-moving hydrogen molecules. The Earth, on the other hand, has been able to 'hold on to' only the slower-moving oxygen and nitrogen molecules because of its feebler gravitational attraction.

Atom: The smallest particle of an element. A complex system of electrons, protons and neutrons.

Aurora: Northern or Southern Lights caused by charged particles from the Sun causing parts of the upper atmosphere to glow. Normally visible only in high latitudes.

Autumnal Equinox: The September Equinox: The First Point of

Libra: One of the points of intersection between the Celestial Equator and the Ecliptic that the Sun reaches when crossing from north to south on or about 23 September.

Axis: The imaginary line connecting the two poles of a planet, and passing through its centre. The line about which a planet rotates.

Azimuth: The horizontal distance between the intersection of the meridian with the horizon (south point) and the intersection of the line from the zenith through the star to the horizon. A co-ordinate of the Horizon system (q.v.), measured in degrees and minutes.

Binary: A double star, where the two component stars are revolving around each other.

Bode's Law: A law connecting the distances of each planet from the Sun with a mathematical progression of numbers. To each number in the series, 0, 3, 6, 12, 24, 48, 96, 192, is added 4 to give, 4, 7, 10, 16, 28, 52, 100, 196, which is the approximate distance, in tens of millions of miles, of each planet from the Sun, from Mercury out to Uranus. This law does not hold good for Neptune or Pluto. The number 28 corresponds to the asteroids' distances from the Sun.

Brightness: The apparent brilliance of a star or planet. Generally the word *magnitude* is used in this context for a stricter definition.

Celestial Equator: A great circle on the celestial sphere (q.v.) mid-way between the celestial poles (q.v.). A projection of the Earth's Equator onto the celestial sphere.

Celestial mechanics: Branch of astronomy which is concerned with the motions and orbits of celestial bodies through space.

Celestial meridian: The great circle on the celestial sphere which passes through the Poles, zenith and nadir, and the north and south points of the horizon. The observer's meridian of longitude projected onto the celestial sphere (q.v.).

Celestial poles: The points on the sky which are directly overhead at the terrestrial poles. The Earth's rotational axis extended into space.

Celestial sphere: The apparent sphere, with the Earth at the centre, on which the celestial bodies appear to be projected.

Centrifugal force: Apparent force, caused by a rotating body. This force tends to cause objects to move in a straight line instead of round in a circle.

Cepheid: Variable star whose period varies directly with its luminosity.

Ceres: Largest of the asteroids (minor planets). Discovered by G. Piazzi in 1801, it is about 430 miles across and orbits the Sun once every 4½ years.

Chromosphere: Region of the Sun's surface lying directly above the photosphere (luminous surface of the Sun).

Circumpolar stars: Those stars which never rise or set, but are always visible from a particular place. At the latitude of London (51½° north), all stars which have declinations of (90°-51½°) or 38½° north or more, are circumpolar. At the Equator, no stars are circumpolar, while at the Poles, all are.

Civil Day: The twenty-four-hour Mean Solar Day.

Cluster: A group of stars or a group of galaxies (q.v.), containing from a few to hundreds of thousands of members.

Coma: The head of a comet, consisting of rarefied gas.

Conjunction: Occurs when two astronomical bodies (e.g. the Sun and a planet, the Moon and a planet, or two or more planets) are at their least distance apart. At New Moon the Moon is in conjunction with the Sun. Because of their slightly different orbital inclinations, planets do not pass one behind the other, but approach to a minimum distance before drawing apart again.

Constellation: A group of stars which are not physically related to one another but merely happen to lie in the same line of sight. Constellations were associated by the ancients with mythological characters, animals, etc., and the stars in them are connected by imaginary lines. On star-maps, the names of constellations are still used, and they have officially defined boundaries, so that the entire celestial sphere (q.v.) is covered by the eighty-eight constellations. Some constellations are large, while others are much smaller; some contain bright stars — Orion, Leo, Ursa Major (the Great Bear), Cygnus (the Swan), and as such, are easily recognized, while others with faint stars are obscure. Constellations are known by their Latin names, and a Greek letter is assigned to the twenty-four brightest stars in each constellation (alpha being the brightest, beta the second brightest, gamma the third brightest, then delta, epsilon, and so on). Those close to the Ecliptic (q.v.) have the same names as the signs of the Zodiac, but are in no way connected with the signs.

Co-ordinates: The means by which the position of a point on a map is defined. On the Earth the two co-ordinates are latitude and longitude, while on the celestial sphere (q.v.) the two co-ordinates are declination (q.v.) and right ascension (q.v.) Other systems may be used, for instance: the Horizon co-ordinate system (altitude and azimuth); the Hour-angle system (hour-angle and declination); the Ecliptic system (longitude and latitude measured along and from the ecliptic); the Helio-centric system (distance from the Sun and position angle); and the Galactic system (longitude and latitude measured along and from the galactic plane).

Corona: The Sun's atmosphere.

Cosmogony: Branch of astronomy concerned with the origin and evolution of particular regions of the universe, such as the Solar system.

Cosmology: Branch of astronomy concerned with the origin, evolution, structure and composition of the entire universe.

Culmination: The meridian (q.v.) passage of a celestial body.

Cusp: The point of division between either signs or houses.

Cycle: A period of time which constantly repeats itself; a recurring series of changes.

Day: The period of time equal to one rotation of the Earth. It can be measured as a Sidereal Day (q.v.), a Solar Day (q.v.) or a Mean Solar Day (q.v.).

Declination: One of the co-ordinates used to fix the position of a star or body on the celestial sphere (q.v.). It is measured in degrees and minutes north or south of the Celestial Equator (q.v.); the angular distance of a body from the Celestial Equator.

Degree: One 360th part of a circle. It is divided up into 60 minutes of arc, and each minute is divided up into 60 seconds of arc.

Deimos: One of the two satellites of Mars (Deimos and Phobos), which orbits Mars every 30 hours and is very small, approximately 5 miles across.

Density: Quantity of matter contained in a unit volume. The densities of stars and planets are measured relative to that of water (= 1), so that the Earth's for example is 5.52.

Dichotomy: Appearance of Mercury or Venus in a telescope, when one-half of the planet's disk is illuminated by the Sun, and it appears like a half-moon.

Direct motion: The normal apparent motion of a planet around the Sun, as seen from the Earth. This motion is eastward, in distinction to retrograde motion (q.v.) which is westward.

Diurnal arc: The measurement in degrees of a planet from its rising to its setting.

Diurnal circle: The apparent path of a celestial body across the sky during daylight hours.

Diurnal motion: The apparent motion of celestial bodies across the sky from east to west.

Doppler effect: Discovered by Doppler in 1842. A source of sound moving towards the observer, compresses the sound waves and the pitch is raised; conversely, when the same source recedes from the observer, the sound waves are rarefied or stretched apart and the pitch is lowered. (The pitch of a sound depends on the frequency of waves, the greater the frequency, the higher the pitch.) In astronomy, the same principle may be applied to light waves, so that, for a star which is approaching us, the lines in its spectrum are shifted to the blue end of the spectrum, while a star receding from us has its spectral lines shifted toward the red end.

Double star: Pair of stars close together in the sky, either in the same line of sight, or physically associated.

Dwarf star: A small, relatively dim star. These make up the vast bulk of the stellar population, being at the relatively small, low-mass end of the population map. (Large, massive stars are known as Giants.) Our Sun is a Yellow Dwarf; there are also White Dwarfs and Red Dwarfs.

Earth: Third planet from the Sun. One of the five 'terrestrial' planets (the others being Mercury, Venus, Mars and Pluto), which all have small sizes and high densities. Of these, the Earth is the largest. Its interior consists of an outer crust, surrounding a mantle of rock, while at the centre, there is an iron-nickel core, liquid molten, but solid at the centre. The tilt of the Earth's axis to the perpendicular to the plane of its orbit (23½°), is responsible for the seasons. Because the equatorial regions receive much more sunlight than the Poles, temperatures increase towards lower latitudes but winds and ocean currents transport heat and cold to different parts of the globe. The continents ride on 'plates' of the Earth's crust, and interactions between these plates build up stresses which are relieved by sudden earthquakes which occur along fault lines between plates. Volcanic eruptions are caused by hot magma forcing its way up through weak points in the Earth's crust. Temperatures in the Earth's core are likely to be as high as 4,000°C. (See also Planetary Data table, Fig. 9.)

Eccentricity: Measurement of the degree of flattening of an ellipse (q.v.), varying between zero for a circle to one for a straight line.

Eclipse: Phenomenon occurring when either (a) the Moon passes in front of the Sun and partially or wholly obscures it (solar eclipse — see Fig. 16) or (b) the Moon passes into the Earth's shadow

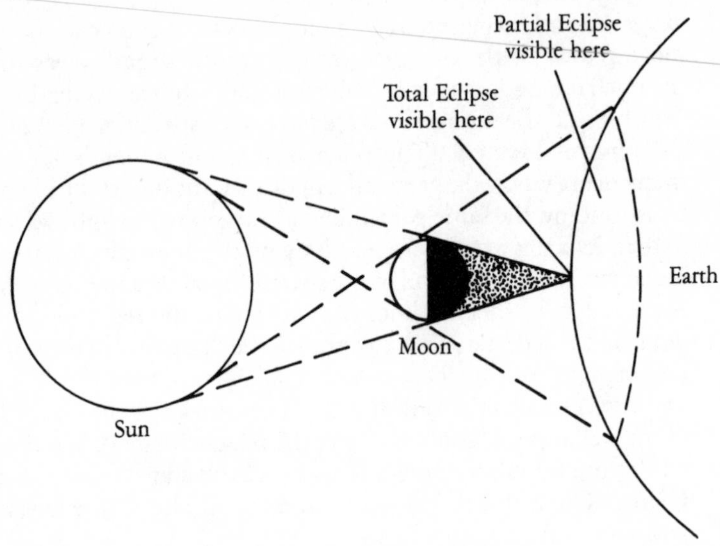

Figure 16 Solar Eclipse.

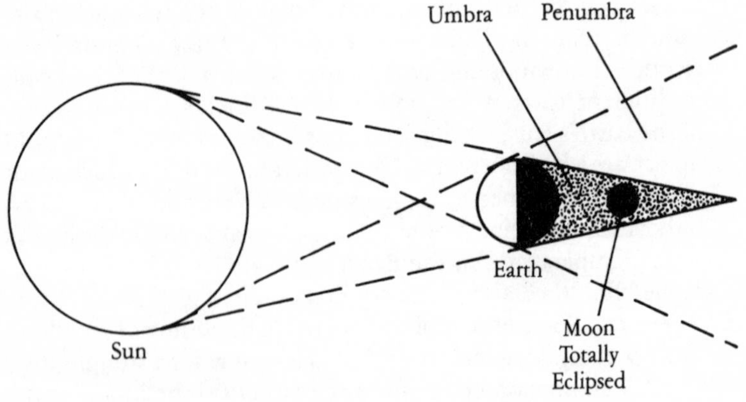

Figure 17 Lunar Eclipse.

and is obscured (lunar eclipse — see Fig. 17). Eclipses of the satellites of Jupiter by that planet's shadow may also be seen. Eclipses occur at six-monthly intervals, when the new and full Moon takes place near one of the Moon's nodes (intersections of the lunar orbit with the Ecliptic).

If the Moon is near its perigee (q.v.) at the time of a solar eclipse, then the eclipse is total (complete obscuration of the Sun), but this total phase lasts always less than 8 minutes as the intersection of the Moon's shadow with the Earth's surface is small in diameter (less than 170 miles), and the Moon's motion through space plus the Earth's rotation cause this shadow to travel quickly over the continents. During a total eclipse, the sky and countryside become dark and the Sun's corona is visible around the black Moon. On either side of totality, and away from the shadow, a partial eclipse is visible. If the Moon is well away from perigee, its shadow will fail to reach the Earth and an annular eclipse results with a ring (annulus) of sunlight surrounding the Moon. When the Moon passes into the Earth's shadow, there is a lunar eclipse (at Full Moon). This may last up to two hours and it can be seen over a large part of the Earth. Sometimes, the Moon is completely obscured by the shadow but, at other times, the Earth's atmosphere refracts sunlight into the shadow causing the eclipsed Moon to appear with a faint coppery glow. If the Moon passes into the full shadow (umbra) of the Earth, it is totally eclipsed, but if it passes into the half-shadow (penumbra), then it is only slightly dulled.

Ecliptic: The Sun's apparent path across the sky during one year, caused by the Earth's orbital revolution around the Sun. The Ecliptic is inclined at 23½° to the Celestial Equator (q.v.).

Ecliptic system: Co-ordinate system, the fundamental plane of which is the plane of the Ecliptic. (See Fig. 4).

Electromagnetic Radiation: Energy in wave form, which comes in several different types, e.g. gamma rays, X-rays, ultra-violet light, visible light, infra-red (heat), and radio waves.

Electrons: Sub-atomic negatively charged particles in orbits within atoms.

Ellipse: Oval-shaped closed curve. Caused by a circle being viewed from an angle or by a cone being sliced in two away from its base. Most astronomical bodies follow elliptical orbits.

Elongation: Maximum apparent separation of the two inferior planets (Mercury and Venus) either east or west of the Sun. For Mercury, this distance is 28° and for Venus it is 48°. This term can also be used to define the maximum apparent separation of a satellite from its planet.

Energy: Quantity which describes movement of an object (kinetic energy) or electromagnetic radiation.

Ephemeris: A publication which lists astrological/astronomical data; essential for the calculation of astrological charts.

Equation of Time: The difference between Apparent Solar Time and Mean Solar Time (q.v.). Varies throughout the year from 0 to 16 minutes.

Equator: Great circle on the Earth's surface which is perpendicular to the polar axis and which is at the maximum distance from both poles. Other planets and stars, including the Sun, also have equators. The Celestial Equator is the projection of the Earth's Equator onto the celestial sphere.

Equator system: Co-ordinate system, whose fundamental plane is the plane of the Equator. (See Fig. 3.)

Equinox: Occurs when day and night are equal all over the Earth when the Earth's axis is in line with the terminator separating the illuminated day and dark night hemispheres of the Earth. This takes place twice a year, on or about 21 March (Spring Equinox in the northern hemisphere) and on or about 23 September (Autumn Equinox in the northern hemisphere). For the southern hemisphere the seasons are reversed. At the March Equinox, the Sun crosses the Celestial Equator from south to north at the point known as the First Point of Aries (q.v.), at the September Equinox it moves from north to south at the First Point of Libra.

Eros: Asteroid (q.v.) with an orbit between that of the Earth and Mars, with a diameter of about 8 miles and an orbital period of 642 days. It passed within 10 million miles of the Earth in 1931.

Escape velocity: Velocity required by a body to escape from the gravitational pull of a planet. For the Earth, this velocity is 7 miles per second.

Europa: One of the four largest of Jupiter's satellites, discovered by Galileo in 1610. It orbits the planet once every 3 days 13 hours at a mean distance of 417,000 miles. It is 1,950 miles in diameter and has an icy surface with a few craters.

Evection: Inequality in the motion of the Moon, caused by variations in its orbital eccentricity (q.v.). This variation can displace the Moon, in longitude, by up to 1.3 degrees.

Faculae: Bright localized regions on the Sun's surface, probably associated with sunspots (q.v.).

First Point of Aries: Position on the celestial sphere (q.v.) where the Ecliptic intersects the Celestial Equator (q.v.). The first point of the Zodiac from which is measured celestial longitude (q.v.) (along the Ecliptic [q.v.]) or right ascension (q.v.) (along the Equator).

Focus of an orbit: The point which is occupied by the primary body, about which a smaller body revolves in an orbit. For open orbits (i.e. parabolae and hyperbolae), there is only one focus, but for elliptical orbits there are two foci, one of the foci being empty.

Force: One of the fundamental properties of mechanics; force is that which is required to cause a change in velocity to a massive object, or to start or stop an object in motion or at rest. Gravitation is one of the four primary forces in the Universe.

Galaxy: A stellar system. A large collection of millions of stars. Our Sun and solar system are in such a system called the Milky Way, which contains about 100,000 million stars arranged in a flattened disc with the central hub from which spiral arms extend outward. (See Fig. 8.)

Ganymede: One of the four largest of Jupiter's satellites discovered by Galileo in 1610. It is 3,200 miles in diameter, and orbits Jupiter once every 7 days 4 hours at an average distance of 666,000 miles. It has an icy, cratered surface.

Gegenschein: Faint glow sometimes seen in the night sky exactly opposite to the Sun, and caused by diffusion of light by the Earth's atmosphere.

Giant: Type of star, much larger and more massive than the Sun, of two types, white or blue, and red, although orange and yellow giants (e.g. Arcturus, Capella) also exist. Giant stars are relatively rare in space.

Gnomon: Rod or plate on a sundial which is used to cast the shadow on to the dial.

Granulation: Mottled appearance of the Sun's surface, when it is seen close-up. Granules are the result of convection currents below the Sun's surface.

Gravitation: Force of mutual attraction between planets, stars or galaxies. Depends directly on the masses and inversely on the square of the distance, between the bodies. The theory of gravitation was developed by Newton.

Greenwich: Suburb of London. Longitude is measured from the Greenwich meridian (0° meridian).

Greenwich Mean Time: (G.M.T.). The local time of the Greenwich meridian. G.M.T. is used as civil time in Britain except from March to October when Summer Time (G.M.T. + 1 hour) is used. Universal time is G.M.T. reckoned on a 24-hour basis, e.g. 19.00 hours = 7.00 p.m.

Gregorian Calendar: The New Style calendar which superseded the Old Style (Julian) calendar.

Helium: Second lightest element and second most abundant one in the Universe.

Hemisphere: One half of a sphere, separated from the other half by a great circle. This term is used on Earth to define (a) northern and southern hemispheres separated by the Equator, (b) eastern and western hemispheres separated by the 0° Greenwich and the 180° meridians of longitude. On the celestial sphere (q.v.), the term is used to define: (a) the northern and southern celestial hemispheres separated by the Celestial Equator (q.v.); (b) the visible and invisible hemispheres separated by the horizon; (c) the two galactic hemispheres separated by the galactic plane (Milky Way).

Hermes: One of the asteroids (q.v.), very small with a diameter of less than one mile. Its eccentric orbit carried it, in 1937, to within 500,000 miles of the Earth.

Hertzsprung-Russell Diagram: Chart showing the absolute magnitudes of stars (luminosity) plotted against their spectral types (colours). Most stars fall into a band (called the Main Sequence) running from top left (brilliant bluish-white stars) to bottom right (dim red stars). Exceptions to this rule are the Red Giants and White Dwarfs. Absolute magnitudes range from −5 to +15 and spectral types run O,B,A,F,G,K,M,R,N,S. The Sun's position is +5,G. (See Fig. 18.)

Hidalgo: One of the asteroids, it follows an eccentric orbit out as far as Saturn during its orbital revolution period of fourteen years.

Horizon: The great circle which marks the intersection of the horizontal plane with the celestial sphere (q.v.).

Horizon system: Co-ordinate system with the horizon plane as the fundamental plane. (See Fig. 2.)

Hour angle: The arc measured westward from the meridian (q.v.). The angle between the hour circle of a body and the celestial meridian (q.v.).

Hour circle: A Great Circle passing through a celestial body and the celestial poles (q.v.).

Hydrogen: Most abundant and lightest element in the universe. It is the lightest of all gases ($^1/_{14}$ that of air) and is the principal constituent of the Sun, stars, nebulae, and of the atmospheres of the giant planets.

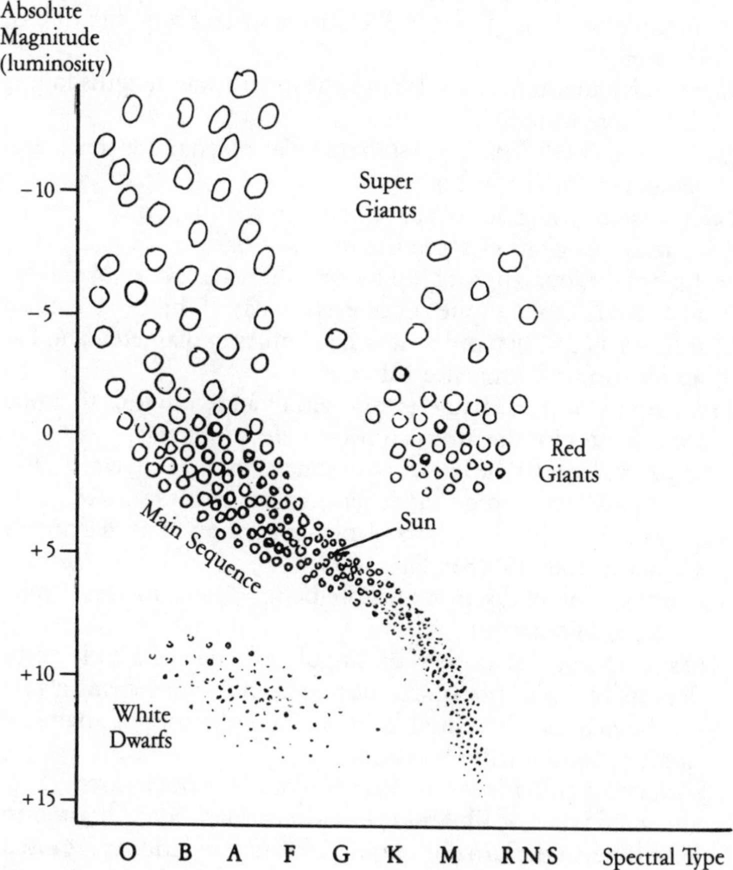

Figure 18 The Hertzsprung-Russell Diagram.

Icarus: One of the asteroids (q.v.), very small (diameter only 1 mile) and following a highly eccentric orbit which carries it within the orbit of Mars.

Inclination (of an orbit): Angle between the plane of the orbit and that of the Ecliptic (q.v.). The Moon's orbit is, for example, inclined 5°8′ to that of the Ecliptic.

Inertia: Term used in mechanics to define an object's resistance to starting, stopping or change in velocity. Depends directly on the object's mass (the greater the mass, the greater the resistance).

Inferior planet: Planet whose orbit lies within that of the Earth. There are two 'inferior' planets, Mercury and Venus. These appear alternately east and west of the Sun but never opposite to it in the sky.

Infra-red: Radiation in the form of heat with wavelengths longer than those of red light.

International Date Line: The 180th meridian of longitude that passes across the Pacific Ocean.

Interplanetary: Regions of space between the planets.

Interstellar: Regions of space between the stars.

Io: One of the four largest of Jupiter's satellites, discovered by Galileo in 1610. It orbits Jupiter once every 1 day 18 hours at a mean distance of 262,000 miles. It is 2,310 miles in diameter, and has an icy surface with active volcanoes.

Ion: Atom which has had electrons either added to it or removed from it, to give the atom an overall electric charge.

Ionosphere: Layer of the Earth's atmosphere, from which radio waves can be deflected to different parts of the Earth's surface.

Kepler's Laws: The three laws of planetary motion as defined by Kepler in 1609-18. (See Fig. 12.)

Kilometre: Unit of distance measurement = 1,000 metres (1 mile = 1.609 kilometres).

Latitude: Celestial latitude is the angular distance of a body north or south of the Ecliptic (q.v.). The Sun has no latitude being always on the Ecliptic. Terrestrial latitude is the distance of any place north or south of the Equator.

Libration: Irregularities of the Moon's motions about its axes. There are three types of libration; libration in latitude; libration in longitude; and diurnal libration. Libration in latitude is caused by the deviation from the perpendicular of the lunar axis, and results in the Moon appearing to rock up and down. Libration in longitude is caused by the Moon's elliptical path through space resulting in the Moon's rotation and revolution becoming out of step with one another, causing the Moon to rock from side to side. Diurnal libration is the result of the Earth's diameter being an appreciable fraction ($^1/_{30}$) of the Earth-Moon distance, so that it is possible to see a short way (1°) around the Moon's edge when it is rising or setting. These various librations enable us to see 59 per cent of the Moon's surface from the Earth, the remaining 41 per cent being invisible.

Light year: The distance that light travels in one year (186,000 miles per second). This distance is equal to six million, million miles.

Local group. Group of galaxies (q.v.) to which our Milky Way Galaxy belongs.

Longitude: Celestial longitude is the distance of a body from the First Point of Aries (q.v.), measured along the Ecliptic (q.v.) towards the east in either degrees and minutes or in signs, degrees and minutes. Terrestrial longitude, in conjunction with parallels of latitude, is used to define the position of a place on the Earth's surface. Lines of longitude run from pole to pole intersecting the parallels of latitude at right angles, and are measured from 0° (the Greenwich meridian) through to 180°, east and west from Greenwich.

Luminosity: Power output of the Sun or of a star, measured in watts per square metre.

Lunation: The time from New Moon to New Moon (29½ days); the sequence of phases of the Moon.

Lune: The portion of the surface of a sphere which is contained within two great semi-circles.

Magnitude (General): A definitive measurement of the brightness of a star or planet. Magnitudes are measured in whole numbers and fractions of ten or a hundred. A star of magnitude 1.00 is exactly one hundred times brighter than one of magnitude 6.00. Stars fainter than the sixth magnitude can only be seen through a telescope or binoculars. This scale operates in the negative direction for stars and planets brighter than magnitude 0 (Jupiter −2.5, Moon −12, Sun −27). *Apparent magnitude* is the apparent brightness of a star as seen from the Earth, according to the definition given above. *Absolute magnitude* is the magnitude (according to the definition given above) with which a star would appear, were it at a standard distance of 10 parsecs or 32.6 light years. At this distance our Sun would have its magnitude of −27 reduced to just +4.8, so that it would be barely brighter than Uranus. At the same distance, some stars would have their magnitudes increased over a thousand times to around −7. A star's absolute magnitude is therefore a true indication of its luminosity, unlike its apparent magnitude.

Main Sequence: A band in the Hertzsprung-Russell diagram (q.v.) along which many of the stars are to be found.

Mass: The total quantity of matter contained in an object, measured in kilograms. An object's weight is the mass × gravitational acceleration.

Mean Solar Day: The interval of time between two successive culminations of the Sun.

Mean Sun: The fictitious Sun which is used as a timekeeper moving along the Equator, as opposed to the True Sun which moves along the Ecliptic (q.v.).

Mean Solar Time: A measurement of time based on the motion of the Mean Sun.

M.C./Medium Coeli (Midheaven): The highest point of the Ecliptic (q.v.) culminating.

Meridian: A great circle which passes through the North and South Poles of the Earth, intersecting the Equator at right angles. Meridians are lines of longitude and are measured from the meridian that passes through Greenwich (0°), east and west. On the celestial sphere (q.v.), meridians connect the north and the south celestial poles and intersect the Celestial Equator at right angles. Celestial meridians are lines of right ascension and are measured from the meridian passing through the First Point of Aries (0°) (q.v.) eastward through 360°. The observer's meridian is a great circle passing through the zenith and the north and south points of the horizon, and each star appears to cross or transit this meridian twice a day (at upper and lower culmination).

Meteor: Small extra-terrestrial particle which burns up in the Earth's atmosphere as a streak of light. Meteors normally arrive in the form of showers.

Midnight Sun: Term used to describe the Sun when it is visible above the horizon at midnight and is circumpolar, north of the Arctic circle, or south of the Antarctic circle.

Milky Way: Faint luminous band of light crossing the sky and forming part of our Galaxy. It consists of millions of faint stars, passing in a great circle across the sky through the constellations Sagittarius, Scorpio, Scutum, Aquila, Vulpecula, Cygnus, Lacerta, Cepheus, Cassiopeia, Perseus, Auriga, Gemini, Monoceros and Canis Major (all visible from Britain). It continues through the constellations Argo, Crux, Norma, Ara (in the southern sky). The Milky Way is uneven in width and brightness, being widest and brightest in the region from Aquila through to Crux, because this is where the centre of the Milky Way Galaxy lies. Conversely, the more northern parts of the band are fainter and narrower, particularly around Monoceros, Gemini and Auriga.

Nadir: The point in the heavens that is directly opposite the zenith (q.v.).

Nebula: A cloud of gas in deep space. External galaxies are sometimes called spiral nebulae.

Neutrons: Sub-atomic particles carrying no electric charge, occupying the centres of atoms with protons. Both protons and neutrons are each 1,840 times more massive than an electron.

Node: The nodes of the Moon's orbit circle around the Ecliptic once in 18½ years (the Saros cycle [q.v.]), and because the positions of the nodes determine the timing of eclipses, there is an 18½-year cycle of eclipses.

Nodes: The two points of intersection of the orbit of a planet, a comet or of the Moon, to the Ecliptic (q.v.). The point of intersection where the orbit is northbound is called the *ascending* or *North Node*, and the intersection where the orbit is southbound is the *descending* or *South Node.*

Nova: A star which appears to brighten dramatically in a very short period (a few days or weeks) and subsequently fades again. Novae are unstable stars near to the end of their lifetimes. Supernovae are really brilliant novae which outshine the planets but which are quite rare (in the past 1,000 years, three have been visible in our part of the galaxy, in the years 1054, 1572 and 1604), although they may also occur from time to time in more distant parts of the galaxy.

Nutation: Effect produced by the Moon on the Earth's axis causing it to oscillate in circles a few hundred feet in diameter.

Obliquity of the Ecliptic: The angle between the plane of the Ecliptic (q.v.) and the plane of the Celestial Equator (q.v.), currently equal to 23°27′. This angle does not remain constant but alters slowly by about 2°-3° over a period of about 40,000 years as the tilt of the Earth's axis changes.

Occultation: Occurs when one astronomical body passes in front of another and obscures it. Normally, this term is used to describe the Moon passing in front of a star or planet.

Opposition: An aspect formed when two planets or bodies are 180° apart. Planets outside the orbit of Mars come to opposition with the Sun at intervals of just over a year, and the Moon is in opposition to the Sun when it is Full.

Orbit: The path taken by an astronomical body (star, planet, satellite or comet) around a more massive body. This path is the result of a balance between two opposing forces, the gravitational attraction between the two objects and the centrifugal force pushing them apart. The resulting orbit may be elliptical, or if the two bodies are only passing in space, one of the two open curves, parabola or hyperbola.

Orbital inclination: The angle at which a comet's or planet's orbit is inclined to the Ecliptic (q.v.) This varies from 0° to 180° where a comet is moving directly retrograde to the Sun's apparent motion.

Oxygen: One of the constituent gases of the Earth's atmosphere.

Pallas: One of the largest of the asteroids (q.v.), second to be discovered (1802). Orbits the Sun once every 1,684 days.

Parallax: Apparent displacement of a distant object compared to more distant objects, when the observer's light of sight is changed. This phenomenon is used to determine the distances of stars and planets.

Parallels: Normally refers to parallels of declination; circles parallel to the Celestial Equator (q.v.).

Parsec: Unit of measurement of distance to the stars. It is the distance at which the radius of the Earth's orbit would subtend an angle of one second of arc, or 3.26 light years.

Penumbra: Half-shadow cast by a planet or by the Moon or Earth. In this region the Sun is partially obscured. The term penumbra is normally used to describe the portion of the half shadow which is cast by the Earth onto the Moon during a lunar eclipse.

Perigee: Occurs where the Moon or an artificial Earth satellite is at its nearest point, in its orbit, to the Earth.

Perihelion: Occurs when the Earth or another planet is at its nearest point, in its orbit, to the Sun.

Phases: Differences in illumination of the Moon or a planet, caused by alterations in position relative to the Sun and to the Earth. The Moon, and the inferior planets, Mercury and Venus, show the whole cycle of phases, but the superior planets beyond the Earth's orbit appear as only Full or slightly less than Full.

Photosphere: Luminous surface of the Sun.

Planet: A body, other than a comet or meteor, that revolves around the Sun as the centre and with it forms the solar system.

Polar Circle: A parallel circle on the celestial sphere or on the Earth, 23½° from the pole. The 'midnight sun' is observed from this latitude at the time of the solstice (Summer); at the Winter solstice, the Sun is only at the horizon at noon.

Polaris (Pole Star): North Star, a bright 2nd magnitude yellow giant star at a distance of 600 light years. At present, this star is within 1° of the North Celestial Pole, but will cease to be the Pole Star a few hundred years from now (see Fig. 15), due to the precession of the Equinoxes (q.v.; see Fig. 14).

Pole/Pole Elevation: The two points on the Earth's surface which are intersected by its axis (North and South Poles). The North and South Celestial Poles are the two points where the Earth's axis, extended into space, intersects the celestial sphere. Polar elevation is the height of the pole above the horizon as observed from any place and is equal to the terrestrial latitude.

Precession: Slow oscillation of the Earth's axis about a mean position. Each pole appears to trace out a circle of radius 23½° in the sky, which causes different pole stars to come directly above the poles, in a cycle lasting 25,800 years. Precession results in a gradual advance of the equinoctial point (Vernal Equinox — q.v.) westward at the rate of fifty seconds of arc per year. Caused by the pole of the Equator revolving round the pole of the Ecliptic (q.v.). (See Fig. 14.)

Prime Meridian: The Greenwich meridian which is the zero point for measurements of longitude on the Earth.

Prime Vertical: The great circle that intersects the horizon at the east and west points passing through the zenith (q.v.) at right angles to the meridian (q.v.).

Prominences: Outbursts of hot gas from the Sun's surface.

Proper motion: Motion of a star across the celestial sphere over years or centuries, measured relative to other stars. Proper motion is the transverse component of a star's true velocity through space and is measured perpendicular to the line of sight.

Protons: Sub-atomic, positively charged particles occupying the centres (nuclei) of atoms.

Pulsar: Very small, rapidly spinning star which sends out regular pulses of radio waves.

Quadrant: Quarter-section of a circle (90° arc). An astronomical instrument that was used to measure the positions of stars.

Quadrature: 90° distance; a square aspect.

Quasar: A very distant and very faint bluish starlike object (quasi-stellar object) much more powerful than an ordinary galaxy and much more distant than an optical galaxy. Powerful source of radio waves.

Radial velocity: The radial component of a star's true velocity through space, measured parallel to the line of sight (toward or away from the Earth). Also used to describe the motions of planets or galaxies.

Radian: Angle which is subtended, at a circle's centre, by the arc which is of equal length to the circle's radius. One radian = 57.296

degrees, and therefore the circumference of the circle = 2π radians.

Radiant: Apparent point of origin of a stream of meteors (shooting stars). As a result of perspective, the meteors appear to diverge from that point.

Radiation: Electromagnetic energy in the form of waves (e.g. light waves).

Radius: Most astronomical objects are not quite spherical but have a greater diameter through their equators than through their poles. There are two types of radius, the equatorial and the polar. The difference between the two, compared to the equatorial radius, gives a measure of the planet's oblateness (deviation from perfect sphericity). The Earth's oblateness is $^1/_{297}$.

Red shift: Phenomenon observed in the spectrum of a receding galaxy. The galaxy's recession shifts the spectral lines toward the red end.

Red Spot: Semi-permanent feature in Jupiter's atmosphere. It is 20,000 miles long by 7,000 miles wide and appears to change colour from time to time over different shades of red. It may be seen in a small telescope.

Relativity (Einstein's Theory of): There are two theories of relativity which were derived by Albert Einstein, the Special Theory (1905) and the General Theory (1916). The Special Theory predicted the non-existence of absolute frames of reference for the measurement of the speeds of astronomical objects through space (particularly galaxies), and the General Theory predicted results for accelerating systems taking into account the factor of force.

Retrograde motion: The apparent westward motion of a body which is contrary to the usual or direct motion. When the Earth 'overtakes' a superior planet (q.v.) near to its opposition with the Sun, that superior planet will, for a time, appear to drift westward against the stars, in distinction to its normal eastward movement. (See Fig. 13.)

Right Ascension (R.A.): A co-ordinate of the Equator system (q.v.) measured from the First Point of Aries (q.v.) eastward to a point which rises with a planet or part of the Ecliptic (q.v.). The distance from 0° Aries along the Equator. R.A. is the celestial counterpart of longitude and is measured in hours and minutes or in degrees and minutes.

Rising and setting: As the Earth rotates on its axis so the various astronomical bodies — the Sun, Moon, planets, stars, etc — will appear to rise and set once a day. Stars and planets are not usually visible when they are within about 2° or so of the horizon because of the dust and haze in the Earth's atmosphere. The place of rising or setting depends upon the object's declination: the greater the declination, the further north or south is the point of rising or setting. Stars which never rise or set and remain perpetually above the horizon are termed circumpolar stars.

Saros cycle: Cycle of eclipses, lasting about 18 years (223 lunations) caused by the slow westward motion of the nodes (q.v.) of the lunar orbit. After 223 lunations, eclipses occur in the same months again.

Satellite: A body which is in orbit around a planet. The Moon is a satellite of the Earth, and there are also artificial satellites. Many of the other planets also have satellites.

Seasons: These occur on any planet whose axis is tilted to the perpendicular plane of its orbit. The Earth's seasons: spring, summer, autumn, winter in each hemisphere alternately are separated by the two solstices and two equinoxes. At the solstices, one or other of the poles is at its maximum inclination toward the Sun, and at the equinoxes the Earth's axis is in line with the day-night terminator and day and night are of equal length over the globe. (See Fig. 19.)

Second of arc: $^{1}/_{3600}$ part of a degree. 60 seconds of arc (60″) = 1 minute of arc (1′), and 60 minutes of arc = 1 degree.

Second of time: $^{1}/_{3600}$ part of an hour. The second can be determined very accurately using quartz and atomic clocks.

Sextant: Astronomical instrument which was used to measure the altitude of the Sun, and is a one-sixth section of a circle, or 60°.

Sidereal Time/Day/Year: Time based upon the rotation of the Earth with respect to the stars; time between two successive culminations of the Vernal Equinox. A Sidereal Year is the period of the Sun's apparent revolution with respect to the stars and coincides with the Earth's revolution around the Sun.

Solar system: The collection of planets and their satellites, the Earth and Moon, asteroids, comets and meteors, all of which revolve around the Sun. Because the diameters of the planets are so small compared to the distances separating them, the solar system is mainly empty space.

Solar Time/Day/Year: The time used for civil purposes based upon the daily motion of the Sun. Solar Day is the time interval between two successive culminations of the apparent Sun; the average value of the Apparent Solar Day is termed the Mean Solar Day; the Solar Year is the Tropical Year (year of the seasons).

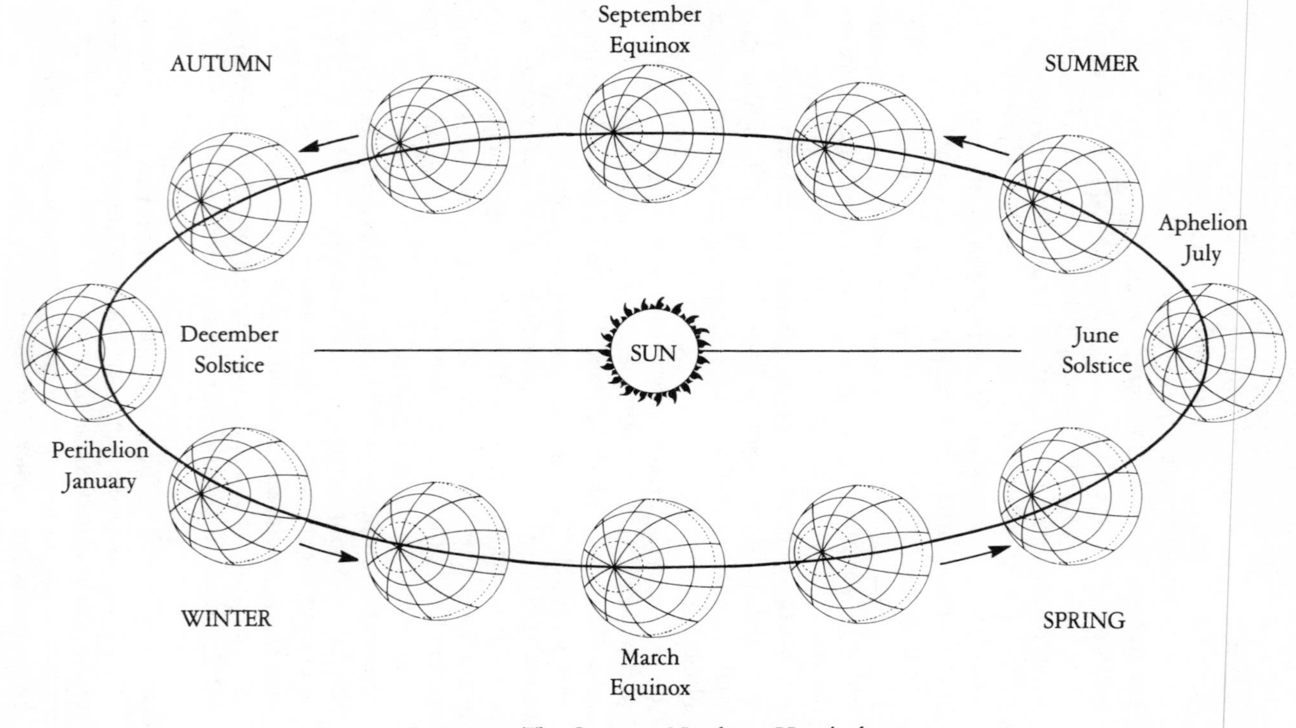

Figure 19 The Seasons: Northern Hemisphere.

Solar Wind: A stream of electrically charged particles moving out from the Sun into space.

Solstices: Points in the Earth's orbit where the Sun's declination is at its maximum of 23½° (north in June, south in December) on or about 21 June and 22 December. The Sun is then farthest from the Equator and appears to 'stand still'.

Space: Term used to describe the vacuum through which astronomical bodies move. It is not quite a vacuum, because there are stray particles such as meteoroids and dust grains, and also different types of radiations from the Sun and stars.

Spectral classification: Stars are classified according to which type of spectrum they possess, the spectral type being related to the star's colour and surface temperature.

Spectroscope: Device used to analyse the spectrum of the Sun, a star, nebula, galaxy, etc.

Spectrum: Rainbow colours obtained when white light is passed through a prism or through a spectroscope. Each star has its own particular spectrum, with dark Fraunhofer lines corresponding to absorption of particular wavelengths of light by various elements or compounds.

Spiral Nebulae: External galaxy with spiral arms.

Standard Meridian: The meridian adopted for time zones.

Standard Time: The local civil time of a standard meridian, which is the time kept for all places within a particular zone; the difference between zones is normally 1 hour or 15° of longitude reckoned from Greenwich.

Sundial: Device used to indicate the time from the shadow cast by a stick (gnomon) onto a horizontal (or sometimes vertical) plate. The plate has the hours marked on it, and the gnomon points due north (or south) to the Celestial Pole. Time measured by sundials is Apparent Solar Time or True Sun Time and differs from Mean Solar Time, the difference being termed the Equation of time. This equation varies throughout the year from 0 to 16 minutes.

Sunspot: Dark blemish on the Sun's surface which is associated with magnetic fields.

Supergiant: The most luminous stars in space. Some supergiants have absolute magnitudes of −5 to −7 and are tens of thousands of times more luminous than our Sun (e.g. Rigel, Deneb, Antares, Beta Centauri).

Superior conjunction: Occurs when any planet passes the Sun on its far side. The planet is then invisible.

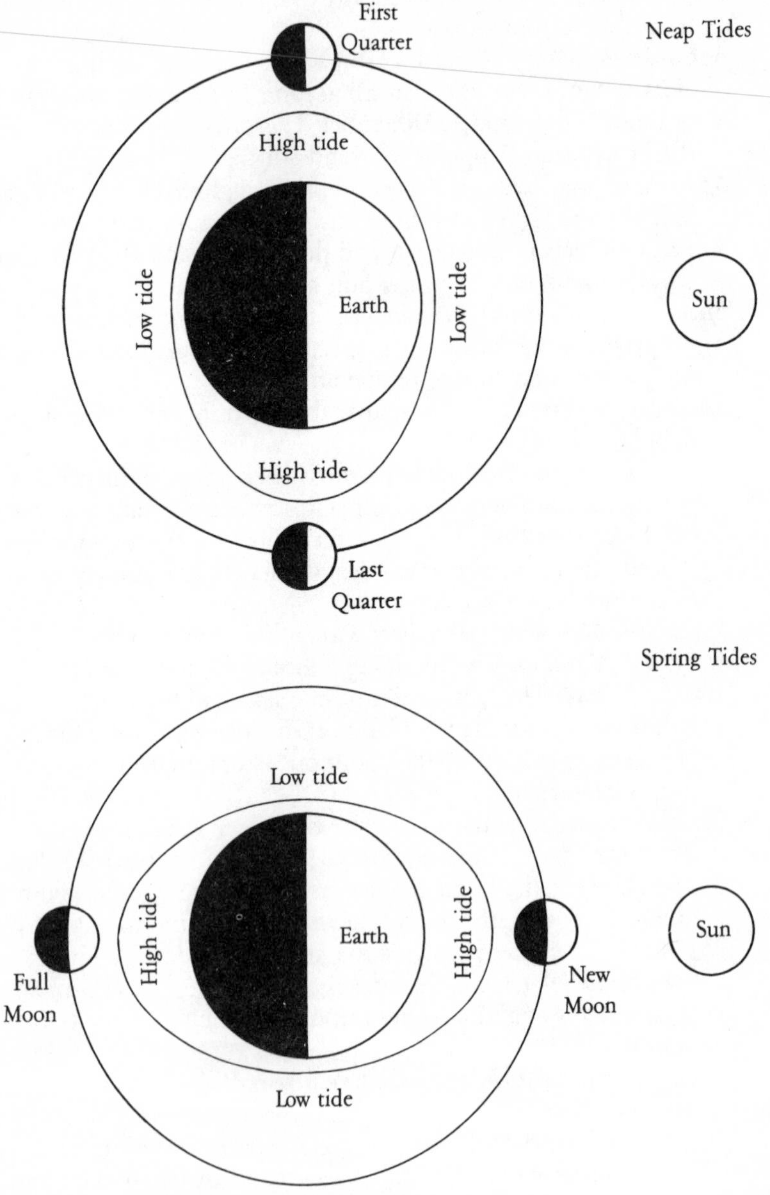

Figure 20 The Tides.

Superior planet: A planet whose orbit lies outside the Earth's (Mars, Jupiter, Saturn, Uranus, Neptune, and Pluto).

Supernova: An exploding star. Ordinary novae experience intermittent outbursts but return to their previous state, but supernovae undergo a complete disruption.

Synodic month: The interval between two successive Full Moons; the length of the synodic month is 29.5306 days.

Syzygy: Occurs when the Earth, Sun and Moon are all in a straight line, that is at every New Moon and Full Moon.

Terminator: The line separating the illuminated and dark sides of the Moon or a planet.

Tides: Periodic rising and falling of the sea level by gravitational attraction of the Sun and the Moon. The Moon's gravitational pull is about twice that of the Sun, so that at New and Full Moon, the tides are much higher because the Sun and Moon are pulling together (Spring tide). Conversely, at First and Last Quarter, the Sun and Moon are pulling at right angles and so the tides are much lower (Neap tide). High tide in the open ocean takes place near upper and lower culmination of the Moon, twice a day, and the two low tides take place six hours later. Around the coasts and rivers, however, the tides are delayed. (See Fig. 20.)

Titan: One of Saturn's satellites, the largest one (3,100 miles in diameter). Orbits the planet at a distance of 760,000 miles from the centre, once every 15 days 22 hours 41 minutes.

Transit: (a) The Sun, Moon, planets and stars all cross the meridian (q.v.) due south once a day. This crossing of the meridian is called a transit. The Sun transits the meridian at local noon. (b) Transits of Mercury and Venus. These two planets on rare occasions appear to cross the Sun's disk when their orbits are in line at the right time. (c) Jupiter's satellites. These often pass in front of Jupiter's disk as they revolve, and such transits can be seen in a small telescope. (See also page 118.)

Triton: Largest of Neptune's two satellites, about 2,500 miles in diameter. It orbits the planet at 219,000 miles from the centre once every 5 days 21 hours.

Tropical year: The year of the seasons; the time required for the Sun to complete one revolution with respect to the Vernal Equinox (First Point of Aries) (q.v.).

Tropics: Region on the Earth's surface where the Sun can be overhead. It is bounded by the Tropic of Cancer and the Tropic of Capricorn at latitudes respectively 23½° north and 23½° south. These two parallels of latitude are equal to the inclination of the Ecliptic (23½°).

Twilight: Time between full daylight and complete night, lasting for about one hour early morning and evening. Astronomical twilight occurs when the Sun is less than 18° below the horizon.

Ultra-violet: Part of the electromagnetic spectrum, just beyond the visible light, and with a shorter wavelength than visible light. Ultra-violet light is dangerous but is mostly blocked off by the Earth's atmosphere.

Umbra: Full shadow cast by an object.

Universal Time (U.T.): Greenwich Mean Time reckoned from mean midnight on the meridian of Greenwich. Used universally in astronomical observations.

Universe: General term used to describe the space which contains the galaxies. The observable universe is about 10,000 million light years in radius.

Variable star: A star which shines with an unsteady light, which fluctuates in intensity.

Vernal Equinox (First Point of Aries): The point of intersection between the Ecliptic (q.v.) and the Equator (q.v.) which the Sun crosses on or about 21 March each year. The point from which Right Ascension (q.v.) and Celestial Longitude (q.v.) are measured.

Vertical circles: Two circles at 90° to one another, one passing through the horizon's north and south points, the zenith and nadir (that is, the observer's meridian), and the other passing through the horizon's east and west points, the zenith and nadir.

Weight: The mass of a body × acceleration of gravity. On earth, this gravitational acceleration is equal to 10 metres per second, per second (32 feet per second, per second), but the weight of objects depends upon the mass of the attracting planet. In orbit or in free fall, objects are weightless.

Year: There are several types of year. The term is used to describe the period of revolution of a planet about the Sun (Earth's year = 365¼ days). The Sidereal year and the tropical year are the two types of year which have special significance, but astronomers also deal with the anomalistic year, the eclipse year and the Besselian year.

Zenith: The point on the celestial sphere (q.v.) directly above the observer, 90° distance from the horizon.

Zodiac: The band about 8° on either side of the Ecliptic (q.v.). Within this circle the Sun, Moon and planets, except Pluto, are always found. The zodiac contains twelve constellations which are no longer aligned with their corresponding signs because of precession. For astrological purposes, the zodiac is divided into 12 signs of 30°.

Zodiacal light: A faint luminous glow extending some distance along the Ecliptic (q.v.), visible either after sunset or before sunrise.

2.
ASTROLOGY: THE TECHNICAL BASIS

Time of Birth

The calculation of any astrological chart is dependent upon certain essential data. These are: *date, time* and *place*, without which an accurate chart cannot be calculated.

Date

The date of birth does not usually present any difficulties, except for births in those countries which did not change from the Julian (Old Style) calendar to the Gregorian (New Style) calendar until the early years of this century. In these instances, the date given needs to be checked as to whether it is the original date given in the Old Style reckoning or whether it has been corrected to the New Style calendar. The error between the two calendars is twelve days for the nineteenth century and thirteen days for the present century, so that a birth date given in the Old Style reckoning would need twelve days added (nineteenth-century birth) in order to coincide with the current calendar (Gregorian). Likewise, twentieth-century birth dates need thirteen days added. Information concerning calendar dates and changes can be found in any good reference work which specializes in time changes (see References).

Time

The time of birth is normally given as the clock time which was in operation at the date and place of birth. Here there can be difficulties because of the common practice of referring to the time in use at a particular locality as Local time. It is true that the time is local for that particular place, but local time, in a technical sense, is other than what is normally understood as local time. So far as astrological charting is concerned, there are various types of time, of which any one kind may be quoted when the birth data are given. Of these, the most common are: Greenwich Mean Time; Standard Time; Daylight Saving (Summer) Time; Local Mean Time and *Local Time.*

Greenwich Mean Time (G.M.T.) is the local mean time of the meridian of Greenwich. The difference between Greenwich Mean Time and Local Mean Time at any instant of time, is the longitude expressed in time (15° = 1 hour). When the birth time is given in G.M.T., no amendments to the time are required if using a Greenwich-based ephemeris.

Standard Time is a system of time reckoning based upon time zones, using a central meridian either east or west from the Prime Meridian of Greenwich. Places east of Greenwich have standard times in advance of the Greenwich time, places west have standard times which are slow on Greenwich. Standard time, is in effect, the local mean time of the meridian that has been adopted for a definite zone or area. All places within that zone show the same standard time, even though their actual local mean time may differ by several minutes.

In large countries such as the United States of America, or Russia, several standard time zones are in operation, and these range from 3½ to 8 hours in North America and from 3 to 13 hours in the Soviet Republics.

Daylight Saving Time (Summer Time) relates to advancing the clock in the early spring (normally by 1 hour), until the Autumn. This practice was introduced during the First World War and has continued each year, but the amount of the advance and the period of its duration has varied, particularly during the war years. Many countries now use Daylight Saving Time, and if the birth time is given in this time, then the appropriate amount of the advance must be *deducted* to obtain the standard time of the country. During the Second World War, North America advanced all time zones and used War Time. In Britain, Double British Summer Time operated for certain months of the year. For all charting, it is essential to consult reliable reference works that list time changes.

Local Mean Time (Mean Solar) is the mean solar time for a definite meridian and differs by four minutes for every one degree of longitude. The Local Mean Time at any place depends upon its distance east or west of Greenwich. For example, when it is noon at Greenwich, the Local Mean Time at New York would be 4 hours 55 minutes and 48 seconds less than the time at Greenwich, i.e. 7.04.12 a.m., because the New York longitude is 73°57′ west which, when expressed in time, is 4.55.48. The Local Mean time at any place is found by expressing its longitude in time (15° = 1 hour) and adding to, or subtracting from, the Greenwich time, depending on whether the place is east or west of Greenwich.

Local Time

It follows from what has been stated that the term 'local time' can be ambiguous because a birth time can be stated as 'local time', which would normally be the clock time, but this clock time could be recording Standard Time and/or Daylight Saving Time. Unless information is given to the contrary, it can be assumed that when the term 'local time' is used, it refers to the clock time in operation at that particular locality.

Place on Earth

Time and place go hand in hand so far as charting is concerned. Neither is much use without the other. It is important whether the place in question is New York, Paris or even some remote island in the Pacific. If the same moment of time is taken, say noon G.M.T. at London, 1.1.84, that moment will have a different astrological significance for New York or the Pacific island. The Earth is a rotating sphere, and the aspect of the heavens change during each twenty-four hours, the change being greater or lesser depending upon the point from which the heavens are viewed. At the Equator all bodies rise vertically, while at the Poles, certain bodies neither rise nor set; i.e. they are circumpolar.

The zodiacal positions — as given in the ephemeris — apply worldwide and if, for example, the Sun is at 10° Capricorn on the 1.1.84 at noon at London, its zodiacal position is the same for New York, the Pacific or any other place in the world at that particular time. The imaginary circle of the zodiac contains all the planets including the Sun and Moon (planets in signs), and their positions are common to all the Earth. When we consider the planet's mundane (house) positions, we realize that as every place on Earth has its own horizon circle and plane and therefore its own 'set of houses', a chart will appear differently for various places although calculated for the same time. This difference, as regards houses, can be illustrated by the data already quoted, namely 1.1.84, noon G.M.T. At London, the Sun at noon is inthe 10th house — it is culminating — the sidereal time at noon being 18.41.20 which gives an Ascendant of 23° Aries: M.C. 10° Capricorn: Sun 10° Capricorn. At New York, five hours earlier, the Sun is about to rise, while at Delhi, five and half hours

Latitude

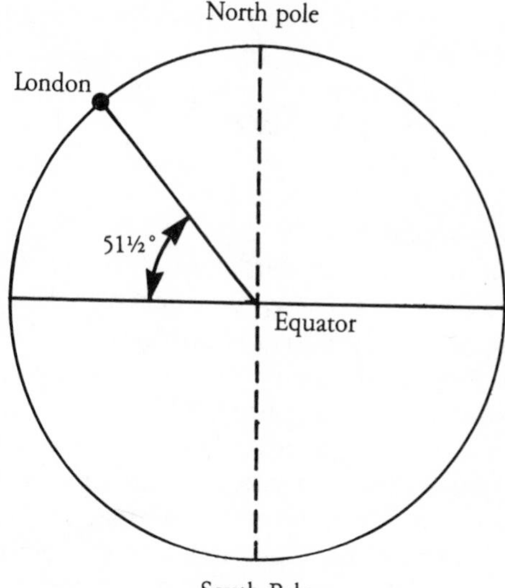

Latitude of a place is equal to its angular distance north or south of the Equator, that is 0° (Equator) to 90° N or S (poles).

Longitude

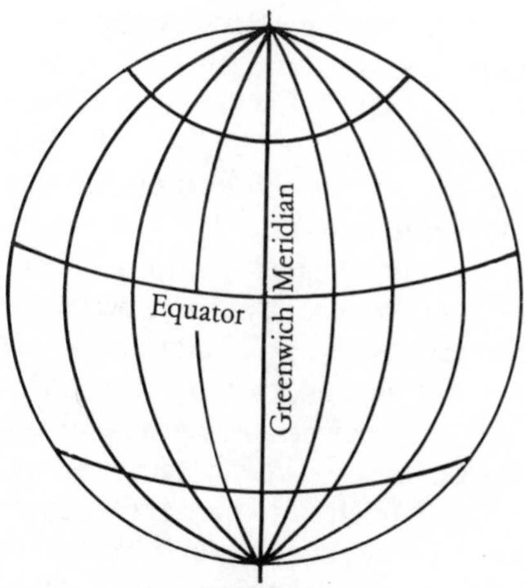

Longitude of a place is equal to its angular distance east or west of the Greenwich meridian, that is 0° (Greenwich) to 180° E or W.

Figure 21

later than G.M.T. noon, it is setting. The house position of a planet is governed by how the houses 'cut' the zodiac, and this apportionment is dependent upon time and place. We therefore, have two sets of locations: (1) planets in signs, and (2) planets in houses, the latter being determined according to the locality of birth.

Latitude and Longitude (See Fig. 21)

The location of any place on Earth can be found if we know its geographical co-ordinates. The great circle which divides the Earth into two hemispheres is the Equator (latitude 0°) and measurement either north or south of this parallel from 0° to 90° is indicated on maps by horizontal lines. Longitude, which is indicated on maps by vertical lines, defines the distance from the Greenwich meridian (Longitude 0°) and is measured in degrees and minutes from 0°-180° either east or west. In the early days of navigation, latitude could be found by measuring the angle between the Pole Star and the horizon, but longitude which is related to time, posed greater problems, particularly as the radius of the Earth was not known. The North Pole, when extended to the heavens, cuts the celestial sphere, and this point is the Celestial North Pole, around which the stars appear to rotate. Latitude, is in effect, the angle between the Equator and the vertical and also the angle between the Celestial North Pole and the horizon. By knowing our latitude, we can determine our position either north or south. The Greenwich meridian (0°) is the zero point for the measurement of longitude. As longitude and time are closely connected, we can define the time at any locality by converting the longitude into time (15° = 1 hour). Alternatively, by converting the time into degrees and minutes, we can determine the longitude of the locality, provided we know the Greenwich time.

If, for example, the time in east longitude is 9.00 p.m., and it is Greenwich noon at this time, then 9×15°=135°=longitude. At 135° west longitude at Greenwich noon, the time is 135° over 15=9 hours less than the Greenwich time, because the longitude is west, i.e. 3.00 a.m. The time referred to here is the *apparent solar time* (see page 82), which is the time required by the Sun to make two consecutive meridian transits. If we were using a sundial which, for instance, indicated 3.00 p.m., and we also knew that at the same instant a Greenwich sundial showed 5.00 p.m., we would know that the two hours difference indicated that our longitude was 30° west (2×15°), as the time indicated was earlier than the Greenwich time. Provided we know our own time and the Greenwich time, we can

WEST — GREENWICH NOON — EAST

	SLOW ON GREENWICH A.M.													FAST ON GREENWICH P.M.											
Degs. of Long.	180	165	150	135	120	105	90	75	60	45	30	15	0	15	30	45	60	75	90	105	120	135	150	165	180
Long. Equiv. Hours	12	11	10	9	8	7	6	5	4	3	2	1	0	1	2	3	4	5	6	7	8	9	10	11	12
Standard Time	Mid-Night	1	2	3	4	5	6	7	8	9	10	11	Noon	1	2	3	4	5	6	7	8	9	10	11	Mid-Night

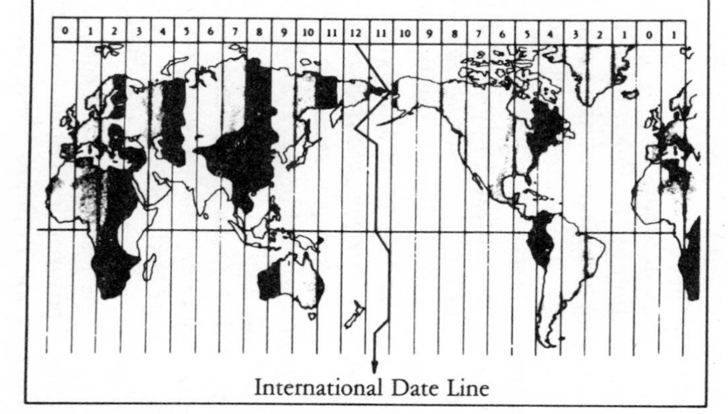

Figure 22 The International Date Line

measure longitude. The problem, in the early days of navigation, was that the Greenwich time could not be ascertained, and it was not until the invention of the marine chronometer by Harrison in the eighteenth century, that the difficulties connected with time and longitude at sea were finally resolved.

Sun Time — Star Time

To an astrologer, time is of the utmost importance, for without a reliable time of birth, a detailed assessment of a chart and its potentialities is difficult to obtain. In discussing time, in so far as astrological calculation is concerned, it is sufficient to deal with the kinds of time normally employed in charting.

The rotation of the Earth upon its axis, with reference to the apparent angular motion of the heavenly bodies, is the basis of time measurement. A day can be defined as the interval between two successive transits of the same object over a particular meridian. In the case of the Sun, it is known as a *Solar Day*, or if a star or the First Point of Aries, a *Sidereal Day*. A great circle (*the observer's Celestial Meridian)*, passing through the north and south points of the *Horizon* and the point directly overhead (*Zenith*), coincide with the observer's *Meridian of Longitude*. The moment at which a celestial body or point is on the meridian of the observer is known as the *culmination, transit* or *meridian passage* of that body or point.

There are two methods of time-keeping based on the rotation of the Earth: (1) *Solar Time,* which is kept with reference to the Sun; (2) *Sidereal Time,* which is measured with reference to the stars. The time required by the Sun to make two consecutive meridian transits is called an *Apparent Solar Day*. This varies with the time of year, and so it is necessary to define the *Mean Solar Day* as the average solar day. The variations in the length of the day are due to two causes: (a) the Sun does not move along the Ecliptic at a uniform rate, due to the varying distance of the Earth from the Sun during the year; and (b) the Sun moves in the Ecliptic and not along the Celestial Equator. Its celestial longitude (measurement along the Ecliptic) is, in general, different from its *Right Ascension* (measurement along the Celestial Equator). Revolution causes the Sun to appear about 1° of arc to the east each day, and therefore the Earth must turn an additional degree of arc (or four minutes of time) to bring the Sun to the meridian the following day. To overcome the variations of the *Apparent or True Sun's* motion, a fictitious *Mean Sun* is used which moves eastward in the Celestial Equator at a uniform speed equal to the average rate of the *True Sun in the Ecliptic.* The time between two successive lower transits of the Mean Sun is defined as the *Mean Solar or Civil Day* which is approximately four minutes longer than a Sidereal Day. Due to the non-uniform motion of the Earth relative to the Sun because of the elliptical nature of the Earth's orbit, and because the real Sun moves along the Ecliptic, whereas the Mean Sun moves along the Celestial Equator, Apparent Solar Time and Mean Time differ from each other. This difference, termed the *Equation of Time,* varies throughout the year, ranging from 0 to 16 minutes. Since it is essential to have an invariable unit of time, the Mean Solar Day is used as the practical unit of time, and clocks are regulated so as to record twenty-four hours in a Mean Solar Day.

Sidereal time (S.T.) is star time and is reckoned by the transit of the First Point of Aries. A sidereal day is the time interval between two successive transits of this point. As the Sun crosses the meridian four minutes later each day, the solar and sidereal days differ. Sidereal time measures the rotation of the Earth relative to the First Point of Aries (Vernal Equinox) and is identical with the Right Ascension of the Meridian. During the course of a Sidereal day, the Earth rotates on its axis in a period of 23 hours 56 minutes 04 seconds of mean time (civil time), and for an observer located at a particular longitude, the sidereal day is equivalent to the apparent rotation period of the celestial sphere. This rotation period can be determined by measuring the interval between two successive upper transits of the First Point of Aries or of a given star across the meridian. Sidereal time at any instant is the hour angle of the Vernal Equinox expressed in time, or in other words, the angle between an observer's meridian and a body or point measured westward from the meridian in a direction parallel to the Celestial Equator. Sometime during the course of twenty-four hours, the First Point of Aries will be on the meridian, and the time of day when this occurs will depend upon the longitude of the observer and the time of year. When the First Point of Aries is on the meridian, its hour angle is zero and the sidereal time zero hours. The constant rotation of the celestial sphere increases this angle, and at, say, 60 degrees, 4 hours have elapsed, and the sidereal time is 4 hours. At 90 degrees, 6 hours and so on until, after 24 hours, the First Point of Aries once again returns to the meridian.

Sidereal time is always *local*; it cannot be otherwise. The difference between Local Sidereal time and Greenwich Sidereal Time corresponds to the longitude of the observer expressed in time, an hour being equivalent to 15 degrees, since the Earth rotates through

15 degrees per hour. Places on the same meridian always have the same local sidereal time. Sidereal time at Greenwich is local for the Greenwich meridian and for all places on that meridian, irrespective of latitude. Other places on Earth, not on the Greenwich meridian, would have a local sidereal time differing from the Greenwich sidereal time, and this difference would range from 0 to 24 hours sidereal time, depending on the longitude of the place either east or west of Greenwich. In determining the local sidereal time for a given time and place, the culminating degree of the Ecliptic and the degree rising can be found.

In astrological charting we therefore deal with two kinds of time, namely Sun time (Mean Solar Time) and star time (sidereal time).

Mean Time Correction

The difference between solar time and sidereal time results from the fact that, apart from spinning on its axis, the Earth also orbits the Sun once a year, and this results in the position of the Sun, against the background of distant stars, changing daily. If, for example, the Sun and a star cross the meridian at the same time, 24 sidereal hours later, the star will again cross the meridian, but, because the Earth has moved on in its orbit, it will take approximately 4 more minutes before the Sun is again on the meridian. The Earth makes a complete revolution around the Sun in one year, so the difference between solar time and sidereal time is exactly one day per year.

From the ephemeris, it will be seen that the sidereal time, as tabulated, appears to increase from day to day by about 3 minutes 56 seconds due to the fact that, in one mean solar day (24 hours of clock time), the rotating Earth turns through 24 hours 3 minutes 56½ seconds of sidereal time, to keep pace with the average daily motion of the fictitious Mean Sun. The difference between mean and sidereal time has to be allowed for, so, a correction (mean time correction) of 9.856 seconds per mean time hour has to be applied.

Chart Calculation

Although this work is designed primarily to assist those who already have some knowledge of astrology and its techniques, it may be useful to outline the basic procedures of natal charting.

An astrological chart is a diagram based on astronomical information which shows the 'pattern of the heavens' as it appears from Earth, for a specified time and place. It follows that a chart can be set up for any event occurring at a particular time and place and, when the event is the birth of a child, the chart is termed the natal or birth chart. Other astrological techniques such as mundane astrology, vocational astrology, electional astrology or comparison astrology all have 'natal' charts or 'foundation' charts.

Calculations

The essential data required for natal charting are the date, time and place of birth. The first step with any natal charting is to ascertain the Ascendant (rising degree), Midheaven (M.C.) and the cusps of the mundane houses, and these are dependent upon the local sidereal time at the birthplace. Next, the positions of the planets for the date and time of birth must be calculated, bearing in mind, that the date and time of birth must be expressed in the Greenwich date and time, if using a Greenwich-based ephemeris. Finally, the aspects and the other traditional astrological factors associated with natal charting are listed. The following examples illustrate the necessary steps for an accurately calculated birth chart:

Example No. 1

Birth data: Date: 15 November 1984; *Time:* 2.15 p.m. G.M.T.; *Place:* London, Lat. 51°32′N; Long. 00°00′

Working:

From Raphael's Ephemeris 1984:		*Hours*	*Mins*	*Secs.*
1. Sidereal time at noon 15 Nov.		15	39	01
2. Time from noon (birthtime)	+	2	15	00
3. Mean time correction 9.86 secs. per hour	+	0	00	22
4. Sidereal time at Greenwich at birth		17	54	23
5. Longitude equivalent		—	—	—
6. Local sidereal time at birth		17	54	23

1 = Sidereal time at noon at Greenwich, as listed in the ephemeris.

2 = The Greenwich time of birth, which in this case is 2.15 after noon. If Summer Time had been in operation, the birth time would have been 1.15 p.m. G.M.T., because the clock time of birth would have been one hour in advance of Greenwich time.

3 = The correction which has to be made at all times when converting mean time into sidereal time (see page 84).

5 = As sidereal time is always 'local' for a particular time and place, the difference between the Greenwich longitude (0°) and the longitude of the birthplace is converted into time (15° = 1 hour) and added or deducted, depending upon whether the place is east or west of Greenwich (see example calculation and page 80).

The local sidereal time of birth having been found, we can extract the Ascendant, Midheaven and cusps of the houses from the appropriate Tables of Houses for the latitude, or nearest thereto, of birth. In this case, the tables for London in Raphael's ephemeris give for a sidereal time of 17.54.23, 27° Pisces Ascendant, and 29° Sagittarius Midheaven. These are the nearest figures listed, but when exactness is required, interpolation is needed. The Tables of Houses list the tenth, eleventh and twelfth houses with the Ascendant (first) second and third houses. These six houses show the degree and sign which are on the cusp. The opposite six houses (fourth, fifth, sixth, seventh, eighth and ninth) will have the same degree but opposite sign. The Local sidereal time is the 'key' for finding what sign is rising, and how the Zodiac is 'distributed' on the various cusps.

Planetary Positions

The positions of the planets, including the Sun and Moon, are given in the ephemeris for Greenwich noon. As the example chart has a birthtime of 2.15 p.m., we require an apportionment of the daily motion in order to find the planets' positions at 2.15 p.m. The easiest way is to use a calculator or, failing that, diurnal logarithms as given on the last page of the ephemeris. As the birthtime is after noon, we take the daily motion from noon on the 15th to the 16th, as listed on page 28 of the ephemeris. Using a calculator, we can obtain a constant of 2.15 over 24, which equals 0.09375, and, by multiplying the daily motion by this constant, we obtain the motion which has occurred in 2 hours 15 minutes. This is added to the noon position of the planet, giving its position for the time required. If the planet is *retrograde*, the amount is deducted for a *p.m. time* but *added* for an *a.m. time.* Using our constant of 0.09375 we have:

Sun's daily motion 60′28″×0.09375 =	0°	5′	40″
Add to noon position	23	18	19
Sun's position — 2.15 p.m. G.M.T. — Scorpio	23	23	59

Moon's daily motion 13°48′26″ × constant	=	1	17	40
Add to noon position		13	12	19
Moon's position — 2.15 p.m. G.M.T. — Leo		14	29	59

The faster-moving planets (Mercury, Venus and Mars) whose positions can change, even in a couple of hours, need to be calculated in the same manner. The slower-moving planets (Jupiter, Saturn, Uranus, Neptune and Pluto) whose motion is comparatively slight, require little or no calculation, and their positions can be obtained by inspection. If using logarithms, the above calculations would be:

Sun's daily motion 60'28″ (1° nearest)	Log.	1.3802	
Time — 2.15 p.m.	Log.	1.0280	add
5′40″ = Log. 2.4050	nearest	2.4082	

Moon's daily motion 13°48′26″ (13°48′)	Log.	0.2403	
Time 2.15 p.m.	Log.	1.0280	add
1°17′40″ — Log. 1.2681	(nearest = 18′)	1.2683	

Charting for Places Abroad (Northern Hemisphere)

The procedure for calculating a chart other than for the Greenwich longitude entails making an adjustment for the longitude of the place of birth, in order to obtain the local sidereal time at that place.

Example No. 2

Birth data: Date: 15 November 1984; *Time:* 9.15 a.m. E.S.T.; *Place:* New York, Lat. 40°43′ N; Long. 73°57′ W.

New York Standard Time is 5 hours slow on Greenwich, therefore the equivalent in Greenwich Mean Time is 2.15 p.m.

Working:

From Raphael's Ephemeris — Greenwich Noon		*Hours*	*Mins*	*Secs.*
S.T. at noon 15 November 1984		15	39	01
G.M.T. interval from noon	+	2	15	00
Mean time correction 9.86 secs. per hour	+	0	00	22
S.T. at Greenwich at birth		17	54	23
Longitude equivalent — West 73°57′ over 15	–	4	55	48
Local sidereal time at birth		12	58	35

From Tables of Houses for New York: Ascendant 23° Sagittarius, M.C. 16° Libra.

In this example, the planets' positions are calculated for 2.15 p.m. G.M.T., as we are using a Greenwich-based ephemeris.

Example No. 3.
Birth data: Date: 15 November 1984; *Time:* 7.45 p.m. Indian Standard Time; *Place:* Delhi, Lat. 28°40′ N.; Long. 77°14′ E.

Indian Standard Time is 5 hours 30 minutes in advance of Greenwich, therefore the equivalent Greenwich Mean Time is 2.15 p.m.

Working:

From Raphael's Ephemeris — Greenwich Noon		*Hours*	*Mins*	*Secs.*
S.T. at noon 15 November 1984		15	39	01
G.M.T. interval from noon	+	2	15	00
Mean time correction	+	0	00	22
S.T. at Greenwich at birth		17	54	23
Longitude equivalent + East 77°14′ over 15	+	5	08	56
Local sidereal time at birth		23	03	19

From Tables of Houses for Delhi: Ascendant 29° Gemini, M.C. 14° Pisces. Planets' positions as at 2.15 p.m. G.M.T.

Charting for Southern Latitudes using Northern Latitude Tables: The Horizon Circle and Plane, along with the Ecliptic Circle and Plane, is the basis of the Houses. Every horizon circle and plane for places in the northern hemisphere has a correspondence with the *antipodal* place in the southern hemisphere. If we consider the horizon plane between the two antipodes as 'cutting' the earth into two equal parts, we have a common horizon with the southern hemisphere side of the plane complemental to that of the northern hemisphere.

The intersection of the planes and circles of the horizon and Ecliptic denote the Ascendant and Descendant points. With this common horizon, the southern hemisphere side of the plane is obverse from that of the northern hemisphere. The southern or northern hemisphere observer uses the same horizon but in an opposite manner. As the intersection of the horizon and Ecliptic denote the rising and setting points (Ascendant/Descendant), it follows that, if the Sun is rising above the horizon in the northern hemisphere, it will be setting on the *antipodal horizon* in the southern hemisphere. Whereas the northern hemisphere observer looks towards the south with regard to the Ecliptic above his horizon, the observer in the southern hemisphere looks northwards regarding the Ecliptic above his horizon. With regard to places within the Tropics (i.e. 23½° north or south), the time of day determines whether the observation is made northwards or southwards. It is only the antipodal places which have a correspondence with their northern hemisphere places. A place in the southern hemisphere on the same meridian of longitude as London, and at the same latitude, will not have an exact correspondence concerning the Ecliptic degree rising or setting for a definite time, because of the different horizon which would be cutting the Ecliptic. For example, 1 January 1984, at Latitude 51°32′ South, Longitude 0° (same as London), at noon, the Ascending degree and sign would be:

	Hours	*Mins*	*Secs.*
S.T. at noon Greenwich	18	41	20
Time from noon	—	—	—
Add 12 hours (southern latitudes)	12	00	00
	6	41	20

From Tables for London 6.41.20 =
7° Libra Ascendant: 9° Cancer M.C. Reverse signs which gives 7° Aries Ascendant: 9° Capricorn M.C. = degree and sign at southern latitude.

At London, the sidereal time at noon 18.41.20 gives an Ascendant of 23° Aries and the M.C. 9° Capricorn.

Due to the obliquity of the Ecliptic at an angle of 23½° to the Equator, some signs of it are to the north and some to the south of the Equator. As the Earth rotates, some signs ascend quickly (short ascension), while their opposites ascend slowly (long ascension). Therefore, signs which ascend quickly in one hemisphere will ascend slowly in the opposite hemisphere and vice versa. The southern hemisphere horizon, with regard to the Ecliptic, acts obversely to the northern hemisphere horizon. This affects the numerical values of the degrees of signs rising so that, for example, Aries will not rise over the southern hemisphere ascendant horizon in the same way as it rose over the London horizon twelve hours earlier. Aries will rise over the southern hemisphere horizon in the same way as Libra will rise over the London horizon. Libra rises at London, as shown in the example, by adding twelve hours to the given sidereal time, and this shows how Aries rises in the southern hemisphere in the same manner as Libra rises in the northern hemisphere, i.e. to the value of 7°. The reversal of signs Libra/Aries is a reversal back to an original. Although the numerical values of the degrees ascending are affected, the degree of the M.C. is not. If we consider an antipodal place to London, which is not only in the southern hemisphere, but also on the opposite side of the world (180° longitude either east or west), we have as an example:

New Moon: 22.12.84, 11.47 a.m. G.M.T. = 11.47 p.m. local time 22.12.84 at antipodal place.

At London:		*Hours*	*Mins*	*Secs.*
S.T. at noon G.M.T. 22.12.84		18	04	54
Time before noon	–	00	13	00
Mean time correction	–	00	00	02
S.T. at London at time of New Moon		17	51	52

Asc. 25° Pisces: M.C. 28° Sagittarius.

At Antipodal place:	*Hours*	*Mins.*	*Secs.*
S.T. at London at time of New Moon	17	51	52
Longitude Equiv. 180° over 15 (East +)	12	00	00
	5	51	52*
Add 12 hours (southern latitudes)	12	00	00
and reverse signs	17	51	52

*When sum exceeds 24 hours, subtract 24.

From Tables of Houses for London 17.51.52. S.T. = Asc. 25° Pisces: M.C. 28° Sagittarius: Reverse signs = Asc. 25° Virgo: M.C. 28° Gemini = degree and sign at southern latitude.

Summarizing the procedure for southern latitude charts, we have:

1. Find the Sidereal Time (S.T.) which is equivalent to the local time of birth.
2. Add or subtract twelve hours to this S.T.
3. From Tables for Northern Latitudes, take the latitude nearest to the birth latitude and extract the S.T. as found in (2).
4. Reverse the signs, but use the same degrees as found with S.T. in (2).
5. Calculate the planets' places for the Greenwich time of birth, if using a Greenwich-based ephemeris.

Example No. 1
Birth data: Date: 1 January 1984; *Time:* 10.00 p.m. Standard Time; Lat. 43°54′ S; Long. 171°46′E. Standard Time 12 hours in advance of G.M.T. — 10.00 a.m. G.M.T.

Working:

		Hours	*Mins*	*Secs.*
S.T. at noon G.M.T. 1.1.84		18	41	20
Time before noon (12.00–10.00 a.m.)	less	2	00	00
Mean time correction	less	0	00	20
S.T. at Greenwich at birth		16	41	00
Longitude Equiv. 171°46′ over 15	East +	11	27	04
Local S.T. at birth		4	08	04
Add 12 hours (southern latitude)		12	00	00
		16	08	04

From Table of Houses 43°40′ (nearest)
16.08.04 S.T. Asc. 12° Aquarius: M.C. 4° Sagittarius.

Reverse signs = Asc. 12° Leo: M.C. 4° Gemini.

Example No. 2
Birth data: Date: 1 January 1984; *Time:* 10.00 p.m. Standard Time, Lat. 43°46′ S; Long. 171°46′ W. Standard Time is 12 hours slow on G.M.T. = 10.00 a.m. G.M.T. 2.1.84 = Greenwich time and date.

Working:

		Hours	*Mins*	*Secs.*
S.T. at noon Greenwich 2.1.84		18	45	16
Time before noon (12.00 – 10.00 a.m.)	less	2	00	00
Mean time correction	less	0	00	20
S.T. at Greenwich at birth		16	44	56
Longitude Equiv. 171°46′ over 15	less	11	27	04
Local S.T. at birth		5	17	52
Add 12 hours (southern latitude)		12	00	00
		17	17	52

From Tables of Houses 43°40′ (nearest)
17.17.52 S.T. Asc.11° Pisces: M.C. 20° Sagittarius.

Reverse signs = Asc. 11° Virgo: M.C. 20° Gemini.

An additional check for all charting is to note the quadrant containing the Sun. From sunrise to noon, it will be (working clockwise) in houses 1-10. From noon to sunset, it will be in houses 9-7. From sunset to midnight, in houses 6-4. From midnight until sunrise, in houses 3-1.

The Ascendant, M.C. and cusps of houses are derived from the *Local time of birth;* the planets' positions from the *Greenwich time of birth,* if using an ephemeris which is Greenwich-based.

The Ascendant. (ASC.)
The Ascendant is the degree of the zodiac rising. Due to the Earth's rotation, all signs of the zodiac rise and set every twenty-four hours (except within the polar latitudes). As each sign contains 30°, the average time for a sign to rise is about two hours (1° every four minutes of time), but in intermediate latitudes, certain signs rise in less than two hours (short ascension), while others take longer (long ascension).

This variation in rising is due to the obliquity of the Ecliptic (the angle between the horizon and the Ecliptic). In the northern hemisphere, the signs of short ascension are Capricorn to Gemini; signs of long ascension are Cancer to Sagittarius. In the southern hemisphere intermediate latitudes, the situation is reversed. At the Equator, the signs rise evenly.

To determine the Ascendant, the time of birth must be known with reasonable accuracy and also the geographical longitude and latitude (see page 80). The sign on the first house cusp is the Ascendant sign (rising sign), and the ruler of the Ascendant is the planet which rules the rising sign (e.g. Aries Ascendant = Mars ruler).

Planets close to the Ascendant — within 6-8° — are strongly placed, and the closer a planet is to the ascending degree, the greater its influence. Although modern astrologers give precedence to the Ascendant and first house, the midheaven and tenth house are also of paramount importance, as indeed are the Descendant (seventh house) and the lower meridian (fourth house). In broad terms, the Ascendant represents 'self', with the opposite point (Descendant) 'relating to others;' while the Midheaven and tenth signify 'public standing and aspirations', with the opposite point (fourth house) denoting 'foundations, security and privacy'.

The Ascendant is geocentric, and it has been suggested that geocentric latitude, and not geographic latitude, should be used for its exact calculation. The geocentric latitude is measured relative to the plane of the horizon and the Equator, and is the angle between the Equator and a radius from the centre of the earth. The difference between the two kinds of latitude is small, but could be important when dealing with precise directions. Most astrologers use the latitude which is tabulated in atlases and gazetteers (geographic).

In any statistical study involving the Ascendant, the factor of 'long and short ascension' has to be considered because, depending upon latitude, there will be a large difference in expectancy.

Interpolation

Calculation of exact Ascendant and M.C. and interpolation between latitudes

When the time of birth is given to the nearest quarter of an hour or so, it is misleading and inaccurate to chart the Ascendant and M.C. by listing the degree and *minute* as extracted from a Table of Houses nearest to the birth latitude. In all cases where there is uncertainty regarding the birth time, it is sufficient to list the degree only, ignoring minutes. However, with precisely timed births, the chart should be calculated with precision and for the exact latitude. Errors concerning the Angles result in Progressions and Directions being 'off mark', so far as the timing of events and conditions are concerned. For determining the exact degree rising and culminating, several methods of calculation are available, and in the following examples, the method using diurnal logarithms and a Table of Houses for Great Britain or a calculator is employed.

1. *M.C.* The degree and minute culminating is the same for all latitudes for a specified sidereal time. It is not affected by latitude, unlike the Ascending degree which varies according to the latitude. Therefore, having found the exact M.C. for the stated sidereal time (S.T.) at birth, no further calculation is required.
2. *Ascendant.* Ascertain the two latitudes nearest to the latitude required, and list the highest and lowest sidereal time nearest to the sidereal time at birth for both these latitudes. Note also the variation over the Ascendant for these two latitudes.
3. Having found the exact Ascendant for the highest and lowest latitudes we can, by interpolation, obtain the exact Ascendant for the required latitude.
4. The easiest method for these calculations is to use a calculating machine. An alternative is to use Diurnal Logarithms, the table of which can be adapted for these calculations by calling the *hours and minutes* as tabulated — *minutes and seconds.*

Example No. 1 (a) — Highest Latitude (54°34′N)
Required to find the exact Ascendant and M.C. at latitude 54°20′N for a sidereal time at birth of *4 H. 26 M. 10 S.*

	(1) *S.T.*	(2) *Asc.*	(3) *M.C.*	(4) *S.T.*
Highest	4.29.11	14.39 Virgo	9 Gemini	—
Required	—	—	—	4.26.10
Lowest	4.24.55	13.56 Virgo	8 Gemini	4.24.55
Difference	– 4.16	0.43	1 (60)	– 1.15

Ascendant

Diurnal Logs.			*Mins.*	*Secs.*		*Log.*	
Col. 4	1.15	=	1	15	=	1.2833	
Col. 2	43.00	=	43	00	=	1.5249	Add
						2.8082	
Col. 1	4.16	=	4	16	=	0.7501	Deduct
						2.0581	

Log. 2.0581 = 13 mins., which added to the Lower Ascendant 13.56 Virgo=14.09 Virgo=exact Ascendant at Latitude 54°34′ N.

Midheaven	*Mins.*	*Secs.*		*Log.*	
	1	15	=	1.2833	
(1 degree)	60	00	=	1,3802	Add
				2.6635	
	4	16	=	0.7501	Deduct
				1.9134	

Log. 1.9134 = 17 mins., which added to the Lower Midheaven 8 Gemini=8°17′ Gemini=exact Midheaven at this latitude and at the required latitude.

Midheaven for a specified sidereal time is the same for all latitudes.

Example No. 1 (b) — Lowest Latitude
From the Tables of Houses for York (lower latitude 53°58′ N), calculate the exact Ascendant. The M.C. calculation is not required as the exact M.C. has already been determined (8°17′ Gemini).

	(1) *S.T.*	(2) *Asc.*	(3) *S.T.*
Highest	4.29.11	14.31 Virgo	—
Required	—	—	4.26.10
Lowest	4.24.55	13.47 Virgo	4.24.55
Difference	4.16	0.44	1.15

Ascendant Diurnal Logs	*Mins.*	*Secs.*		*Log.*	
Col. 3	1	15	=	1.2833	
Col. 2	44	00	=	1.5149	Add
				2.7982	
Col. 1	4	16	=	0.7501	Deduct
				2.0481	

Log. 2.0481=13 mins., which added to the Lower Ascendant 13°47′ Virgo=14°00′ Virgo=exact Ascendant at latitude 53°58′ N.

Having found the exact Ascendant for the two latitudes nearest to the one required (54°20′ N) we can, by interpolation, obtain the exact Ascendant at the required latitude.

	(1) *Lat.*	(2) *Exact. Asc.*	(3) *Lat.*
Highest	54.34	14.09 Virgo	—
Required	—	—	54.20
Lowest	53.58	14.00 Virgo	53.58
Difference	0.36	0.09	0.22

Diurnal Logs.	*Mins.*		*Log.*	
Col..3	22	=	1.8159	
Col. 2	9	=	2.2041	Add
			4.0200	
Col. 1	36	=	1.6021	Deduct
			2.4179	

Log. 2.4179=5 mins., which added to Lower Ascendant 14° Virgo=14°05′ Virgo=exact Ascendant for the required latitude 54°20′ N.

At latitude 54°20′ N, for a sidereal time of 4.26.10 the Ascendant is 14°05′ Virgo and the M.C. is 8°17′ Gemini.

Use of Calculator

Example No. 1: Highest Latitude 54°34′ N. S.T. 4.26.10
(Part A)
The difference between the highest and lower S.T. as shown in the Tables is: 4′16″ and the difference between the lower S.T. and the required S.T. is 1′15″, with a difference between the highest and lowest Ascendant of 43 mins. Therefore, if 4 mins. 16 secs. = 0.43 mins. over the Ascendant, 1 min. 15 secs. = ?

$$1.15 = \frac{1.25 \times 0.7166 \text{ (43 mins.)}}{4.2667 \text{ (4 mins. 16 secs.)}}$$

= 0.20995 = 13 mins.
Exact Ascendant 14° 09′ Virgo

(Part B) Lowest Latitude 53°58′ N

$$\frac{1.25 \times 0.7333 \text{ (44 mins.)}}{4.2667 \text{ (4 mins. 16 secs.)}}$$

= 0.21483 = 13 mins
Exact Ascendant = 14° Virgo

(Part C)

Latitudes		*Deg.*	*Min.*	*Exact Ascendant*
Highest	=	54	34	14° 09′ Virgo
Lowest	=	53	58	14° 00′ Virgo
Difference		0	36	00 09
Required Lat.		54	20	
Lowest Lat.		53	58	
Difference		0	22	

Therefore, if 36 mins. difference in latitudes = 9 mins. over the Ascendant, 22 mins. will =

$$\frac{22 \times 9}{36}$$

= 5 mins.
nearest which, added to the lower Ascendant 14° Virgo = *14°05′ Virgo = exact Ascendant at the required latitude 54°20′*

Midheaven — (Degree and minute culminating)

Mins.	*Secs.*	
4	16	= 1 degree (60 mins.)
1	15	= ?

$1.15 = \frac{1.25 \times 60}{4.2667} = 17$ mins. nearest which added

to lower M.C. = 8°17′ Gemini = exact M.C. for the required S.T. 4.26.10.

At latitude 54°20′ N, for a S.T. 4.26.10., the Ascendant is 14°05′ Virgo and the M.C. is 8°17′ Gemini.

Ascending Degree and Minute Decreasing between Latitudes

Example No. 2 (A): Find the exact Ascendant for latitude 59°53′N. S.T. 7.18.13.
From Tables of Houses for latitude 59°56′ N. (Highest Lat.)

	(1) *S.T.*	(2) *Asc.*	(3) *M.C.*	(4) *S.T.*
Highest	7.22.18	12.48 Libra	19 Cancer	—
Required	—	—	—	7.18.13
Lowest	7.18.01	12.08	18	7.18.01
Difference	4.17	0.40	1	0.00.12

Ascendant

Diurnal Logs.			*Mins.*	*Secs.*	*Log.*	
Col. 4	0.00.12	=	0	12	2.0792	
Col. 2	0.40.00	=	40	00	1.5563	Add
					3.6355	
Col. 1	0.04.17	=	4	17	0.7484	Deduct
					2.8871	

Log. 2.8871 = 2 minutes, which added to lower Asc. 12°08′ Libra = *12°.10′ Libra = exact Asc. at latitude 59°.56′ N.*

Midheaven	*Mins.*	*Secs.*		*Log.*	
Col. 4	0	12	=	2.0792	
Col. 3 (1 degree)	60	00	=	1.3802	Add
				3.4594	
Col. 1	4	17	=	0.7484	Deduct
				2.7110	

Log. 2.7110=3 mins., which added to lower M.C. 18° Cancer= *18°.03′ Cancer=exact M.C. as required.*

Example No. 2 (B): Lowest Latitude 59°0′ N.

	(1) *S.T.*	*(2)* *Asc.*	*(3)* *M.C.*	*(4)* *S.T.*
Highest	7.22.18	13.00 Libra	19 Cancer	—
Required	—	—	—	7.18.13
Lowest	7.18.01	12.20	18	7.18.01
Difference	0.04.17	0.40	1	0.00.12

	Mins.	*Secs.*	*Log.*	
Col. 4	0	12	2.0792	
Col. 2	40	00	1.5563	Add
			3.6355	
Col. 1	04	17	0.7484	Deduct
			2.8871	

Log. 2.8871=2 minutes, which, added to lower Asc. 12°.20′ Libra=*12°22′ Libra=exact Asc. at latitude 59° N.*

The M.C. for a specified sidereal time is the same for all latitudes.

Having found the exact Ascendant for the two latitudes nearest to the one required (59°53′ N) we can, by interpolation, obtain the exact Ascendant at the required latitude:

	(1) *Lat.*	(2) *Exact Asc.*	(3) *Lat.*
Highest	59.56	12.10 Libra	—
Required	—	—	59.53
Lowest	59.00	12.22 Libra	59.00
Difference	0.56	0.12*	0.53

* 12 minutes difference decreasing towards higher latitudes.

	Mins.	*Logs.*	
Col. 3	53	1.4341	
Col. 2	12	2.0792	Add
		3.5133	
Col. 1	56	1.4102	Deduct
		2.1031	

Log. 2.1031 = 11 mins., which is *deducted* from the lower Asc. 12°22′ Libra as the ascending degree and minute is decreasing from latitude 59° N to latitude 59°56′ N. The exact Ascendant as required in latitude 59°53′ N is therefore 12°11′ Libra (12°22′ less 11 mins.)

Use of Calculator

(A) Highest Latitude 59°56′ N. S.T. 7.18.13

Min.	*Sec.*		*Min.*	*Sec.*
4	17	=	40	00 over Asc.
0	12	=	?	

$$\frac{0.2 \times 0.666}{4.2833} = 2 \text{ minutes}$$

Exact Ascendant=12°10′ Libra.

(B) Lowest Latitude 59° N.

Min.	*Sec.*		*Min.*	*Sec.*
4	17	=	40	00 over Asc.
0	12	=	?	

$$\frac{0.2 \times 0.666}{4.2833} = 2 \text{ minutes}$$

Exact Ascendant=12°22′ Libra.

(C) *Latitudes*		*Deg.*	*Min.*	*Exact Asc.*
Highest	=	59	56	12° 10′ Libra
Lowest	=	59	00	12° 22′ Libra
Difference	=	0	56	0° 12′ Note Decrease
Required	=	59	53	
Lowest	=	59	00	
Difference	=	0	53	

Therefore, if 56 minutes difference in latitudes = *12 minutes decrease* over the Ascendant, 53 minutes in latitude will =

$$\frac{53 \times 12}{56}$$

= 11 minutes nearest, which *deducted* from the lower Ascendant 12°22′=*12°11′=Exact Ascendant at 59°53′ N. as required.*

Midheaven
The degree and minute culminating for any specified sidereal time can be found by proportion or from Tables of Right Ascension (R.A.)

Right Ascension Tables

S.T.	*R.A.*	*Longitude M.C.*
7.20.00	110°00′	18°28′
7.16.00	109°00′	17°32′
4.00	1°00′	0°56′

Required S.T.

7. 18. 13
7. 16. 00 less
0. 2. 13 $= \dfrac{2.2166 \times 56}{4} = 31$ minutes,

which added to M.C. 17°32′=18°03′ Cancer=M.C. required.

Check that 18°03′ is the correct M.C. for a S.T. of 7.18.13:

$$(2.13)\ \frac{2.2166 \times 60}{4} = 33 \text{ mins. } 15 \text{ secs.}$$

added to R.A. 109° = 109°33′15″. Divide by 15 to convert to sidereal time

$$= \frac{109.5541}{15} = 7.3036 = 7.\ 18.\ 13.\ \text{S.T. as required.}$$

An additional check is:

$$7 \times 15 = 105°: \frac{18}{4} = 4°30′: \frac{13}{4} = 3′15″$$

Deg.	*Min.*	*Sec.*	
105	00	00	
4	30	00	Add
0	3	15	
109	33	15	Right Ascension = 7.18.13. S.T. or 60 mins. R.A. =

56 minutes difference in longitude, therefore

$$\frac{33.15 \text{ R.A.} \times 56}{60} = 31 \text{ minutes,}$$

which added to 17°32′ = 18°03′ Cancer = M.C. required.

House Division

The zodiac and the circle of the twelve mundane houses are the principal frames of reference and, although both have many similarities and correspondences, there is a distinction to be made concerning their meaning and importance. The Sun, Moon and planets keep within the zodiacal belt and are, according to astrological concepts, 'coloured' by the sign they occupy. The basic attributes of the planets do not alter, irrespective of the sign occupied. Mars is always Mars, active, aggressive and forthright; the Moon, tenacious, negative and withdrawn; Saturn, slow, ponderous and conservative. Although the inherent nature of a planet does not change, the expression of its characteristics is governed, to a greater or lesser degree, according to the sign occupied. There is an accentuation or modification, due not only to the sign emplacement, but also to its aspectual strength or weakness, (see Aspects) and to its mundane (house) position. The houses are 'fields of action and experiences' wherein the planet, 'coloured' by the sign it is in, expresses its intrinsic nature. The traditional association of the twelve houses, with all aspects of human activity and experience, has validity, and there is a correlation between signs and houses. As Aries is the first sign of the zodiac, so the first house has a basic Aries influence, the second house a Taurus influence, and so on for the twelve houses.

It follows that in attempting to judge the significance of a particular planetary pattern (planet, sign and house) we need to consider not only the actual emplacement, but also how the configuration is related to the natural sign and ruler of the house in question.

The first house will always have a basic sub-influence of Mars/Aries; the second house of Venus/Taurus and so on for the other houses. If, for example, Mars is in Libra in the tenth house, we can judge that it is a 'toned down' Mars because of the Venus influence, but being in the tenth, it has a Saturn/Capricorn contact, and this will curb the natural impulsiveness so often associated with Mars. The intrinsic nature will not have altered, but the Martian qualities will operate in a more controlled and deliberate manner. It is still an active, vigorous influence as befits its nature, but the energies are channelled in a more constructive and purposeful way. Activities connected with personal prestige, security, and other matters traditionally associated with Saturn/Capricorn, will be approached less stridently or aggressively than if Mars was in Aries or some other outgoing sign. As with many other things, astrology has its fashions, and yesterday's hero is today's villain and vice versa. A few decades ago, considerable controversy existed concerning the relative merits of various methods of house division, and periodically new systems, which in the main are not new at all, but merely variations of existing methods, are proposed. What the innovators of the various systems of house division often fail to realize, is that the Zodiac cannot be 'draped' on to the cusps of the twelve mundane houses, due to the fact that the signs of the Zodiac are intercepted according to the angle of the obliquity of the Ecliptic and the system employed.

House division is an important astrological concept, as it is the only factor which alters in a short space of time. Without this division, the relationship of man to his environment would be difficult to ascertain. Recent research by M. and F. Gauquelin has shown significant statistical evidence in relation to houses, with certain areas designated zones of high intensity. These areas close to the traditional angles of the first, tenth, seventh and fourth houses are in agreement with traditional astrological teaching.

Systems of House Division

There are three commonly accepted classifications of house division:

1. the Ecliptic systems;
2. the space systems;
3. the time systems.

The Ecliptic Systems

The Equal House Method

This system is attributed to Ptolemy and is described in his *Tetrabiblos*. The basis of this system is to determine the Ascendant in the usual way and to add 30° of the zodiac, in order to obtain the cusps of the houses. With this system, the Ecliptic is the foundation circle and is divided into twelve equal parts by six great circles passing through the poles of the Ecliptic. Each house is partly above and partly below the plane of the horizon, except when the poles of the Ecliptic coincide with the north and south points of the horizon, in which case the houses are entirely above or below the horizon. The circles forming the boundaries are circles of latitude. This equal division of the Ecliptic results in the tenth house being in exact square (90°) to the Ascendant, but does not necessarily coincide with the degree of the zodiac then culminating.

The principle of this sytem is the tri-section of a quadrant of the Ecliptic commencing with the degree ascending.

The Porphyry System

This system is a modification of the Equal House system, and dates from about the third century AD. The Ecliptic is the basic circle, and its division is effected by six great circles passing through its poles. The arcs of the Ecliptic, enclosed between the meridian and horizon circles, are each divided into three equal parts. The houses are equal when the right ascension of the Midheaven (R.A.M.C.) is either six or eighteen hours. Otherwise, only those of opposing quadrants are equal.

The principle of this system in the tri-section of the arc of the Ecliptic intercepted between the horizon and meridian.

The Natural Graduation System

This system was introduced by Colin Evans in the 1950s and is a variation of the Porphyry system. As with Porphyry, this system is deficient in that it seeks to divide the Ecliptic unequally. Details concerning this system are included in the work by Evans, *New Waites Compendium of Natal Astrology*.

M- House Method

This method of house division originated in the early 1950s and uses a starting point from the culminating degree of the Ecliptic, similar to the Equal house method which uses the Ascendant. The name 'M- House' is derived from the fact that the system is based on the Midheaven as a starting point. The great circles forming the boundaries of the house lunes pass through the poles of the Ecliptic. With this system, the Ascendant is not normally the cusp of the first house, but as with the Equal House method and the Midheaven, is regarded as a significant point.

The Space Systems

The Campanus House System

This system of house division was devised by Johannes Campanus, a thirteenth-century mathematician. With this method, the Prime Vertical is employed as the foundation circle. If the Prime Vertical is divided into twelve equal parts, with six great circles of the sphere from the north or south points of the horizon passing through the dividing points on the Prime Vertical, we obtain the cusps of the twelve Campanus houses. This division gives the six houses above the horizontal plane and six below which appear like lunes, and in which all the bodies must be contained. Two of these circles are coincident with the planes of the horizon and meridian respectively. The houses are all equal in point of magnitude and entirely above or below the horizon. This method of division has much to commend it, because the houses are equal and the Angles are house cusps.

The principle of this system is the tri-section of a quadrant of the Prime Vertical (which is a great circle passing through the zenith point, and at right angles to the meridian) by great circles mutually intersecting at the north and south points of the horizon; the cusps of the houses being the degrees of the Ecliptic cut by these circles.

The Regiomontanus House System

Johannes Müller (Regiomontanus) was a professor of astronomy at Vienna, and his system of house division is a modification of that of Campanus. The foundation circle of this method is the Equator, which is divided into twelve equal parts by six great circles intersecting in the north and south points of the horizon. As with the Campanus system, the houses are either entirely above or below the horizon; likewise planes of the horizon and meridian coincide with the planes of two great circles. The houses, which are complementary to one another, are equal in point of magnitude.

Although this system was recognized and gained favour and is still in use today, it has not attracted the same attention as the Campanus method.

The principle of this system is the tri-section of a quadrant of the Equator, comprised between the horizon and meridian, by great circles mutually intersecting at the north and south points of the horizon; the cusps of the houses being the degrees of the Ecliptic cut by these circles.

The Morinus House System

Jean Baptiste Morin was a physician and professor of mathematics at the Paris University during the seventeenth century. The system attributed to him is similar to the method advocated by Regiomontanus, in that the Equator acts as the basic circle, which is divided into twelve equal parts by six great circles intersecting in the poles of the Ecliptic. The houses are partly above and below the horizon with one exception that is, when the poles of the Ecliptic coincide with the north and south points of the horizon, then the houses are entirely above or below. The opposite pairs are equal in point of magnitude.

The principle of this system is the tri-section of quadrants of the Equator by great circles through the poles of the Ecliptic.

Time Systems

The Alcabitius House System

This method, devised by the Arabic astrologer Alcabitius, is probably one of the earlier examples of a time system of house division. The basis of this system is that the Ascendant is determined in the usual way; the sidereal time at which this degree reaches the cusp of the tenth house is next determined, and the difference between it and the sidereal time at birth is divided into three equal parts, which are successively added to the sidereal time at birth. The degrees then found culminating are the cusps of the eleventh, twelfth and first houses. A similar procedure with regard to the cusp of the fourth house will give the cusps of the third, second and first houses, deduction being used in place of addition.

The principle of this system is the tri-section of the semi-arcs, diurnal and nocturnal, of the Ascendant.

The Placidus House System

Placidus de Tito was an Italian monk and professor of mathematics in the seventeenth century. The Placidean system was originally introduced into Britain during the seventeenth century by a Dr Francis Wright, who brought it to the notice of Lilley, Gadbury, Coley and other leading members of the astrological fraternity, but they rejected the system. However, another astrologer, named Partridge, advocated its use, and eventually R. C. Smith (Raphael), an almanac publisher, included the tables in his 1821 publication.

The method of Placidus, commonly known as the 'Semi-Arc system' is very similar to the method of Alcabitius. Basically, the system consists of taking the time for any degree to move from the Ascendant to the Midheaven, and to equally tri-sect this time to ascertain the time at which this degree will become the cusps of the twelfth and eleventh houses. Likewise, the semi-nocturnal arc from the lower meridian (I.C.) to the Ascendant is tri-sected, and the times are those at which the same degree will become the cusps of the second and third houses. The following example illustrates the method.

At London — Latitude 51°32′ north		*Sidereal Time*		
		Hours	*Mins.*	
Midheaven (M.C.)	= 4° Gemini	4	08	
Lower Meridian (I.C.)	= 4° Sagittarius	16	08	
Ascendant	= 4° Gemini	20	13	
Therefore semi-diurnal arc =		4	08	
Less		20	13	
		7	55	÷ 3
	=	2	38	
and semi-nocturnal arc =		20	13	
Less		16	08	
		4	05	÷ 3
	=	1	22	
M.C.	= 4° Gemini	4	08	
11th cusp	= 4.08–2.38	1	30	
12th cusp	= 1.30–2.38	22	52	

Ascendant at		20	13
2nd cusp	= 20.13–1.22	18	51
3rd cusp	= 18.51–1.22	17	29

The above example shows that, although the time that a degree may spend in a particular quandrant may be unequal, the motion is uniform due to the apparent rotation of the celestial sphere. It therefore reaches the points of tri-section (I.C.–Asc. and Asc.–M.C.) at precisely one-third of the time which is required to complete the total arc of the particular quadrant. Any degree of the Ecliptic makes a complete revolution in one sidereal day, and the time at which it reaches those points on the semi-diurnal and semi-nocturnal arcs which tri-sect them is the time at which the degree becomes the cusp of the particular house.

As with all methods of house division which use the Ascendant as the zero point, distortion occurs in high latitudes, and at the polar circle latitude (66½°), a degree of the Ecliptic will become circumpolar for the first time. Above the polar circle, certain degrees will not rise, and therefore systems, such as the Placidean whose basis is the tri-section of semi-arcs, present problems. Only experience, using charts with well-attested data, will confirm whether a particular system has validity or not.

The principle of the Placidean system is the tri-section of the Semi-Arc of each degree of the Ecliptic. By successively adding one-third semi-arc (diurnal) of any degree to the sidereal time of its ascension, the degree on the cusp of the twelfth, eleventh and tenth houses is found; similarly, by adding one-third semi-arc (nocturnal) to the sidereal time of its descension, the degree on the cusp of the sixth, fifth, and fourth houses is found.

The Birthplace House System

This method of division was devised by Dr Walter Koch, and tables were published in the early 1970s. It is similar to the method of Alcabitius and uses the oblique ascension of the birthplace. Whereas Alcabitius uses the arc from the Ecliptic to the meridian, the Birthplace system uses the arc of oblique ascension from the horizon to the Ecliptic.

The Topocentric House System

In the early 1960s, Wendel Polich and A. P. Nelson Page of Buenos Aires published this method, and a detailed exposition of this system (somewhat mathematical) appeared in the sidereal astrology publication *Spica* Vol. 3, No. 3, 1964 and Vol. 5, No. 3, 1966. This system is similar to the time system of Placidus but, whereas Placidus relates time to the Ascendant, the Topocentric relates the poles of the houses to that of the geographic latitude of birth.

The various methods of house division that have been discussed are a few of the methods available. The whole question of house division is a complex and contentious matter and, although some systems have more claim for consideration than others, no firm agreement as to the correct method has yet been achieved.

Definitions

Angles: the four cardinal points. The first, tenth, seventh and fourth house cusps. In a birth chart, the places where the horizon plane of the birth locality and the meridian plane intersect the Ecliptic. The houses of which these angles form the cusps are known as Angular houses.

Antiscion: A point that is equidistant with a given planet from either solstice point (0° Cancer or 0° Capricorn) but on the opposite side. For example, a planet at, say, 10° Leo has its antiscion point at 20° at Taurus. For planet at 18° Sagittarius, the antiscion is 12° Capricorn. The contrascion is a point equidistant with a given planet from either equinoctial point (0° Aries or 0° Libra) but on the opposite side; e.g. for a planet at 25° Virgo, the contrascion is 5° Libra. These points are significant when activated by progressions or transits.

Ascendant: The degree of the Zodiac rising on the eastern horizon of the birthplace at the time of birth. The eastern angle or first house of the birth chart. The eastern point intersection of the horizon and Ecliptic. The planet 'ruling' the sign rising is the Ruler of the Ascendant and is often considered as the ruler of the chart.

Ascension, long and short: At intermediate latitudes, due to the Obliquity of the Ecliptic (23°), the angle between the horizon and Ecliptic varies, causing some signs to rise faster than others. Signs which rise faster (short ascension) are Capricorn through to Gemini; those which rise slower (long ascension) are Cancer through to Sagittarius. This applies to the northern hemisphere; in the southern hemisphere intermediate latitudes the situation is reversed.

Ascensional difference: If a star is not on the Equator, it will, when it rises, form an angle with that part of the Equator which is rising at the same time; this is termed its Ascensional Difference, which, added to its right ascension if it has south declination, but subtracted if it has north declination, will give its oblique ascension. For places in *southern latitudes, reverse* the rules; add instead of subtracting, and subtract instead of adding.

Axial rotation: The spinning of any celestial body around its axis. The Earth's rotation results in the apparent rising, culmination and setting of the Sun, Moon and other celestial bodies.

Axis: The imaginary line round which a solid body rotates, and which is perpendicular to the direction of rotation. The Earth's axis extends from the North Pole to the South Pole (both terrestrial and celestial) and is perpendicular to the Equator (terrestrial and celestial).

Ayanamsa: Sanskrit word for 'precession'. The vernal point of the tropical zodiac is moving backwards along the Ecliptic path — against the order of the constellations — at a rate of approximately 50 seconds per year, this rate being known as general precession. This point has now so far receded from the initial point of the fixed zodiac, that they are now approximately 24° apart. This separation in their respective positions is known as the *ayanamsa.* Deducting the value of the *ayanamsa* from 360° gives the sidereal longitude of the Vernal Point. The *ayanamsa* used by Western astrologers is that formulated by C. Fagan and D. Bradley.

Cadent: (falling.) Term used to describe those houses which 'fall away' from the angles (third, sixth, ninth and twelfth). Formerly regarded as weak mundane positions, but modern research, particularly by the Gauquelins, suggests otherwise. Planets located in these houses are termed Cadent.

Campanus system: A method of house division.

Caput Draconis (the Dragon's Head): The north node of the Moon. (See *Nodes*, Chapter 1 Definitions.)

Cardinal houses: First, tenth, seventh and fourth (the Angles).

Cardinal points: The north, south, east and west points of the heavens.

Cardinal Signs: Aries, Cancer, Libra and Capricorn.

Cauda Draconis (the Dragon's Tail): The south node of the Moon. (See *Nodes,* Chapter 1 Definitions.)

Cazimi: A term used to describe a planet when its longitude is within 17 minutes of the Sun. This position within the 'heart of the Sun' was considered to fortify the planet as much as combustion (within

8½° of the Sun) debilitated it.

Celestial co-ordinates: (See page 12.)

Circles of position: An astronomical term used in calculating the polar elevation of a planet. Small circles having the same relationship to the meridian circle as the parallels of latitude do to the Equator.

Co-latitude: 90° less the latitude of birth; e.g. co-latitude of London = 90° less 51°32′ N. = 38°28′. (See Vertex.)

Combust: A planet is said to be 'combust' when its longitude is within 8½° of the Sun. (See *Cazimi.*)

Cosmical Rising/Setting: When a planet or star rises with the Sun in the morning or sets with the Sun in the evening.

Culmination: The meridian passage of a body. The arrival of a star or planet at the upper meridian or Midheaven. It has then attained its greatest elevation.

Cusp: Normally the boundary or edge of a house in the birth chart. Some astrologers consider that the cusp does not mark the beginning of a house, but that it designates the middle point of the house. A term also used to identify the division between signs, e.g. 'a cuspal', relating to the Sun at the end of one sign and about to 'enter' the next sign.

Daily motion: The angular distance along the Ecliptic that the Sun, Moon and planets have moved in twenty-four hours. Measured in degrees, minutes and seconds. (See page 124.)

Decreasing in light: The Moon passing from the Full to the conjunction (New) is decreasing in light. Planets decrease in light when they approach the Sun after having passed the opposition. Venus and Mercury decrease in light as they move nearer to the Sun, after having reached their greatest elongation.

Degree rising: The exact degree of the zodiac rising at the time of birth. (See Ascendant.)

Descendant: The point opposite to the Ascendant (q.v.); the western angle or cusp of the seventh house.

Direct: The opposite of retrograde. When a body is moving forward in the zodiac in the order of the signs from Aries to Pisces.

Draconic Period: The period between one transit of a planet or the Moon over its ascending node with the Ecliptic. (See page 21.)

East Point: The point where the eastern horizon intersects the Prime Vertical and the Celestial Equator. The Ascendant is a point where the eastern horizon intersects the Ecliptic; the two should not be confused.

Elevation: The distance of a celestial body above the horizon. (See *Altitude,* Chapter 1 Definitions.) A term applied to a planet that is elevated over another. The most elevated planet is the one nearest to the Midheaven (q.v.).

Embolismic: In every year, there are twelve Moons of 29½ days each and 11 days over, and when these odd days amount to 30, they make an additional, or Embolismic lunation.

Face: Outmoded term relating to a sixth part of a sign (5°).

Fiducial: A term used in sidereal astrology; a 'marker' for ascertaining the *ayanamsa* (q.v.), in order to obtain the sidereal celestial longitude.

Fixed stars: Stars which appear to remain fixed, unlike the planets which 'wander' against the background of the constellations. The ancients considered that some fixed stars were important when they formed significant configurations with the natal chart. In noting aspects to fixed stars, the *celestial longitude* and the *celestial latitude* of the star and the planet have to be taken into account. There appears to be some validity for 'influence' of the fixed stars and their degree areas.

Fixed zodiac: The sidereal, starry, non-moving, non-precessional zodiac of the constellations.

Geocentric: Viewed from, or having relation to the Earth. All astrological positions are geocentric, because they relate to the Earth. The Ptolemaic system, in which the Earth was the centre of the universe, was superseded by the Copernican (heliocentric) system in the sixteenth century. Although some advocates have adopted 'heliocentric astrology', the geocentric references are, in most cases employed in relation to birth charts.

Great circle: Any circle whose plane (level) passes through the centre of a sphere, e.g. Earth. A *small* circle is, in contrast, a circle whose plane does not pass through the centre of a sphere. The horizon, Equator and Ecliptic are three great circles. Other circles of importance in astrology are meridians of longitude (terrestrial and celestial), the Prime Vertical, and meridians of right ascension.

Heliacal: Related to the Sun. Heliacal rising is when a star or planet that was hidden by the Sun's rays becomes visible, either to the east or west of the Sun; heliacal setting is the disappearance from view of a body, as it approaches a conjunction with the Sun. The Moon is said to rise or set heliacally when 17° distant from the Sun.

Heliocentric: Taking the Sun as centre. The heliocentric system of Copernicus — a Sun-centred universe — replaced the geocentric

— Earth-centred — universe of Ptolemy. Although astrology in the main is concerned with the geocentric framework, heliocentric astrology has its advocates. The two systems produce widely different positions, because one is Sun-centred and the other Earth-centred. With the heliocentric astrology, many of the familiar factors associated with geocentric charts such as the Ascendant, Midheaven, houses, Sun and Moon, are not applicable. Whatever the merits or disadvantages of heliocentric astrology, some of its supporters suggest that it is not an exclusive approach but is complementary to the geocentric system.

Hemisphere: Half the sphere or circle. Divided into upper and lower hemispheres by the horizon, and into eastern and western hemispheres by the meridian. The visible hemisphere is that which is always in view; the hidden or lower hemisphere is that which is beneath us. The eastern hemisphere is that part of the circle extending from the cusp of the fourth house (I.C.) to the Midheaven; the western hemisphere extends from the cusp of the Midheaven to the fourth house cusp. Astrologically, planets posited in the eastern hemisphere are said to be associated with positive personal attitudes, while those in the western hemisphere indicate compliance and acceptance. This doctrine, like many others in astrology, is highly suspect, and although planets above the horizon (particularly those close to the Midheaven or rising) are always important, the chart as a whole needs to be considered.

Horoscope: ('Scope of the hour'). Originally, the Ascendant or more particularly, the degree of the Zodiac rising on the eastern horizon at the time and place of birth. Subsequently, the term was used to describe the complete chart of the heavens. Sun sign forecasts, found in popular journals and the like, use the term horoscope but this — as with so much of 'instant astrology' — is misleading.

Houses: The twelve divisions into which the circle of the heavens is divided and whose boundaries intersect the Ecliptic and determine the cusps of the houses. (See page 102.)

Immum Coeli: The lower heaven. The fourth house cusp in most systems of house division. It is the point at which the lower meridian intersects the Ecliptic; this point is always directly opposite the Midheaven. The lowest point below the horizon is the nadir, which is opposite the zenith, and these points should not be confused with the Immum Coeli and Midheaven.

Increasing in light: When any planet is leaving the Sun and is not yet arrived at the opposition; after which it decreases in light.

Increasing in Motion: When a planet moves faster every succeeding day.

Intercepted: A sign is intercepted if it is contained within a house without occupying the cusp. When a sign is intercepted in a house, the opposite sign will also be intercepted in the opposite house. Interception is due to the inclination of the Earth's axis in relation to the Ecliptic, which causes the number of degrees passing over the horizon to vary according to the time of year and the latitude of the birthplace. Equal house division, which is really equal ecliptical division, does not produce interception.

Lights: The luminaries — the Sun and Moon.

Local Mean Time: (See page 77.)

Logarithms: A series of numbers in arithmetical progression answering to another in geometrical progression, whereby it is possible to perform multiplication by addition and division by subtraction. Diurnal Proportional Logarithms found in astrological ephemerides and, until the advent of the calculator, widely used by astrologers are logarithms of the minutes in twenty-four hours or degrees (1440) less the logarithm of the minutes in the given time.

Example: 5 hours 14 minutes or 5°14′ = 314 minutes = 0.66144 Log. which has been found as follows:

Log. 1440	=	3.15836	
Log. 314	=	2.49692	less
	=	0.66144	= Log. of 5 hours 14 minutes.

It is not essential to know how these logs are calculated in order to use them. The planets' positions at any given time can be found by using the tables, as listed in an ephemeris such as Raphael's.

Example: Find the Moon's longitude at 1.20 p.m. G.M.T. 7 March 1985.

Working	*Log.*	
Moon's daily motion 7th/8th March 15°05′	0.2017	
Time from noon 7th March - 1 hour 20 mins.	1.2553	Add
	1.4570	

Log. 1.4570 = 50 minutes = Moon's motion in 1 hour 20 minutes.

Moon's Noon position 7 March	22°35′	
Add motion in 1 hour 20 mins.	00°50′	
Moon's position at 1.20 p.m.	23°25′	Virgo

Lunar mansions: An ancient division of the Moon's orbit. A sidereal month is 27.3217 mean solar days, so there are twenty-seven or twenty-eight lunar mansions. The length of each mansion is

$$\frac{360}{28} = 12.8571$$

or 12°51′25″ of celestial longitude. It is probable, as some writers have suggested, that these 'Mansions of the Moon' may have an important function in determining 'critical' degree areas and the significance of the Pre-Natal Epoch. (See Pre-Natal Epoch.)

Lunar year: A period of 354.367 days (12 lunar months) based on the synodic period of the Moon, or 29.5306 days (29 days, 12 hours, 44 minutes 2.7 seconds).

Lunation: The period of time between two successive New Moons. The synodic month of 29.5306 days. Astrologically, the term is used to denote the New Moon (conjunction of Sun and Moon), the charts of which are important in mundane astrology.

Matutine: Appearing in the morning. A star or planet that rises before the Sun in the morning. The Moon is matutine until she has passed her first quarter.

M.C. (Medium Coeli): The point at which the upper meridian intersects the Ecliptic. Not to be confused with the point directly overhead — the Zenith.

Midheaven: See *M.C.*

Nonagesimal: The point of the Ecliptic that is above the horizon and 90° from the Ascendant. In the equal ecliptical division (Equal House system), the nonagesimal is the tenth house cusp and rarely coincides with the Midheaven.

Oriental/Occidental: Planets found between the fourth house and the Midheaven are classified as oriental (eastern) and rising, although actual rising is when a planet is close to the Ascendant. When a planet has passed the Midheaven and until it reaches the fourth house, it is considered occidental (falling), although actual setting is when a planet is close to the Descendant or seventh house cusp.

Parallels: When taken in the zodiac, these are equal distances from the Equator, or having the same declination. When taken in the world, they are equal distances from the meridian or horizon — in proportion to the semi-arcs of the planets which form them. *Rapt parallels* are parallels formed by the motion of the Earth on its axis, whereby both bodies are rapt or carried away by the same until they come to equal distances from the meridian.

Paran (Paranatellonta): The relationship between *two planets* that come simultaneously to *adjacent angles.* These positions, which could be called mundane squares, are very potent aspects. The calculation of a paran requires the use of spherical trigonometry as it involves the planet's celestial longitude, celestial latitude, right ascension and declination.

Placidean system: House system, tables for which are published in Raphael's ephemeris.

Quadrants: The four quarters of the heavens. A quadrant in a birth chart is defined by the cusps of the four angular houses; in the quadrant systems of house division by the intersecting axes of meridian and horizon. Old texts refer to the oriental quadrants as the first to tenth houses and seventh to fourth houses, the reverse of these being the occidental quadrants. In the zodiac, the oriental quadrants are from the beginning of Aries to the beginning of Cancer, and from the beginning of Libra to the beginning of Capricorn. The opposite are the occidental quadrants.

Radical (Radix): The original chart. A birthchart, mundane chart, foundation chart or any chart that represents the 'birth' of a person or event.

R.A.M.C.: Abbreviation for the right ascension of the Midheaven. (See *Right Ascension,* Chapter 1 Definitions.)

Regiomontanus system: A system of house division.

Secondary Progressions: See Progressions.

Semi-arc: See House Division and Progressions, pages 102 and 198.

Short ascension: See *Ascension, long and short.*

Slow of Course: A planet moving slower than its mean motion.

Solar arc: See Progressions, page 198.

Solar chart: When the time of birth is uncertain or unknown, a solar chart, using the Sun's longitude at noon on the birthday, can be taken in lieu of a properly calculated chart. The cusps of the solar chart are at 30° intervals from the solar ascendant (Sun's longitude) and this chart, with the planets in the signs they occupy but located in the 'solar houses', will give a broad generalization. No assessment is possible concerning the mundane (house) positions, but the interplanetary aspects can prove helpful. The solar chart is not the same as a sunrise chart, which is a chart cast for sunrise at the birth latitude, the cusp of the first house being the degree of longitude of the Sun at sunrise. Although it is generally accepted that no assessments can be made concerning mundane positions, some astrologers consider that the solar chart can be interpreted symbolically in relation to the sign on the cusp of each house. For example, a solar chart with Scorpio as the first house cusp (Sun sign Scorpio) would have Leo on the tenth cusp, and all matters relating to the tenth would have some Leo connotation. Likewise, with the other cusps according to the sign. Obviously, without a properly calculated chart no exact progressions or directions can be made. But a broad survey regarding future trends is possible by noting the various planetary alignments which may be formed subsequent to the birthdate. No details concerning progressions to angles can be obtained, because of the uncertain or unknown birthtime.

Southern hemisphere charts: (See page 89.)

Speculum: A table giving details of planetary positions and all relevant information such as latitude, declination, right ascension, etc., necessary for the calculation of Primary directions. (See page 198.)

Star: A heavenly body, especially one visible by night whose place appears fixed (fixed stars — q.v.). Sometimes loosely applied to include planets and other celestial bodies. The phrase 'one's stars', 'the science of the stars' is sometimes used by the uninformed when referring to astrology.

Stationary/Stations: The term applied to a planet when, observed from Earth, it appears to stand still prior to reversing its motion. The point in its orbit, where it apparently stands still, is called its station. A planet can be stationary retrograde (going from direct to retrograde), or it can be stationary direct (going from retrograde to direct). The Sun and Moon are never stationary.

Succedent: The houses that follow or succeed the Angular houses, namely the second, fifth, eighth and eleventh. These houses correspond to the fixed signs (Taurus, Leo, Scorpio and Aquarius), and the term is also applied to planets occupying these houses.

Synetic Vernal Point: The sidereal longitude of the Vernal Point, as proposed by Donald Bradley, a notable exponent of the sidereal system of astrology. (See *Ayanamsa.*)

Tables of Houses: Tables, essential for the calculation of charts, which list the signs and degrees of the zodiac upon the cusps of the mundane houses for every degree of right ascension, or for every four minutes (approximately) of sidereal time. The tables are obtainable for various latitudes, and *Raphael's Ephemeris* includes those for London, Liverpool and New York.

Time: For the various 'kinds of time' used in astrological calculation, certain conversions or adjustments are usually necessary before a chart can be erected. (See page 76.)

Transit: The movement of a planet through a sign of the zodiac. Normally, the term refers to the current passage of a planet over a sensitive or important point in a natal or progressed chart. Transits are found by referring to the ephemeris for the year required and noting the planets' positions at the appropriate date. The transits of the major planets are significant when they aspect or contact important areas of a chart. Astronomically, a transit is the passage of a body over the meridian, i.e. its culmination either upper or lower.

Vertex: The point where the Prime Vertical intersects the Ecliptic in the west. The opposite point in the east is termed the Anti-Vertex. The Vertex is determined as follows:

1. 90° less the terrestrial latitude = co-latitude.
2. Add 12 hours to the sidereal time of birth and extract the Ascendant from the table of houses for the co-latitude.
3. This Ascendant position is the Vertex.

Vespertine: Setting just after the Sun. The reverse of Matutine (rising before the Sun). The Moon is vespertine after she has passed her first quarter.

Via Combusta: The combust way. An area of the Zodiac from 15° Libra to 15° Scorpio considered by the ancients to be unfortunate because of the 'violent' fixed stars (q.v.) associated with this area.

Void of Course: If a planet forms no major aspect before leaving the sign it occupies, it is said to be 'void of course'. Generally associated with the Moon and used mainly in horary astrology, although the term is now being applied in natal and mundane astrology.

West point: The point where the western horizon intersects the Celestial Equator and the Prime Vertical.

Zone Time: See page 81.

3.
THE BRANCHES OF ASTROLOGY

Natal Astrology

Most forward-looking astrological students and practitioners have long realized that the astrology which sufficed for previous generations is not, in some instances, applicable to the present age. This is not to say that all the traditional teachings should be abandoned, but that astrology should be reappraised and restructured, in order that its real significance can be appreciated and its truths applied for constructive growth and development. In the light of psychological and psychiatric developments and the application of therapeutic techniques, astrology demonstrates the most revealing means of understanding the complexities of human behaviour. Man is part of the universe, and he does respond in varying degrees to cyclic phenomena according to his fundamental nature.

A natal chart, when it is analysed in detail, will disclose certain basic information which is common to all born at a particular time and place. This information needs to be considered firstly in broad terms and then each factor, taken in isolation, studied in relation to its overall importance in the chart. Gradually a pattern will 'come into focus' and this pattern, with its various combinations, will show potentialities which, subject to appropriate stimulus and in accordance with environmental factors, will be expressed in terms of the chart as a whole.

Traditionally, character, disposition, personality, mentality and the affections were portrayed by the Sun, Moon, Ascendant, Mercury and Venus. These bodies, with their signs and any aspects they received, were considered the significators of these qualities. Although this has some validity, it does not do justice to the intrinsic meaning of the planets, a knowledge of which is essential if an adequate synthesis of a chart is to be made. Astrology must be studied in operation, that is, in day-to-day existence, and it will then be seen how rich and diversified planetary symbolism can be. The following is a broad outline of planetary significators.

Sun ☉
Symbolizes the life-force; the core of the individual; the ego; what we are at heart; vitality, desires, the urge to power, recognition, honour and acclaim.

Moon ☽
The habits, mannerisms, feelings and moods; signifies fluctuation, emotional responses, the protective instinct and the desire for security; health and sexuality.

Mercury ☿
Communication skills; verbal expression; perception; our ability to comprehend the outside world; how we express our need to know about and relate to that which is external to us; our ability to absorb knowledge and ideas and to co-ordinate learning and experience.

Venus ♀
Co-operation and unity; love, marriage, intimacy, affections, social contacts, peace and harmony. The ability to express and receive affection; our need for appreciation and sharing.

Mars ♂
Physical activity; initiative and action; the ability to meet challenges and overcome obstacles; our need to assert our will and obtain our demands; how we are stimulated physically.

Jupiter ♃
Expansiveness, joy, abundance and confidence; our need to reach out beyond our immediate environment; Optimism, faith and hope; our ability for progress and achievement; the acquisition of those things which increase our sense of well-being, preserve us from injury or contribute to a widening of our knowledge and understanding.

Saturn ♄
Consolidation, conservative approach, constriction, fears and frustrations. Emotional repressions; sense of inadequacy; inhibitions; the urge to throw up barriers, either physical or psychological, to prevent unwanted intrusions. Our ability to pursue well-defined aims

with discipline and concentrated effort; our need for well-structured foundations to counteract adverse influences and effects.

Uranus ♅

Our sense of originality; the desire for freedom and independence; our wilfulness and craving for novelty and change; the hankering after the new at the expense of the old; the urge to be different; the rejection of the commonplace and familiar; our ability for self-discovery and awareness.

Neptune ♆

The ideals we strive for; our sense of limitation or confinement; imagined feelings of guilt; the urge to escape; our visions of perfection; our flight from reality; our attraction to the dream-world; our fantasies; our world of make-believe.

Pluto ♇

Our ability to penetrate below the surface; our attitude towards enforced changes and upheavals; our sense of isolation and detachment; our capacity to endure loneliness; our anti-social tendencies; our ability to rise, phoenix-like, from the ashes of destruction and regenerate and transform ourselves. Our attitude towards beginnings and endings and birth and death, either actual or symbolic.

The significance of the planets, and how the urges or energies denoted by them will be expressed, are governed by their sign emplacement and by their house position. Regarding sign position, it may be that the elements should be considered in greater detail, in combination with the basic meanings of the signs and houses. For example, in the case of Mars in Gemini, the emphasis is on fire/air, and the energies of Mars will be expressed in a diffuse Geminian manner — mentally agile, but somewhat inconsistently. In Virgo, however, the 'mixture' of fire/earth enables the energies to be expressed in a realistic and practical manner. With this placement, the preoccupation with detail, essential for a craftsman, would be acceptable, whereas Mars/Gemini would lack the necessary patience which fire/earth provides.

Signs and Symbols

Sign	*Symbol*	*Name*	*Ruler*	*Symbol*
1st Aries	♈	The Ram	Mars	♂
2nd Taurus	♉	The Bull	Venus	♀
3rd Gemini	♊	The Twins	Mercury	☿
4th Cancer	♋	The Crab	Moon	☽
5th Leo	♌	The Lion	Sun	☉
6th Virgo	♍	The Virgin	Mercury	☿
7th Libra	♎	The Balance or Scales	Venus	♀
8th Scorpio	♏	The Scorpion	Mars Pluto	♂ ♇
9th Sagittarius	♐	The Archer	Jupiter	♃
10th Capricorn	♑	The Goat	Saturn	♄
11th Aquarius	♒	The Waterbearer	Uranus Saturn	♅ ♄
12th Pisces	♓	The Fishes	Neptune Jupiter	♆ ♃
The Moon's Nodes:				
North	☊	Caput draconis (dragon's head)		
South	☋	Cauda draconis (dragon's tail)		
Part of Fortune:	⊕			

Elements and Qualities (Substance and Energy)

Traditionally, the signs of the zodiac and the twelve mundane houses are classified into two main categories: Elements (Triplicities) — Fire, Earth, Air and Water; and Qualities, (Quadruplicities) — Cardinal, Fixed and Mutable or Common. In addition, the four elements are considered as either Positive or Negative (the Polarities). The following table shows the various classifications:

Sign	*Element*	*Quality*	*House*
Aries ♈	Fire (Positive)	Cardinal	1 Angular
Leo ♌		Fixed	5 Succedent
Sagittarius ♐		Mutable	9 Cadent
Capricorn ♑	Earth (Negative)	Cardinal	10 Angular
Taurus ♉		Fixed	2 Succedent
Virgo ♍		Mutable	6 Cadent

Libra ♎		Cardinal	7 Angular
Aquarius ♒	Air (Positive)	Fixed	11 Succedent
Gemini ♊		Mutable	3 Cadent
Cancer ♋		Cardinal	4 Angular
Scorpio ♏	Water (Negative)	Fixed	8 Succedent
Pisces ♓		Mutable	12 Cadent

The concept of Elements and Qualities has to be considered in broad general terms, for it does not follow that all Leos are fiery or that all Capricorns are earthy. Neither is it established that Positive signs are associated with extroversion and Negative signs with introversion.

Although the positive signs are generally considered as direct and outgoing, and the negative signs as receptive and passive, this is a broad generalization, and each chart must be studied according to the planetary groupings, patterns and house positions. Leo may be fiery, positive and creative, but an unsympathetic combination of sign and planet will not be conducive to the natural exuberant nature associated with Leo. As with Leo, so with the other signs.

The twelve houses of the chart are divided into three groups:

1. Angular houses (1, 10, 7 and 4).
2. Succedent houses (2, 11, 8 and 5).
3. Cadent houses (3, 12, 9 and 6).

The Angular houses are the most important houses, and planets in them, particularly if close to the Angles (cusps 1, 10, 7, and 4), exert their maximum influence depending on the sign containing the planet and the aspects which the planet receives. (See also Zones of High Intensity, below.)

Traditionally, the houses are related to the signs, in that the first house has a relationship with the first sign, Aries, the second house to Taurus, the third to Gemini and so on. The Angular houses have a correspondence with the Cardinal signs, the Succedent houses with the Fixed signs, and the Cadent houses with the Mutable signs. This traditional relationship appears to have some justification, and planets in a particular house often display certain facets, not only of the house where they are posited, but also of the natural sign of that house.

Basically, the three divisions of the houses, Angular, Succedent and Cadent, represent the Qualities of the signs naturally associated with them. Each sign and house has a correspondence with its opposite, and this fact has to be considered in any chart synthesis.

For example, Aries and the first house (self) Libra and the seventh house (others). Taurus and the second house (personal assets of all kinds) Scorpio and the eighth (other person's assets). (See Polarity, page 168.)

Each sign has a ruler (in some cases two), and these rulers have an affinity with the sign(s) with which they are associated. Aries, for example, has Mars as its ruler, Taurus has Venus, Gemini has Mercury, and so on. The modern planets, i.e. those discovered in modern times, Uranus, Neptune and Pluto, are classified as co-rulers of the signs Aquarius, Pisces and Scorpio. (See Rulers, page 169.)

Zones of High Intensity

Due to the Earth's rotation round its axis once every twenty-four hours, the celestial bodies — Sun, Moon, planets and stars — appear to rise in the east, reach their culmination point and then descend to set in the west. A planet will culminate at the time which corresponds to its right ascension, but its rising and setting is dependent upon its ascensional difference. The actual time at which a planet bodily crosses an angle can be found from its sidereal time of rising and setting. In the same way that there is a solar day, so also there are 'planetary days' which can commence and end at anytime during the 'normal day', depending upon the planet's co-ordinates (latitude, declination and longitude) at any given time, and the place of observation (locality).

Astrologically, the place of rising is the Ascendant (first house), and the opposite point — Descendant (seventh house) is the setting point. Culmination is the meridian passage of a body; upper culmination — the high point in the sky — coincides with the tenth house, while lower culmination coincides with the opposite point and the fourth house. These houses and places closely adjacent to them are the zones of high intensity. M. and F. Gauquelin in their indefatigable researches concerning planetary temperaments and personality, have shown that certain planetary positions are prominent at the moment of birth, far more often than chance would allow. A planet is in a zone of high intensity when it is rising, at upper culmination, setting and at lower culmination, the rising and culmination zones being more powerful than the setting and lower culmination zones. A person born with a planet in one of these zones will show the characteristics associated with that planet. If more than one planet is in one of these zones, then there will be a combined influence, modified or accentuated according to the planets in combination and their relative strengths.

The angular houses have always been considered the most important areas, particularly when planets are close to their cusps, and the findings of the Gauquelins' confirm this fact. In the initial assessment of any chart, it would appear that these zones should be given priority and the chart as a whole related to them.

The Elements

Fire

In astrological symbolism, fire indicates energy, action, ardour and creativity. It is the life-giving force, scintillating and radiant. The three Fire signs (Aries, Leo and Sagittarius) exhibit these qualities in varying degrees. In Aries, 'primitive' fire corresponds with the dynamic, enthusiastic spirit which is initiatory and exploratory. It is uncontrolled fire which is all-consuming unless it is checked, harnessed and channelled into constructive outlets. In Leo, fire is 'fixed', burning with a steady constant glow which warms and illuminates all that it contacts. There is a true beauty with Fixed Fire, symbolizing as it does, the concepts of life and creativity. The third sign of the fiery trigon, Sagittarius, combines the qualities of Aries and Leo in a purified and more expansive form. Whereas Aries is initiatory in a primitive way and Leo seeks to shine with undiminished radiance, Sagittarius strives for sublimation and a sense of spirituality.

Earth

As fire signifies creative energy, so Earth represents the concrete and physical. The practicality of Earth is well-illustrated in Capricorn, whose awareness of time and its ravages, impels it to provide secure foundations by conserving and utilizing material assets. In Taurus, the solidity of Earth is expressed in a realistic appreciation of, and delight in, the physical aspects of existence. In Virgo, Earth resembles 'fine dust' which has been ground, in order that its constituent properties may be analysed in minute detail. All the Earth signs are concerned with the material world; Capricorn with stability and structure, Taurus with basic foundations, and Virgo with adaptability and application.

Air

Perception, communication, relationships and reasoning are the functions of Air. Libra symbolizes the need to communicate and establish relationships which are complementary and which assist in achieving a 'balance'. Equilibrium, often as a compensatory factor, characterizes its action, whereas Libra often seeks a one-to-one relationship, Aquarius is more concerned with collective relationships: 'as free as air', aptly describes the Aquarian approach. Aquarius has a detached attitude in which ideas, visions, hopes and expectations are more important than personal commitments. Exchange and intercourse with others are stimulating, but it must not fetter the Aquarian sense of universalness. Gemini, 'the child of the zodiac', is in a sense, 'primitive' Air. It is inquisitive, curious, always seeking to know 'why and how'. It represents the beginning of perception and understanding and the formation of personal attachments, usually those of the immediate environment. All the Air signs have a cold logical approach to life and view both things and persons from the intellectual standpoint.

Water

Emotion, feeling and intuition are the chief attributes of Water. It is introspective — inward-looking — as opposed to Fire, which is forward-looking and thrusting. In Cancer, the instinct is towards protection of the feelings and the desire to nourish and sustain at all costs. Cardinal Water has the tenacity to wear away a rock if it is necessary, but usually, it is content to build, defensive structures, either physical or psychological, to ward off actual or imagined dangers. In Scorpio, Water runs deep. As with all the Water signs it is introspective, but unlike Cancer and Pisces its emotions are not paraded, but held in firm check, which in turn gives intensity and depth. It seeks to fathom the unknown, and is the most tenacious of all the twelve signs in pursuing its objectives. It has a natural affinity with the processes of life and death and an instinctive feeling for the unknown. Whereas Air arrives at conclusions by logical deduction, Water, particularly Scorpio, can sense and assess the true nature of persons and conditions.

Pisces, the third sign of the Water trigon, is boundless Water. It symbolizes the ocean wherein all experiences are merged, and the individuality is renounced for some ideal. It indicates the dissolution of forms, and the desire for communion with the mystical and abstract. With Pisces, there is the endless ebbing and flowing in the search for some indefinable ideal. In this sign, the striving for oneness with God and nature is paramount.

The Houses

The twelve mundane houses are divisions of the celestial sphere, formed by tri-secting the quadrants formed between the meridian and the horizon. From time immemorial, these divisions have been assigned certain qualities and considered to have dominion over various conditions and activities common to man. Modern research has shown that planets in significant areas do indicate a correspondence with certain traits, activities or psychological responses.

Basically, we can consider the twelve houses as areas of action and experience. The fundamental basis of each house has to be considered, not only in terms of the sign and any planet which may be located in it, but also in relation to the natural sign and ruler(s) of the house. The first house, for example, has a relationship with Aries and Mars, the second with Taurus and Venus, the third with Gemini and Mercury. So, in analysing the significance of a particular house, we need to combine several factors before we can establish what the reaction will be.

Another point which may be of value is that the ascending sign (rising sign) may colour our viewpoint as to how we see and respond to matters denoted by the various houses. If, for example, Virgo rises, we may regard fifth house matters such as romance, creativity or leisure activities, not only from the sign on the cusp, say Capricorn, but as Leo/Capricorn filtered through a Virgo Ascendant. Likewise with the other houses. It follows that the analysis of any chart is no simple matter; one factor is part of the whole, and no isolated factor can have significance until it is related to the whole. Traditionally, it is the Angular houses which are the most important and this is true, although recent research by the Gauguelins has shown significant areas which embrace part of the Cadent houses. The Angular houses (first, tenth, seventh and fourth) have a correspondence with the Cardinal signs (Aries, Capricorn, Libra and Cancer), and planets located in them, particularly when close to the angles, exert their maximum strength and power. The next series in importance is the Succedent houses (second, fifth, eighth and eleventh) which correspond to Taurus, Leo, Scorpio and Aquarius. Finally, the Cadent houses (third, sixth, ninth and twelfth) correspond to Gemini, Virgo, Sagittarius and Pisces.

The essential point which has to be grasped regarding houses is that they are fields of experience and action. When other factors such as planets, rulers of signs and important aspects are activated, the house and those matters connected with it 'come alive' in terms of the bodies and contacts involved. Many of the traditional meanings assigned to the twelve houses are archaic, and the rigid approach concerning the houses and their meanings has contributed to an 'event-based' astrology, whereby the deeper and richer expression of the houses has been neglected.

In the same way that the planets and signs denote energies and the expression of those energies, so the houses show the field of action where the individual will seek to experience and express those energies. Whether the experiences have meaning and assist in growth and development, or result in stultifying regressive attitudes, will depend upon the quality of the whole chart and the person's level of awareness. To say that because Neptune in Leo is in the fifth house, one is likely to be deceived in love, is meaningless. A person with this placement may be deceived through foolishness or treachery, but the more apt analysis would be that the principles associated with the fifth house would be viewed and experienced in an idealistic manner. If there are stresses in the natal chart, then the Neptunian/fifth house experiences might prove sensational or enervating. Alternatively, a well-integrated chart would suggest that this placement gave the capacity for an appreciation of the creative arts and the desire to respond to an unfettered imagination.

The Angular Houses

These houses and their correspondence with the Cardinal signs indicate active, outgoing principles. The first house (Aries) is concerned with self and our attitude towards life and everything which affects us personally. The tenth house (Capricorn) indicates our striving for a place in the world; the image we wish others to see and admire, thereby increasing our self-esteem and public standing. Hence it is related to ambition; 'getting on in the world'; our approach to structured organization; what we would like to be publicly or professionally. All the Earth signs are concerned in one way or another with the material world, and Capricorn/tenth shows how we strive to achieve our goals and ambitions. The significance of the tenth house goes far beyond such terms as 'career and reputation'. Many persons have no career as such, but they do have a sense of identity — however much this may be affected by 'authority figures' — and it is by seeking to fulfil themselves as persons, through work or achievements, that they obtain a feeling of personal worth.

The seventh house (Libra) is complementary to the first house

(Aries). It shows, with its ruler Venus, the need and the ability for close personal relationships. Through social intercourse we exchange ideas, enhance our perception and establish bonds. In doing this, we share experiences of a mutual nature and this, in turn, assists us in 'forgetting self' and enables us to compensate, in some degree, for our own shortcomings. The seventh house, with its sign and ruler, signifies all forms of co-operation and unity, which embraces all manner of love, marriage, intimacy, affection and social contacts. The fourth house (Cancer) is the opposite to the tenth and Capricorn. With the tenth house, we strive for recognition; with the fourth house we seek refuge. Cancer and the fourth house is the private domain whereby we seek to nourish, sustain and protect ourselves from a hostile environment. Crab-like we retreat, either physically or psychologically, and embrace the familiar in order to feel secure. Security and protection characterize this sign and house, and it is here that we feel safe. Hence the association with habit, the family and home, and privacy.

The Succedent Houses

These houses and their correspondence with the Fixed signs indicate all forms of resources and assets. The second house (Taurus) is concerned with all material out of which something can be made, fashioned or adapted. It is associated with foundations, particularly economic ones, which enable material security to be obtained. The second house can be likened to a storehouse or treasure chest, within which assets of all kinds are freely available as and when circumstances demand. If Cancer and the fourth house demand emotional security, so Taurus and the second house need physical resources to conserve and value.

The fifth house (Leo) shows the creative resources and the need to express the individuality in a highly personalized way. All Fixed signs and houses have some relation to power and its exercise, and in the fifth house and Leo, this power is often displayed through creative enterprises designed to confirm one's self-worth. Approbation and applause through projecting the self is admirable, provided it does not lead to over-confidence or egocentricity.

The eighth house (Scorpio), like its opposite sign and house (Taurus/second), is concerned with resources, but whereas the second house indicates that which is personal, the eighth shows those resources and assets which are acquired either through joint action with or on behalf of others, or as a result of acquiring knowledge, not only of the physical world, but also of that beyond our immediate perception. It is in this sector of the chart that one confronts the reality of life and death and seeks to understand the mysteries of existence. Both these houses, the second and eighth, are concerned with security: Taurus with material security; and Scorpio with emotional security.

The eleventh house (Aquarius) is the opposite of the fifth (Leo). In the fifth, we are concerned with our creative resources and their expression. In the eleventh, we are interested in impersonal relationships which cannot bind us. The urge is towards complete freedom of expression and the need to experience novelty and change. The desire to be different, a yearning for uniqueness and originality, is related to the eleventh house. Ideas, visions, hopes and aspirations — what we would like to achieve if we have complete freedom of action: all these are contained within the realm of this house.

The Cadent Houses

These houses correspond to the Mutable signs, Gemini, Virgo, Sagittarius and Pisces. The Mutable signs and houses are predominantly concerned with perception and understanding. The third (Gemini) is intimately connected with the immediate environment and the acquisition of learning skills. It indicates the need to communicate; to ask questions; to satisfy the curiosity.

The sixth house (Virgo) indicates the application of learning skills. In the same way that Gemini and the third want to know, so Virgo and the sixth want to differentiate, analyse and comprehend the basic structures of life. Unlike Sagittarius, which looks to the far horizons, Virgo is preoccupied with the minute and routine. It analyses the parts but fails to visualize the whole. In its striving for perfection, it automatically displays the critical faculty in an effort to function efficiently through either work or service.

The ninth house (Sagittarius) is concerned with the expansion of consciousness. Whereas Gemini and the third are concerned with the local environment, and Virgo and the sixth with the small and practical, Sagittarius and the ninth look far beyond the present and the immediate. The ninth house endeavours to visualize the future through philosophical speculation, abstract thought and symbols. It seeks a wider, deeper understanding of life which involves faith, compassion, morality and justice.

The twelfth house (Pisces) shows the striving for idealism and the desire to escape from everything which tends to hold or bind. The urge for spiritual communion with all aspects of existence and the appreciation of the divine involve the renunciation of the material and of the self. It is this sector which denotes the 'dream world' where, in isolation, we can indulge in fantasy and observe the world as we wish it to be — not as it actually is. Through fantasy and delusion, we seek to escape from the hard practicalities of life and, by adopting disguises of one kind or another, strike various kinds of poses, project false images, become enamoured of various cults and crazes which pander to our vanity, all this in a vain attempt to escape the bonds of reality.

Although the vague, subtle, illusory and deceptive elements of life often distort our perception, they are in a sense essential, in that they act as a safety valve, whereby the stresses and tensions of everyday life can be reduced or mitigated. The important thing in our quest for the ideal is that we do not mistake elusive shadows for the substance.

Aspects

Aspects (see Fig. 23) or configurations are angular relationships either between planets or important points on the Zodiac. The integration of a chart depends upon its aspectual strength or lack of it. Planets may be well-placed mundanely (in the houses) but lack strong contacts. Conversely, strongly aspected bodies may be weak mundanely. When strongly placed and aspected, there is ease of expression in matters connected with the planet and/or house, and the person has the ability to realize potentialities. Weakly placed and aspected may cause difficulties and frustrations and, although the aspirations and expectations may be as important as for a person with an 'easy chart', their realization demands energy and courage to meet challenging situations and conditions. As with all chart analysis, assessments require that the chart is studied in its entirety. No one factor can be studied in isolation.

The astrologers of antiquity classified aspects, or 'familiarities' as they termed them, either as *benefic* or *malefic*. The modern approach is to consider such terms as archaic, and the trend is now to use words such as hard or soft, helpful or challenging, to distinguish between the two categories once thought of as either good or bad. According to Ptolemy, there were six aspects, namely the conjunction, sextile, square, trine, opposition and the zodiacal parallel. To these, Kepler added many more minor aspects and divided the classification into two categories — major and minor aspects. The major aspects (see Fig. 23) are:

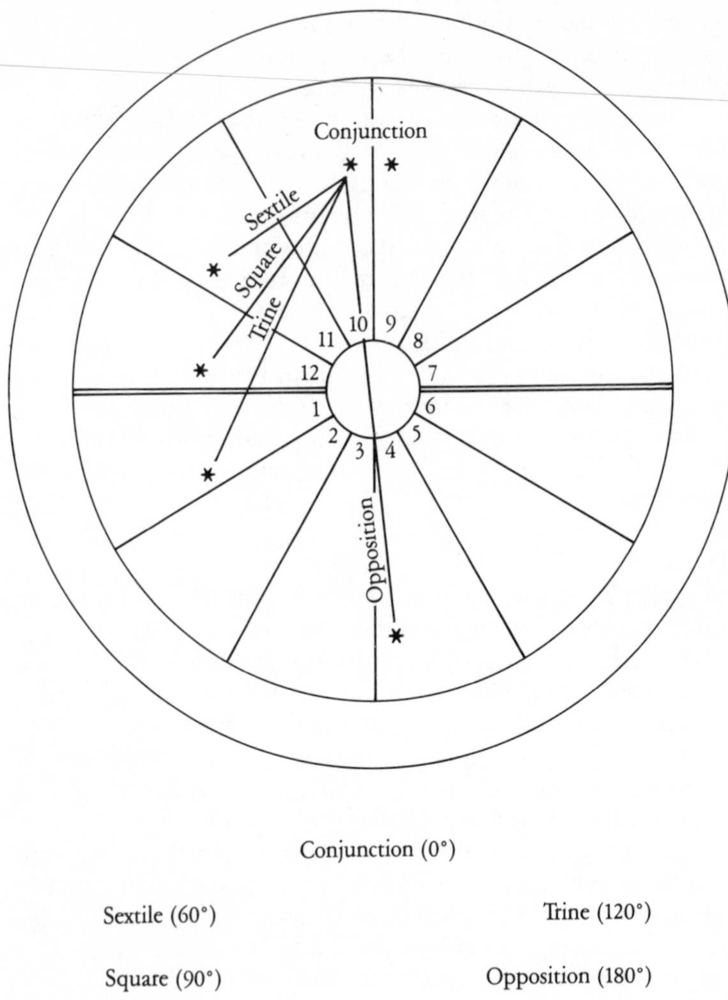

Figure 23 Aspects.

The *conjunction,* when two or more planets are in the same sign and degree. As planets are allowed orbs, a conjunction can occur between planets in different signs, e.g. Mars in the last few degrees of Gemini: Moon in the first few degrees of Cancer.

The *sextile,* when in the same degree but two signs distant (60°).

The *square*, when in the same degree but three signs distant (90°).

The *trine*, when in the same degree but four signs distant (120°).

The *opposition*, when in the same degree of an opposite sign (180°).

These major aspects are exact when the same degree is aspected, but an orb is allowed ranging from 0° to 10° depending upon the bodies or points in aspect. (See below.) The minor aspects include:

the semi-sextile (30°);
the decile (36°);
the semi-square (45°);
the quintile (72°);
the sesquiquadrate (135°);
the biquintile (144°);
the quincunx (150°).

The orb allowed for these minor aspects is normally about 2°.

Although all aspects are allowed orbs which vary according to the type of aspect and the planets in aspect, there is no hard and fast rule regarding the size of the orb, but the following are usually allowed:

Conjunction	8°
Sextile	4°
Square	8°
Trine	8°
Opposition	8°

Table of Aspects
(Major)

360° circle divided by:	*Degree*	*Aspect*	*Symbol*
1	360 or 0	Conjunction	☌
2	180	Opposition	☍
3	120	Trine	△
4	90	Square	□
6	60	Sextile	✶
		(Minor)	
5/12	150	Quincunx	⊼
2/5	144	Bi-Quintile	[illegible]
3/8	135	Sesqui-Quadrate	⚼
5	72	Quintile	Q
8	45	Semi-square	∠
10	36	Decile	⊥
12	30	Semi-sextile	⊻

Each chart needs to be considered in totality and allowance made for aspects which are *applying* (approaching exactitude) or *separating* (departing from exactitude). Also, the strength of the planets in aspects, their house positions, particularly if angular (first, tenth, seventh and fourth angles), and whether forming part of a stellium or some other significant formation, all need to be considered.

Aspects can be either zodiacal or mundane. Zodiacal aspects are measured along the Ecliptic in celestial longitude, whereas mundane aspects are measured along the Celestial Equator in right ascension. Mundane aspects are formed from the distance between the angles, and are often referred to as aspects in *in mundo* (in the world), while zodiacal aspects, which are formed in the zodiac, are termed *in zodiaco* (in the zodiac). If, for example, a planet is conjunct the Midheaven in 2° Pisces, and a planet is conjunct the Ascendant in 8° Cancer, they are in zodiacal trine, but in mundane square. Mundane aspects depend upon the distance in the mundane houses, and are measured, not by the zodiacal degrees on the cusps of the houses, but by the proportional parts of a planet's semi-arc (the time it is above the horizon — diurnal semi-arc — or the time it is below the horizon — nocturnal semi-arc). A planet's semi-arc measures three mundane houses for that planet; two-thirds of its semi-arc, two houses; and one-third of its semi-arc, one house. Any planet which by the Earth's rotation arrives at the cusps of the twelfth, eleventh, tenth, etc., houses will be then in mundane semi-sextile, sextile or square to the Ascendant, as the case may be. Mundane aspects are based upon the Earth's diurnal rotation, whereas zodiacal aspects are based on the sub-division of the planet's orbits along the Ecliptic.

The Nature of Aspects

The planetary principles denote the urges or drives which seek expression via the signs and houses. The quality of this expression is, however, governed in no small measure by the relationship that one planet has with another and/or its configurations with the angles of the chart. The traditional teaching regarding 'good and bad' aspects need to be reviewed because, if we consider the intrinsic nature of the planets and what they represent both consciously and unconsciously, we will find that many of the so-called bad aspects are not so evil, nor are the so-called good aspects always beneficial.

Aspects, broadly speaking, can be divided into two main groups: (a) those that are constructive and assist in ease of expression; and

(b) those that are inhibiting and act as restraints. Now it does not necessarily follow that all constructive aspects will produce good and all inhibiting aspects will produce evil. On the contrary, many so-called constructive aspects may be detrimental in so far as effort and initiative are concerned, whereas the inhibiting aspects may be productive of good, in that the challenging and difficult conditions often associated with them have to be resolved in one way or another.

Traditionally, the Sun, Moon, Mercury, Venus and Jupiter are associated with beneficial conditions and responses, whereas Mars, Saturn, Uranus, Neptune and Pluto denote adverse circumstances and reactions. This traditional teaching is highly suspect, because it does not follow that the so-called beneficial planets will always correlate with easy harmonious conditions, nor will the so-called malefic planets always correspond with difficult, inhibiting or restraining conditions. Mars, for example, is a highly energetic force, often rash and impetuous, hence it may often be prominent at the times of accidents or when one suffers physical injury, but as with all the planets, its mode of operation accords with its intrinsic nature. The severity or otherwise of its action depends upon its sign placement, its aspects and its mundane position. The constraints imposed by a prominent Saturn, however frustrating they may appear, are often beneficial in that one is prevented from acting ill-advisedly or hastily. Over-caution can, of course, lead to missed opportunities, delays and disappointments. It all depends on the planetary aspects, not only natally, but also progressively, and how these patterns are responded to, either actively or passively.

Naturally, the responses to aspects will be governed to a greater or lesser degree by the nature of the personality and the environmental conditions. Aspects involving the outer planets (Jupiter, Saturn, Uranus, Neptune and Pluto) often indicate progress and growth through accepting demanding and challenging conditions. Jupiter enables us to recognize opportunities and to widen our horizons. Saturn may be restrictive, but it does act as a stabilizing influence and assists in restructuring that which may be in danger of collapse. Uranus is a separative influence but this is not necessarily bad, because change is essential for development and progress. Neptune can be inspirational or it can mean unmitigated disorder and a flight from reality. Pluto may take us to the depths of experience or to the very heights, but its action, whatever it may be, will always leave us with a feeling of finality. Progress and growth are not accomplished without effort and confrontation, but the results are often satisfying and enable us to strive to realize our potentialities whatever they may be. So, the challenging aspects, the square and opposition can be productive of good as well as bad, depending upon the planets in aspect. Likewise, the constructive aspects may not always be as beneficial as one has been led to believe.

Although we can determine the significance of each planet and what it represents, the question of aspects and the interpretation of their effects presents a considerable problem. Basically, we can give a theoretical meaning to the various types of contacts, but when we study the effects of planetary contacts and configurations in actual life, we often discover that the same aspect may manifest in a variety of ways. All aspectual contacts need to be related to the person concerned, in so far that each and everyone of us will respond according to our needs, personality and environmental conditions.

It has, in the past, been an accepted teaching that certain aspects are inimical and that others are beneficial. The opposition (180°) and the square (90°) have been regarded as difficult, if not dangerous, contacts, whereas the trine (120°) and the sextile (60°) have been considered beneficial. The conjunction (0°) partakes of the nature of the bodies in contact, good or bad, as the case may be. This doctrine is true up to a point, but it requires qualification in that the planets in aspect will determine how the aspect may be expressed, and this expression is governed according to the nature of the appropriate planets. Mars opposition Saturn is a far more potent contact than, say, Moon opposition Venus, and although both these contacts may be expressed in a variety of ways, the Mars-Saturn opposition will, other things being equal, indicate difficult and demanding situations or severe and restrictive actions. Moon-Venus on the other hand may be concerned with personal relationships and associations which one seeks to preserve. Mars-Saturn may be hard reality, Moon-Venus, emotional responses.

The simplistic view that all oppositions are bad and that all trines are good needs reappraisal. The most important aspect is the conjunction (planets in the same degree of longitude or close to an angle). Again, it is the nature of the planets in aspect which will indicate how the aspect will be expressed. Conjunctions are the most powerful of all contacts, particularly when they affect the angles of a chart, and their effects are very significant. In general, certain planetary contacts appear to act passively, while others are more active and vigorous. Uranian contacts, for example, are invariably disruptive and often coincide with the desire for change and the abandonment of conventional attitudes. Uranus has the unnerving quality of forcing us to extricate ourselves from any rut that we may be in, however, pleasant that rut may be!

In the same way that Uranus acts dramatically, so Neptune acts passively, and its contacts are often associated with escapism in one form or another. Often these contacts stimulate the imagination, but just as often they result in vague, illusory conditions — one visualizes things as one would wish them to be — not as they actually are. Although Neptunian contacts often correspond with treacherous conditions, one is not always aware of the true state of affairs until some time subsequently; hence its contacts can, in some cases, be rather insidious. Not all Neptunian aspects result in chaotic conditions. Well-placed and well-aspected, it gives refinement and inspiration. In contact with Venus, it often indicates idealistic feelings, devotional attitudes or, more often than not, a sense of 'being out of this world', such as one experiences when falling in love.

There is little doubt that certain contacts are expressed forcibly, while others operate almost imperceptibly. Often there is a subtle undertone of impending change and a psychological reappraisal concerning attitudes and responses to life. In some cases, a particular aspect or configuration appears to remain 'dormant' and its significance only becomes apparent when it is excited or galvanized into life through progressions or transits.

It seems unlikely that an unaspected planet does not have importance; all planets form part of the whole and, even if it lacks strong contacts or has no contacts at all, it cannot merely operate as a 'dumb' note. A lack of zodiacal contacts can often be compensated for by a strong sign or house position, and the planet will display its qualities in terms of the sign and house in a 'purer' manner than would otherwise be the case if it formed part of an aspectual pattern.

Each individual responds according to his own pattern, and it is therefore impossible to lay down hard-and-fast rules as to how a particular aspect will be expressed. We know what each planet represents, and we are also aware that certain aspects denote either challenging and disruptive conditions or constructive and progressive conditions. But we cannot determine with certainty how or in what manner a given aspect will operate. An overall study of the natal chart will indicate the strengths and weaknesses of the individual. This, in turn, will show what the likely responses may be, either psychologically (signs and planets) or to the world at large (houses).

A person with a well-integrated chart can often survive the most difficult and formidable challenges and, conversely, also take advantage of opportunities for progress and development. A less well-integrated chart may show the inability to act determinedly when confronted with demanding situations or to respond when opportunities arise. Fortunately, we are all a mixture of many factors and our responses to planetary action will be influenced by our natal make-up.

Mundane Astrology

The ancients classified astrology into three main branches:

1. *Natal astrology,* which is concerned with personal birth charts and which was formerly called genethlialogy astrology.
2. *Horary or judicial astrology,* which is a divinatory branch of astrology. Although some practitioners find horary astrology useful, others reject it completely, possibly due to its connotations with fortune-telling.
3. *Mundane astrology*, which concerns the study of nations, mundane events, the rise and fall of dynasties, disasters and all those matters which affect society collectively.

The study of mundane astrology demands a broad knowledge of history, politics, economics and geography, coupled with a keen interest in current affairs. A student who wishes to specialize in mundane astrology requires the ability and the patience to undertake time-consuming research into a mass of scattered data in order to determine definite times and dates for the foundation of countries, states or institutions. As a keen observer of current events, the mundane astrologer is always on the look-out for data which, although it may not be of immediate interest, may in future years prove extremely valuable. Astrological journals do from time to time record interesting data, but much more could be done, particularly on a worldwide basis. As with all data, it is essential that the source is quoted, and also that when an event occurs, not only are the time, date and place recorded, but also that it is cross-referenced to any other data with which it may have some relationship, e.g. the death of the monarch in relation to the accession chart and/or any other national chart.

The study of political processes plays an important part in mundane astrology, and it is essential that in the analysis of political data, every endeavour is made to assess the results completely divorced from any political bias. An impartial approach is essential; an astrologer should strive to present the truth as he sees it, unclouded by 'party bias'.

Charts Relevant to Mundane Astrology

It has been the accepted fact that certain categories of material provide the most useful tools for the study of mundane astrology. These have been classified in various ways, such as:

the national chart;
the monarch's personal chart;
the monarch's accession chart;
the political party's foundation chart;
the political leader's personal chart;
the prime minister's/president's personal chart.

These charts, used in conjunction with the chart for when a government assumed power, coupled in the case of Great Britain, with other national charts, are deemed to show the political life of the country. Political astrology, although classified as mundane, does have a relationship with natal astrology, and should be studied not only from a national viewpoint but also in connection with the charts of the monarch, president and other leading politicians. So far as the British system of government is concerned, the Lords and Commons, have, for centuries, met at Westminster, and the charts for the Houses of Parliament often figure prominently at the time of notable occurrences which affect British political life.

Apart from the political charts relating to nations, mundane techniques are employed in the study of meteorology, earthquake incidence, and economic and business trends. Weather forecasting is a precarious activity due to the many variables which exist. Although earthquake prediction has yet to become a reality, it is possible in retrospect to see that these disasters do, in fact, correlate with celestial phenomena. Economics and business trends appear to follow cycles, and a country's 'economic health' seems to be related to various cycles which operate in conjunction with various other important charts of the country concerned.

Astrological/Astronomical Factors

The astrological/astronomical factors used in mundane astrology are fairly numerous, the principal phenomena being:

New and Full Moons;
Eclipses;

Solar and Lunar Ingresses;
Great Conjunctions;
Comets.

It is unlikely that one phenomenon on its own has much significance, but when it is related to other appropriate charts and configurations, its effects may be considerable. The Ingress charts (Sun into Aries, Cancer, Libra and Capricorn) have always been regarded as important, but research has tended to confirm that the Capricorn Ingress is extremely powerful and deserves more attention than has hitherto been accorded to it. In sidereal astrology, it is regarded as the 'master chart of the year' and quite rightly so, as it has demonstrated its worth particularly when it is progressed for a particular date and locality.

New and Full Moons which occur each month are significant if they fall on important points in a chart, particularly the position of the Sun, Moon or angles. The same applies to solar and lunar eclipses, which from remote antiquity have been regarded as the 'shadow of things to come'.

Great Conjunctions are those formed between the major planets, Jupiter, Saturn, Uranus, Neptune and Pluto. These conjunctions must be studied as part of world cycles, but they can be related to individual charts where they become significant if forming prominent contacts. The conjunction of Jupiter and Saturn occurs every twenty years and will, for a considerable time, fall in the same triplicity. Eventually, the conjunction occurs in a fresh triplicity, the first conjunction in the new triplicity being termed a Mutation Conjunction. When falling in the Fire element, it is termed a Great Mutation. There is little doubt that these Great Conjunctions can be correlated with mundane events and conditions, and their significance observed over many decades. The appearance of comets is traditionally associated with dire events and calamities. Astrological literature contains examples of their reputed evil when sighted in certain signs of the zodiac. As with all celestial phenomenon, they need to be considered in conjunction with other factors. The return of Halley's Comet in late 1985, early 1986, may prove illuminating in more ways than one!

Great Britain: the Relevant Data

As already indicated, the study of mundane astrology requires a wide interest in the history and development of nations. If the foundation chart for a nation, state or institution is definite (and in some cases the reliability is often suspect), then the foundation chart in conjunction with the charts of the country's leaders may prove

Charts of England and the United Kingdom
(Planetary correspondences)

	♈ - ♎	♉ - ♏	♊ - ♐	♋ - ♑	♌ - ♒	♍ - ♓
Coronation of William I True Noon 25 December 1066 Westminster	Asc. 22 ♈	♆ 22 ♉	♅ 28 ♐	M.C. 9 ♑ ☉ 10 ♑ ☿ 16 ♑ ♀ 29 ♑	♂ 8 ♒	♇ 5 ♓ ♃ 8 ♍ ♄ 17 ♍ ☽ 29 ♓
Union of Scotland and England 00.00 hours L.T. 1 May 1707 O.S. Westminster	♀ 7 ♈ ♆ 22 ♈	☿ 11 ♉ ☉ 20 ♉ M.C. 21 ♏	♄ 5 ♊	Asc. 16 ♑ ♂ 20 ♋	♅ 9 ♌ ♇ 21 ♌ ♃ 22 ♌	☽ 28 ♍
The United Kingdom 00.00 hours L.T. 1 January 1801 Westminster	♅ 2 ♎ Asc. 7 ♎	♂ 12 ♉ ♆ 19 ♏	☿ 17 ♐	M.C. 9 ♋ ☉ 10 ♑ ☽ 19 ♋	♃ 2 ♌ ♀ 16 ♒ ♄ 23 ♌	♇ 2 ♓

Figure 24 Charts of England and the United Kingdom.
(Planetary correspondences)

valuable in judging the state of the nation at a particular time and period.

It has been the accepted practice that there are three main basic charts applicable to Great Britain (see Fig. 24):

1. The coronation of William the Conqueror: noon, 25 December 1066, Old Style.
2. The Union of England and Scotland: midnight (00.00 hours) 1 May 1707, Old Style.
3. The Union of Great Britain and Ireland: midnight (00.00 hours) 1 January 1801, New Style.

These charts are normally set for Westminster, the seat of government.

In addition to these three charts, other charts can be considered, such as the coronation of Edgar the Saxon king in May 973. Why the time of a transfer of power as the result of the Norman invasion should be so significant is not clear. England under the Saxons had its own monarchy, feudal system and laws, and the Norman invasion did not drastically alter the laws and customs which had prevailed for centuries prior to 1066. Nevertheless, the 1066 chart seems to indicate the basic characteristics and development of the English nation.

The present century has seen constitutional changes connected with Irish independence and the formation of the Irish Republic. The legal union of Great Britain and Northern Ireland, the Statute of Westminster, the Debating Chamber of the House of Commons — all have foundation charts which, when studied and related to the charts of Britain and the formation of the major political parties, often indicate the course of political history.

The Nations and the Zodiac

The traditional teaching concerning various countries and their association with a particular sign of the zodiac requires a cautious approach. It may be that certain countries or areas reflect the attributes of a particular sign, but detailed evidence is required to substantiate the claims made concerning countries and their astrological affinities. England is reputedly 'under Aries' with a mixture of Capricorn. Ireland is Taurean, the United States has Geminian influences, although much of American life and thought appears highly Sagittarian. The transits of the major planets through the signs is often indicative of a country's sign and, at the time of important events or crises, there is often an emphasis connected with the sign(s) prominent in the foundation chart. The polarity of Gemini/Sagittarius is certainly obvious so far as the United States is concerned, as a study of its history and the transits through Gemini/Sagittarius amply prove.

Political and Economic Astrology

The study of mundane astrology with respect to political processes is valuable, provided that no one chart is taken in isolation, but is considered in conjunction with all other charts which may have some bearing on it at a particular time or period. Political astrology, is of course, only one branch of mundane astrology, and important though it is, other aspects of mundane study, such as astro-economics, can be related to it. Stock Exchange prices rise and fall in response to supply and demand which, in turn, appear to respond to cyclic phenomena. As with so much of mundane astrology, the forecasting of commodity prices must be assessed in the light of not only the country's charts, but also the appropriate companies and their charts if known. Detailed study and a comprehensive knowledge of trading practices are essential, if the astrology of economics is to have any practical use.

Meteorology

From politics and economics, we can turn to meteorology, with which economics is closely associated. The weather affects life in varying degrees; extremes of climate can cause economic chaos, apart from its effect on living organisms. In the realm of weather prediction, various astrological aphorisms have been handed down, but many of these do not stand critical analysis. As with political and economical processes, the astro-meteorologist needs to be thoroughly conversant with his subject, and to understand the technicalities of weather; how, why and where the various patterns of weather operate. Provided he has the basic technical knowledge, a study of cycles for a given period at a particular locality may give indications of recurring patterns which operate according to planetary laws. An exceptionally cold winter or an excessively hot summer might be shown astrologically by mundane charts cast for the locality. Ingress charts, lunations, conjunctions of major planets — all need to be considered and studied in relation to what is normal for a particular area. Exceptional and unusual configurations at the time of an Ingress, particularly the Capricorn Ingress, may denote exceptional conditions.

The difficulty in assessing mundane charts is that it is not always possible to decide exactly how a certain astrological pattern will manifest. Saturn prominent may correlate with severe weather; alternatively, it could denote a hard time for the government of the day or restrictive legislation affecting the population in general. So it follows that no one chart can be taken singly, but reference must be made to a series of charts, which, when analysed and related to each other, will present a pattern from which certain deductions can be made.

There is little doubt that the various aspects of weather are governed in some way by cosmic laws, but it is only by detailed research undertaken by those who are not only well-grounded in astrological principles, but also fully conversant with the fundamentals of the subject with which they wish to relate to astrology, that progress will be made. Weather patterns vary enormously, particularly in the British Isles, but it is highly probable that a scientific analysis over a period of time might indicate some connection with solar, lunar or planetary motion. If climatic changes are related to cosmic phenomena, and cursory observations suggest that there may be some correlation in conjunction with other factors, then the advantages of being able to forecast approximate weather changes and the type of weather likely to be experienced weeks or months ahead would be invaluable.

Calculation

The calculation of mundane charts does not present any special difficulties, as the procedure is similar to that used for any other type of chart. The times of the solar and lunar ingresses, astronomical phenomena, are normally given in the ephemeris, so it is a simple task to calculate the appropriate chart for any locality. If, for example, the chart for the total solar eclipse which occurs on 12 November 1985 at 2.20 p.m. G.M.T. was required, we would merely calculate from this data which is shown on page 29 of *Raphael's Ephemeris*; likewise, the time of the ingresses as shown on page 39, or the times of New or Full Moon as listed at the head of each page for the appropriate month.

Interpretation

The interpretation of mundane charts is governed by the symbolism which attaches to the Sun, Moon, planets, signs and houses, and the relationship that a particular chart may have with other charts which have some connection with it, e.g. the head of state and the national chart; the birth of aviation and the development of space exploration. All charts are subsumed, and it is interesting to note how mundane charts, and indeed personal charts, demonstrate various subtle, interlocking connections. The Sun is the principal planet in any chart, and its condition will convey the 'heart of the matter'. The following brief descriptions outline the significance of the planets when dealing with mundane charts.

Sun
The Sun denotes authority — the head of state, the monarch, the sovereign body, those in command.

Moon
The Moon represents the masses, the common people, women in general, all matters of a public nature.

Mercury
Governs communications of all kinds, trade and commerce, education, information given or received.

Venus
Venus denotes the female sex, unity and harmony, pleasures, social intercourse, the arts, peace and contentment.

Mars
Mars represents the defence and security forces and all matters connected with them. It is associated with violence, wars, fires and all aggressive and destructive elements.

Jupiter
Indicates the law, religion, financial institutions, foreign relations, the prosperous elements of society.

Saturn
Government institutions, landed property, the established order, tradition and conventions, law enforcement and discipline, agriculture, mining, mineral wealth.

Uranus
Associated with the reactionary elements of society, innovations, new technology, change and upheavals, non-conformist attitudes,

inventions and discoveries, reforms, strikes, riots and anarchy.

Neptune
Abstract ideals, subversion, fraud, vice, scandal, delusions, confusion, waste, chemicals, oil, the sea, the caring institutions, hospitals, charities, prisons, anything which distorts or deceives, the projection of false images.

Pluto
The hidden or obscure elements of society, the anti-social elements, organized crime, regimentation, compulsion, clearance and removals, birth and death — actual or symbolic, the forgotten past which periodically resurfaces.

The Houses
Although the significance of the planets must be assessed according to the signs occupied and the aspects received, the house position is important, and all factors — planets, signs and houses — should be considered together. The house position of a body is always important, both in mundane and natal astrology. The angles, first, tenth, seventh and fourth are sensitive points and for those foundation charts for which the time is not precise, a progressed or transiting body may, in some cases when passing over an angle, indicate the 'true chart'. Houses should always be considered, not only by the sign occupying the cusp, but also according to the natural sign and ruler, e.g. the first house — Aries/Mars, etc. In mundane astrology, the houses are traditionally classified as follows:

The First House
Represents the nation as a whole. It denotes, according to the sign rising and any planets in it, the image and characteristics of the nation. The British 1066 chart has Aries rising and, whereas the original Aries aggressive pioneering spirit was prominent in earlier centuries, the 1801 chart with Libra rising appears to indicate a more sophisticated, compromising nature coupled with a concern for freedom, liberties and rights (Uranus rising).

The Second House
The resources of the nation are shown by the second house. It indicates all manner of assets and how a nation values, not only its material resources, but also its 'invisible assets' such as heritage, aptitudes

and expertise which contribute to the well-being of the nation.

The Third House
Indicates communications of all kinds: all methods of transit: roads, railways, postal services, periodical publishing, schools and education, radio and television, data services, storage and retrieval of information. Close neighbours and kin. Relationships with other countries, particularly regarding trade and commerce.

The Fourth House
The 'foundations' of a nation: land, the 'common people', nationalism, the 'mother figure', hearth and home, the private and personal interests of a people, as opposed to the public and authoritarian demands of the state — as indicated by Capricorn and the tenth house. The political Opposition.

The Fifth House
Leisure activities: sports, entertainments, social functions, creative pastimes, all forms of amusements, speculation undertaken for pleasure, the birth rate, children and schools when regarded from the personal angle, as opposed to Gemini and the third house which shows education and the imparting of information.

The Sixth House
Routine work. Services of all kinds which contribute to the efficient operation of the state. Health and well-being of society and those services and persons associated with the private and public health of the nation. Organizations and associations connected with employment, e.g. trade unions, professional bodies. Those that 'serve the state' — civil servants, armed forces.

The Seventh House
Alliances, mutual undertakings and relationships with foreign countries. International affairs. War and peace. Indicates how a nation regards its 'potential enemies' often as a compensatory factor for its own shortcomings.

The Eighth House
Death and public mortality. The assets of the dead. Taxation and financial transactions and all matters connected with state income and receipts.

The Ninth House
Morality and religious beliefs. Justice and the wider aspects of the law. Foreign relationships and contacts. Publishing and higher education.

The Tenth House
The Government, including monarchs, presidents, landed 'ruling class', and all those that exercise power on behalf of the nation. National prestige and the image a nation wishes to project.

The Eleventh House
The legislature: House of Commons and Parliament in general. Local government administration, although the civil service and local government officials are probably denoted by the sixth house. The nation's aspirations and good neighbour policies.

The Twelfth House
The isolated elements of society: hospitals, religious houses, prisons and all those that cater or minister to the needs of the underprivileged. The secret enemies of the state and those that seek to subvert the national interest or established order.

The Signs and Aspects
As with natal astrology, all charts need to be studied in relation to house- and sign-position and the various aspects which the planets and angles may have. Using the foundation chart as the 'basic chart', we can assess current trends by a study of progressions, transits and other cyclical phenomena.

It has become the fashion in some quarters to play down the importance of the signs, but a study of the major planets through the signs provides clear evidence that they reflect the *Zeitgeist* or spirit of the age. The slower-moving planets, Uranus, Neptune and Pluto, whose sign positions are common to millions born in certain years, will show their intrinsic natures via the sign emplacement when the generation 'comes of age'.

Mundanely, there is a correlation between nations and planets during the years that the planets are passing through a sign and this can be related to the times. Those born during a particular period will in the course of time experience the effects of the various planetary combinations which were prominent in the years of their birth. This 'national and personal' correspondence shows how mundane charts need to be combined with the charts of the principal figures active in government at any particular time. The 'generation influence' will, in some way, be important both natally and also mundanely. Other factors also need to be considered, such as the individual's personal progressions and transits coupled with other mundane data. But if sufficient data are employed, an assessment of the probable trends can be made relative to the state of the nation or institution.

If there should be any doubt regarding the efficacy of the zodiacal signs, a survey of the history of the twentieth century, or for that matter, any other century, will demonstrate that the signs are expressed in the conditions and events of a particular age. The Pluto (Gemini) and Uranus (Sagittarius) transits during the late nineteenth and early twentieth century, ushered in the rapid advancement of communications, the birth of aviation and technological science, which eventually led to space exploration. The Uranus (Capricorn) opposition Neptune (Cancer) contact which occurred in the first decade of this century was experienced not only in the conflict of the First World War with all its attendant horrors, but also in the social upheavals and depressive conditions which followed the war.

The major conjunctions and oppositions are indicative (according to their sign emplacements) of the 'mood or spirit' of the period and this, of course, embraces all aspects of national life which directly or indirectly have repercussions on the individual.

Objections can, of course, be made that, if we use enough charts of one kind or another, then almost anything can be made to work. This may be true if we are indiscriminate in the data we use. But, provided we work with well-authenticated charts, there should be some common pattern that emerges which will give similar indications. Mundane charts should 'lock-in', in that charts relative to a specific country, state or institution should exhibit some common relationship when compared with the various charts used in mundane astrology such as Ingresses, Lunations, Conjunctions or Eclipses. The most useful way in so far as mundane studies are concerned, is to record the events and conditions over a period of time and to relate these not only to the 'foundation chart', but also to the various mundane charts which may be appropriate to the foundation chart. In this way, a history is obtained and the nature of planetary action confirmed or, in some cases, discounted.

Elections and Inceptionals

Electional astrology is concerned with electing a propitious time for the commencement of a new undertaking. The time selected is sometimes controlled by circumstances in that there are certain limits within which action must be taken. Alternatively, there may be no constraints as to when action may be taken and the choice of a suitable time has greater flexibility.

If the commencement of a matter is arranged to be at a definite time and the question of choice does not arise, the chart cast for that time is termed an *inceptional chart.* The precepts and aphorisms concerning the selection of suitable times for action require cautious acceptance. Doubtlessly, some of the ancient teachings have value, but others appear to lack credibility.

In the choice of suitable times, it is essential that not only is the election chart favourable, but also that it has beneficial correspondences with any other charts which may have some relationship with it. In the case of personal matters, the natal chart, the current progressions and transits must be studied and compared because, no matter how favourable an election time may be, unfavourable progressions or a stressful natal chart will not be conducive to a successful outcome.

Election charts have the advantage in that they can be chosen either for a definite time or within a particular period. The formation of the Faculty of Astrological Studies occurred at 6.50 p.m. G.M.T. Monday, 7 June 1948 at Queen Square, West London 51°31′ N, 0.07′W. The decision to form this organization was taken at a committee meeting of the Astrological Lodge, and the time selected was chosen in order that there would be a first house Jupiter. As a teaching and examining body, the first house Jupiter, coupled with several planets in Gemini, is highly appropriate. Not only is it indicative of the subsequent history of the Faculty, but it also shows the importance of selecting times which reflect the nature and operation of the proposed enterprise.

Regarding the assessment of charts such as these, the same principles as used with natal charts are employed. The charts of those active in the organization will show correspondences and much can be learned from a study of, not only the organization's chart and its progressions, but also whether those actively concerned with the organization will in the long run prove either beneficial or inimical to the organization's interests.

Election and inceptional astrology is a highly interesting field of research which, when used in conjunction with other techniques such as synastry (see Chapter 4), is extremely valuable. The same reasoning applies in cases of an impersonal nature such as the formation of an organization, business or club. The chart for enterprises such as these should be related to the natal chart and the current and future progressions of the individual(s) who will

German Battleship Bismarck:
Launched at Hamburg, 14 February 1939 (Inner circle)
11.15 a.m. C.E.T. 'Birth Chart'
10.15 a.m. G.M.T.

Sunk by the Royal Navy, 27 May 1941 (Outer circle)
08.40 a.m. G.M.T. Transits Death chart
Lat. 49° N Long. 9° W.

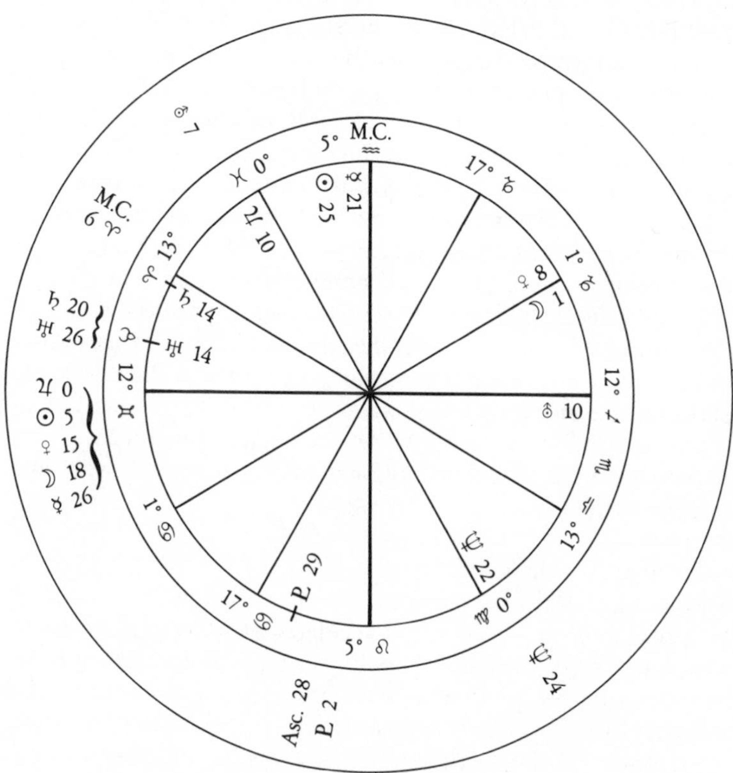

Figure 25 Progressions (Secondary) 16.2.1939 = 13.3.41 (Not listed).

be exercising control or deciding policy. Even with the most favourable election chart, which in these cases is the birth chart of the organization, success and prosperity are by no means certain unless there are firm, mutual contacts of a significant nature between the chart of the organization and those prominently connected with its affairs.

An inceptional chart is not governed by choice, and therefore it is purely fortuitous whether the arranged date and time is favourable or not. Examples such as the launching of a ship, the official opening of a building or the laying of a foundation stone — occasions which are often arranged months in advance and according to circumstances — illustrate, by their subsequent history, the importance of 'fortunate' times for the commencement of enterprises or activities. The German battleship *Bismarck* was launched at Hamburg on 14 February 1939, 10.15 a.m. G.M.T. and was sunk on 27 May 1941 at 8.40 a.m. G.M.T. in latitude 49° north, longitude 9° west. (See Fig. 25.) The launching data are her 'birth positions' and the sinking data her 'death positions'. If inceptional charts have value, then this example should show certain astrological correspondences between the chart for her launching and the time that she was sunk. There is, of course, always an interplay with charts such as these between the commanding officer, the crew, and the national charts of the country. However, a cursory examination of the Bismarck's data shows how cosmic laws appear to operate at certain times and places.

At the time of sinking, the Ascendant was 28° Cancer with Pluto closely involved. The positions at the date of sinking are in fact transits, but the interesting point is that, when the *Bismarck* 'died', the place of the natal Pluto (29° Cancer) was rising. Also, the secondary Moon (Capricorn) was closely opposed to the natal Pluto and the 'event' Ascendant, with the secondary Mars within a degree of the natal seventh cusp.

Vocational Astrology

The question of which profession, trade or occupation is most suitable for a person is not always easily decided. Many people embark on a particular career for which they have no special aptitude or talent and subsequently spend years in uncongenial employment, unable to realize or achieve their ambitions. The reasons for this are varied. Sometimes it is the result of circumstances beyond their control, perhaps economic necessity or due to parental or family influences. Often though, they simply make the wrong choice.

In deciding which vocation is most suitable for a person, a broad indication can be obtained from the natal chart. Whether a person is able to pursue a definite vocation as indicated by astrology will, of course, depend upon other factors and circumtances over which he may have little or no control. However, in general terms, the natal chart can be useful in deciding matters related to the vocation.

The planets, signs, houses and elements all have their significance in vocational matters, but as with all assessments, the natal chart has to be studied as a whole. As a basic starting point, the natal chart should be studied with particular reference to:

1. Planets angular (particularly the Midheaven);
2. Unusual groupings and their aspects;
3. The houses — second house (earning capacity and assets); sixth house (routine work and services), tenth house (ambition, striving and public standing);
4. The Elements and how the planets are distributed in them.

The Angles and Aspects

The angles of the chart, first, fourth, seventh and tenth are important and planets in conjunction with, or close to them, particularly the tenth, are often representative of the vocational interests. The tenth house always gives prominence, and the sign on the Midheaven and any planet(s) in the tenth play an important part in the choice of suitable careers. Planets which aspect the Sun and Midheaven have much influence, as do planets rising and beneficially aspected. Success and security are denoted by a 'strong' Sun, Jupiter or Saturn, well-placed by sign and house.

The Planets

Astrological literature has plenty to say regarding vocation and employment, but as with so much of the traditional teaching, it needs to be approached critically. In general, the planets, along with their natural signs and houses, are considered to indicate the particular vocations and interests outlined below.

The Sun

Persons in authority, entertainments, sports, public relations, creative professions, dealers in precious commodities.

Moon
Caring professions, catering services, antiques, archivist, marine trades and professions.

Mercury
All commercial pursuits, teacher, agent, all forms of communication, printing, publishing.

Venus
Luxury trades, clothiers, particularly those catering for women, fashion trade, horticulturists, artists, musicians, designers.

Mars
Armed forces, security services, mechanical trades, smiths, surgeons, investigators.

Jupiter
Physicians, lawyers, churchmen, bankers, university teachers, librarians, foreign trade and interests.

Saturn
Land and property dealers, agriculturalists, geologists, administrators, historians, politicians, scientists.

Uranus
Local and central government officials, sociologists, inventors, technologists, group organizers, psychologists, aviators.

Neptune
Fine arts, theatre, dancers, films/cinema, cosmetic and paint trades, pharmacy, the Church, welfare services, medical services, oil and tobacco trade.

Pluto
Underground workers (mining, sewers, railways), medical research workers, psychiatrists, archaeologists, secret agencies, waste disposal and recycling trades.

The Houses
Any house which has a large grouping (satellitium) of planets will be important. If, for example, the second house was prominent, the

interest could centre on finance, economics and allied matters; the fifth house could show anything from entertainment to child care; the third house, communications of one kind or another — the realm of the teacher, journalist or advertising executive; the twelfth house, occupations connected with the caring professions, charity organizations, the prison service.

The Elements

The signs — when considered according to the elements — may supply further evidence concerning the choice of occupation.

Fire

The fire element is associated with pioneering enterprises and creative endeavours of the practical kind. Sagittarius, the third sign of the Fire element, often displays enthusiasm and vision concerning long-term projects.

Air

The Air element is associated with intellectual activities, and with literary and artistic pursuits. All the Air signs are gregarious and are attracted to occupations which not only satisfy the exercise of their intellectual abilities, but also allow them to form relationships of one kind or another.

Earth

The Earth element indicates material foundations from which the means of production and the creation of wealth are developed. The signs of this element (Taurus, Virgo, Capricorn) have a relationship with solid matter, and are interested in occupations which use natural resources and assets, such as land and mineral deposits.

Water

The Water element is associated with the nurturing and caring professions and these, of course, range from social welfare services, child care and medical care, to all forms of protection and security services. Of the three Water signs, Cancer and Pisces are probably more concerned with people and their welfare, while Scorpio deals more with the tangible matters such as finance, insurance and the protection services.

Vocational astrology has great value in that it can show the talents and aptitudes of a person. In the assessment of a child's chart, it can assist in deciding the type of training or education that the child should have in order to realize its full potential. It is not an easy area of astrology to define with confidence but, if we take the chart as a whole, study its implications with particular reference to the house positions, we should be able to extract something of value.

The most prominent planet(s) will indicate the most likely interests and talents; the house position will show the area where these can operate with the most effectiveness, and the sign(s) will provide the finer shading — how we operate.

Astrology and Health

The ancients formulated numerous rules, aphorisms and conditions concerning health and the diagnosis of disease. Concealed within the mass of ambiguities which have been handed down concerning health and its relationship with astrology, there is undoubtedly some truth.

In the study of health and disease from the astrological angle, the birth chart of a person may indicate particular weaknesses, so that, although the planets and zodiacal signs have a basic affinity with various parts of the body, only a detailed examination of the natal chart will show whether there is a liability to suffer from diseases or ailments normally associated with a particular sign or planet. Obviously, no astrologer unless he is a qualified medical practitioner can prescribe treatment or cures. What he can do is to indicate, in the most cautious manner, the tendencies which he thinks exist, and to refer the person concerned to a qualified practitioner.

Many illnesses are of a psychological nature, and it is here that the birth chart can be of immense value. An assessment of the chart will indicate the psychological make-up of the person and this, in turn, can show what factors may result in ill health.

The Elements

Probably one of the most important features of any chart is the location of the planets, Ascendant and Midheaven in the four elements (Fire, Air, Earth and Water). An emphasis on a particular element will have not only psychological implications, but will also indicate potential strengths and weaknesses in relation to health.

Fire

Fire (Aries, Leo, Sagittarius) is energetic, and the Fire types often 'burn themselves out' through excessive activity. A proneness to accidents, feverish complaints and a tendency for not knowing 'when to stop' are indicative of this element.

Earth

Earth (Taurus, Virgo, Capricorn) is not wasteful of energy — often quite the reverse — and Earth types normally take good care of themselves, particularly Virgo whose preoccupation with health and well-being often borders on hypochondria. As practical and realistic signs, they conserve their energies but often suffer as the result of their rigidity and lack of mobility.

Air

Air (Gemini, Libra, Aquarius) often shows a pronounced restlessness — always on the go — either mentally or physically. As a result, these types can experience problems, if their abundant nervous energy is not directed into constructive and satisfying activities.

Water

Water (Cancer, Scorpio, Pisces) is associated with emotionalism and the keen sensitivity which is a characteristic of the Water signs, and which often causes these types to have ill-founded fears and worries concerning health. Problems are often caused through worry and, of the three Water signs, probably Cancer and Pisces are inclined to worry the most, resulting in despondent attitudes and a lowered vitality.

The distribution of the planets in the various elements provides an indication of how a person will respond to the circumstances of life, and how this will affect that person's health.

Physiological Rulerships

It has been the accepted teaching that the parts of the body are said to be 'ruled or governed' by the different zodiacal signs. Some of this teaching is suspect and requires updating in the light of modern research. The traditional classifications are:

Aries ♈	Head and cerebral system.
Taurus ♉	Throat and neck.
Gemini ♊	Hands, arms, shoulders, nervous and respiratory system.
Cancer ♋	Breasts, stomach, alimentary system.

Leo ♌	Heart, spine and cardiac system.
Virgo ♍	Abdomen, intestines, visceral system.
Libra ♎	Renal system and lower back.
Scorpio ♏	Sexual organs and generative system.
Sagittarius ♐	Hips and thighs.
Capricorn ♑	Skeletal system, bones, teeth and skin.
Aquarius ♒	Lower leg, circulatory system.
Pisces ♓	Feet.

These are, of course, brief descriptions of what have become the traditional relationships concerning the body and signs. To these we need to add the planets and houses, because these will have significance in the assessment of any chart.

If, for example, there is a satellitium of planets in Cancer, this may indicate health problems connected with the breasts or stomach, but if the ruler (Moon) is well-placed and aspected and the remainder of the chart does not indicate undue health problems, then there is little to fear in this respect. Conversely, if the ruler is not well-placed or aspected and the chart in total indicates problems, then the Cancer emplacement may result in health difficulties connected with the parts of the body signified by Cancer and its ruler, the Moon; likewise with all the other signs and their indications.

The Houses

When we turn to the houses, we need to consider in particular, the first, sixth, eighth and twelfth, as these houses have a bearing on physical well-being, sickness in general, death and confinement. These houses often show the 'state of the body', not only the basic state, as shown by the natal chart studied in its entirety, but also when the body may be subjected to affliction and disease, as shown by the progressed chart during the course of a lifetime.

Association by Polarity

A further point worth mentioning is that the signs often reflect their opposites (polarity). Taurus/Scorpio, for example, may signify sexual or throat diseases. Leo/Aquarius, heart or circulatory complaints. Virgo/Pisces, intestinal or foot complaints. In other words, diseases normally associated with a particular sign may be denoted by the opposite sign. Taurus may display symptoms normally associated with Scorpio; Leo may show Aquarian complaints; Virgo may suffer from foot trouble.

Time Factors

Apart from the vulnerability to certain diseases and their consequences, the time that a person falls ill is important. If a chart is computed for the time or onset of the sickness (decumbiture), it will show — according to the planetary placements and aspects — the progress of the sickness. In acute diseases, the aspects of the Moon will indicate the crisis dates, while with chronic diseases, these will be shown by the motion of the Sun.

Traditional teaching states that in diseases which run a short course, the crisis occurs when the Moon arrives at 45° distance from her longitude at decumbiture, normally within three to four days depending on the Moon's motion. In diseases which run a longer course, the crisis occurs when the Moon is 90° distance (square) from her longitude at decumbiture, normally six to eight days. This is the critical crisis. In diseases which run longer than eight days, the great crisis occurs when the Moon is at the opposition (180°) to her place at the decumbiture, which is normally from the thirteenth to the fifteenth day. With diseases which run longer than fifteen days, the third crisis occurs when the Moon is 270° (opposition plus a square) from her place at the decumbiture, which occurs between the twentieth and twenty-second day. The fourth and last crisis in diseases which run longer than twenty-one days occurs when the Moon returns to her original place at decumbiture. At this final crisis, the disease either ends or degenerates into a chronic or long-lasting one.

The chart for the commencement of an illness — if the time can be ascertained — should show the subsequent developments of the illness. But this chart, important though it is, requires additional testimony from not only the natal chart and its progressions, but also from subsidiary charts such as the current solar return and lunar returns. A combined assessment using these techniques, should give some indication of the subsequent development of the illness.

The Aspects

Although the parts of the body are said to be 'governed' by the various signs, it is highly probable that the planets and their aspects, in combination with their house positions, play a major part in determining the kind of illness or disease. The various epidemics which periodically afflict mankind vary in their intensity. Sometimes they are virulent and malignant; at other times, mild. Why this should be is not clear. The answer probably lies to some extent with the alignments (conjunctions and oppositions) of the major planets.

The nature and intensity of an epidemic appears to be controlled or governed by seasonal changes, atmospheric disturbances, weather and environmental conditions. These factors, combined with planetary action, probably produce the 'high and low' of epidemics. This again is an interesting area for research and could, if properly conducted, confirm or deny the traditional beliefs concerning planetary action and epidemics.

Astrology and Sex

A brief survey of astrology and health would not be complete without some reference to the importance of human sexuality. It cannot be emphasized too strongly that a natal chart must be considered in totality, even though in the initial analysis individual parts are extracted in order to obtain some indication of fundamentals.

All the planets are significant and their placement according to sign, house and aspects indicates in broad terms our physiological and psychological make-up. If the planets are considered as significators of needs, drives or urges, then Mars and Venus are important in matters of sex and sexual behaviour. The Moon also has to be considered, due to her association with instinct, moods, fancies and receptivity. The general 'tenor' of the natal chart will show the needs and responses of an individual. If the planets normally associated with sexual behaviour (Mars and Venus) and the houses usually connected with relationships (fifth and seventh) are emphasized, the approach to sexual matters can be determined. The attitudes, opinions and responses will be influenced by the whole chart, but.Mars and Venus and the fifth and seventh houses are good starting points in matters of this kind. Whether the thoughts and behaviour are along conventional lines or otherwise depends on other factors, not least of which are the contacts of the outer planets:

Jupiter gives a healthy, if somewhat exaggerated, attitude in these matters.

Saturn can be restrictive and inhibiting, with the tendency towards self-denial caused through circumstances or a sense of duty.

Uranus often inclines to eccentric behaviour, with a predilection for experimentation. Often out-of-step with the current mode, whatever that may be.

Neptune seeks the ideal and enjoys the fantasy role, whereby the imagination is allowed to run riot. Often seeks the 'pure' relationship with a tendency to be in 'love with love'.

Pluto, always intense, does not readily become involved in partnerships. This planet probably denotes the avid interest which the sexual processes engender.

From the natal chart and its progressions, we can deduce, in broad terms, the potential weaknesses and health hazards likely to be experienced. But if preventative action is taken in time, many of these will not manifest as damaging physical or psychological conditions.

Horary Astrology

Horary astrology is used mainly to answer questions or to find solutions to problems. The method is to erect a chart for the moment that a question is asked or a solution to a problem is required. Basically, this branch of astrology is a form of astro-divination and, while some astrologers appear very adept in its use, others eschew it completely, probably because of its connotations with fortune-telling.

The underlying principle of this form of astrology is that there is some correspondence between the heavens at the time a question is asked, and the human mind. Provided the question is not frivolous, the chart, if studied according to well-defined horary rules, will indicate a possible answer to the question or the probable outcome of the matter under review. Horary astrology uses basic terms, and although the chart is said to give satisfactory answers to valid questions, its indications need to be studied in relation to the querent's natal chart and progressions. The querent is the person who asks the question and is generally represented by the first house, the Ascendant, any planets in the first house and the ruler of the Ascendant. The quesited is the person, event or thing inquired about. Here it is important that the appropriate house, its ruler and any planets in it are determined. Other rules, such as the state of the Ascendant — less than three degrees of a sign on the Ascendant renders the chart unfit for judgement — need to be considered. If the Moon is 'void of course' (forms no aspect before it leaves the sign it is in), nothing good will come to the querent and the condition will remain the same. There is a wide literature on this branch of astrology, but considerable experience is necessary if this type of astrology is to be practised with confidence.

Definitions

Affliction: Outmoded term for a planet or the cusp of a house inharmoniously aspected.

Air Signs: Gemini, Libra and Aquarius. The third, seventh and eleventh signs respectively.

Anareta: A term seldom used which relates to the 'killing planet' or destroyer of life. A so-called malefic planet in unfavourable aspect to the Hyleg (Arabic term for the significator of longevity) or the Apheta (giver of life). These terms are no longer significant in modern astrology.

Application/Applying: The approach to exactitude of any planet to the body or aspect of another, or to the cusp of any house. A separating aspect is when a faster moving body is moving away from the aspect point.

Aquarius: The eleventh sign of the zodiac. It is a Fixed, Air, Positive sign, ruled by Uranus and probably still retains something of Saturn, by whom it was ruled prior to the discovery of Uranus.

Arabian Parts: Parts or points obtained by taking the differences in celestial longitude between two planets and referring them to the longitude of the Ascendant. The chief part in current use is the Part of Fortune (Fortuna) obtained by taking the longitude of the Ascendant plus the longitude of the Moon, less the longitude of the Sun. For example, with Ascendant 18° Gemini, Moon 6° Virgo, Sun 4° Taurus, the Part of Fortune is found thus:

	Signs	*Deg.*	*Mins.*	
	3	18	00	(18° Gemini)
Add	6	6	00	(6° Virgo)
	9	24	00	
Less	2	4	00	(4° Taurus)
	7	20	00	= 20° Libra = Part of Fortune.

This part is the place where the Moon would be if the Sun was rising. Some authorities question the method of calculation and suggest that, if the part is valid, it should obtained using right ascension.

Aries: The first sign of the zodiac. It is a Cardinal, Fire, Positive sign, ruled by Mars.

Aspect: Angular relationship between two planets or significant points in the zodiac. Aspects are determined by measuring off certain portions of the 360° circle, e.g. 180° (opposition or half the circle); 120° (trine or one-third of the circle); 90° (square or one-quarter of the circle). The various types of aspects are classified as either major or minor.

Aspectarian: A table, usually included in ephemerides, that lists all the major planetary aspects for a given period. The time when the aspect reaches exactitude is normally quoted in the time for which the ephemeris is computed.

Barren signs: An outdated term that was applied to Gemini, Leo and Virgo.

Benefics: A term applied to planets, particularly Venus and Jupiter, or to aspects regarded as having a favourable influence. Modern astrologers are disinclined to use terms such as 'benefic' or 'malefic' and tend to consider planets as forces, drives or energies whose expression is dependent on how they are used.

Besieged: A term used to describe a planet when placed between, or within orbs of, two other planets. A planet between Mars and Saturn was considered 'evilly' besieged; between Venus and Jupiter, it was 'favourably' besieged.

Bestial signs: A similar term relating to Aries, Taurus, Leo, Sagittarius and Capricorn, presumably because of their animal symbolism.

Bi-corporeal signs: The signs Gemini, Sagittarius and Pisces, because these signs contain two different animals. The term now generally used is *double-bodied signs.*

Bi-quintile: An aspect of 144° (two-fifths of 360°) normally classified as a minor aspect (q.v.).

Bitter signs: Term found in old texts relating to the fiery signs (Aries, Leo and Sagittarius), said to be hot and bitter.

Boreal signs: The six northern signs, Aries to Virgo.

Cancer: The fourth sign of the zodiac. It is a Cardinal, Water, Negative sign, ruled by the Moon.

Capricorn: The tenth sign of the Zodiac. It is a Cardinal, Earth, Negative sign, ruled by Saturn.

Chiron: A small asteroid body located between Saturn and Uranus, discovered in November 1977 by Charles Koval. Associated astrologically with healing, through the mythological Chiron, a wise centaur who taught the healing arts.

Climacterical periods: Every seventh and ninth year is considered a climacterical period, due to the Moon's position in the natal chart; every 7th day, or year, she squares (90°) her own place, and every 9th day, or year, forms the trine aspect (120°), and thus, the following become the climacterical years: the 7th, 9th, 14th, 18th, 21st, 27th, 28th, 35th, 36th, 42nd, 45th, 49th, 54th, 56th, and 63rd years. The 49th and 63rd years are often very significant, (7×7 and 7×9).

Common Signs: The Mutable signs, Gemini, Virgo, Sagittarius and Pisces.

Configurations: The relative positions of the planets and their aspects.

Debility: A planet in a weak or 'afflicted' position either by sign or house. The opposite of 'Dignity' when a planet is well-placed either by sign or house. The terms Debility, Detriment, Fall or Cadency all require to be accepted with some reserve.

Decanates: A 10° sub-division of each sign. There are three divisions of each sign termed decanates (first, second and third). Each decanate is assigned a ruler in accordance with the sign and the other signs of the same element, e.g. Aries — the first decanate 'ruled' by Mars; the second by the Sun (Leo); the third by Jupiter (Sagittarius). Similarly, the sign Cancer would have the Moon as 'ruler' for the first decanate; Mars/Pluto (Scorpio) for the second decanate, the Neptune/Jupiter (Pisces) for the third decanate.

Delineation: The analysis, assessment and intepretation of an astrological chart.

Detriment: Term used to describe a planet when in a sign opposite to that which it rules; e.g. Mars in Libra; Venus in Scorpio. See table which follows.

Planet	*Exalted*	*Fall*	*Detriment*
Sun	Aries	Libra	Aquarius
Moon	Taurus	Scorpio	Capricorn
Mercury	Virgo	Pisces	Sagittarius/Pisces
Venus	Pisces	Virgo	Scorpio/Aries
Mars	Capricorn	Cancer	Libra/Taurus
Jupiter	Cancer	Capricorn	Gemini/Virgo
Saturn	Libra	Aries	Cancer/Leo

Uranus, Neptune and Pluto have no definite allocation in this scheme of exaltation, fall and detriment, but if the general classification is adopted then Uranus will be in its detriment in Leo (the opposite sign to which it rules), Neptune's sign of detriment will be Virgo, and Pluto's will be Taurus. Exaltation and fall regarding these planets is not known owing to their comparatively recent discovery.

Dignity: Term relating to the strength of a planet either by sign or house. 'Essential dignity' is when a planet is in its own sign; in a sign of the same element as the sign it rules, or in the sign of its exaltation. 'Accidental dignity' refers to house position — the angles, angularity or the house of which the planet is the natural ruler.

Dispositor: A planet which rules a sign in which another planet is placed; e.g. Sun in Aries, Mars is the dispositor; Venus in Gemini, Mercury is the dispositor. In some charts, there is a final dispositor of all the other planets.

Domicile (Domal dignity): A planet in its own sign; e.g. Mars in Aries; Sun in Leo. Traditionally held to indicate ease of expression of the principles associated with the planet. Also applicable to a planet in its natural house; e.g. Venus in the seventh; Saturn in the tenth.

Double signs: (See Bi-corporeal signs.)

Earth signs: Taurus, Virgo and Capricorn, which form the Earth Triplicity.

Equinoctial signs: The signs Aries and Libra which the Sun 'enters' at the Vernal and Autumnal Equinoxes (Aries — Vernal Equinox on or about 21 March and Libra — Autumnal Equinox on or about 23rd September). This applies to the northern hemisphere. In the southern hemisphere, the entry of the Sun into these signs on those dates marks the commencement of autumn (21 March) and the commencement of spring (23 September).

Evil aspects: Outmoded term for the opposition aspect (180°), square aspect (90°), semi-square aspect (45°) and certain minor aspects. Now normally considered 'challenging'.

Exaltation: Planets are said to be exalted in certain signs and thereby 'strengthened'. The sign or degree opposite the place of a planet's exaltation is termed its *fall.* The concept of dignities and its significance requires to be related to the chart as a whole. See table under *Detriment.*

Fall: See under *Detriment.*

Feminine signs/planets: The even or negative signs (Earth and Water) are reputed to be feminine in nature. The Moon and Venus are traditionally classified as feminine. The term negative — when applied to signs and planets — denotes receptiveness, responsiveness and sensibility.

Fire signs: Aries, Leo and Sagittarius, which form the Fire triplicity.

Fixed: One of the three Qualities of the signs of the Zodiac, the other two being the Cardinal and Mutable. The four fixed signs are Taurus, Leo, Scorpio and Aquarius. Their natural houses are the Succedent houses, second, fifth, eighth and eleventh, respectively.

Fortuna: See *Arabian Parts.*

Fortunes: Term found in old texts to describe Jupiter (Greater Fortune) and Venus (Lesser Fortune). The Sun also, when free from 'affliction', was considered fortunate.

Frustration: Term normally used in horary astrology (q.v.) to indicate a 'cutting off' or the prevention of anything shown by one aspect by the means of another. If one planet is applying to an aspect with another planet but before the aspect is complete, another planet forms an aspect with the latter, the indications signified by the first aspect are 'frustrated'.

Gemini: The third sign of the zodiac. It is a Mutable (Common), Air, Positive sign, ruled by Mercury.

Genethliacal: The branch of astrology concerned with the astrology of the individual (natal astrology).

Geniture: Old term for the birth moment/chart.

Horary astrology: A branch of astrology used principally for answering questions or seeking solutions to problems.

Human signs: The signs Gemini, Virgo, Aquarius and the first half of Sagittarius are said to give a 'human' disposition.

Humanistic astrology: A 'person-oriented' astrology which reflects the influence of depth psychology as propounded by Jung, as opposed to the traditional 'event-oriented' astrology. The approach to this type of astrology was developed by Dane Rudhyar, an American astrologer, author and composer.

Hyleg: Arabic term for the significator of longevity or the 'giver of life'. Rules concerning the hyleg and hylegiacal places are obscure and complex, and little attention is now paid to this doctrine. (See Anareta.)

Impeded: A term applied to the luminaries (Sun and Moon) and sometimes to the other planets, denoting 'affliction' through inharmonious aspects.

Inconjunct: Another term for the quincunx aspect of 150°.

Infortunes: Mars (Lesser Infortune) and Saturn (Greater Infortune) were classified as the infortunes due to their reputed association with destruction and calamity. The term is outmoded in the light of modern astrology.

Ingress: The entry of the Sun, Moon or a planet into a sign of the zodiac, details of which are normally listed in ephemerides. Charts calculated for the exact time of an Ingress, particularly those of the Sun and Moon, are important in Mundane astrology.

Jupiter: (See Natal astrology.)

Kite: A configuration in which three planets form a Grand Trine, with a fourth planet at the mid-point of one of the trines, forming sextiles to two factors of the trine and an opposition to the third.

Leo: The fifth sign of the zodiac. It is a Fixed, Fire, Positive sign ruled by the Sun.

Libra: The seventh sign of the zodiac. It is a Cardinal, Air, Positive sign, ruled by Venus.

Locational astrology: By employing various astrological concepts and techniques, a suitable place to live may be chosen. A usual practice is to compute a natal chart for the birth time but to use the new, proposed locality (latitude and longitude). If this locality is far removed from the birthplace, the natal mundane positions will 'move' into different houses. Comparisons are also made with various mundane charts such as those for the country, state or city to which it is intended to relocate. These comparisons will show the degree of compatibility or prosperity likely to be experienced in the new locality, or alternatively, the difficulties with which one may be confronted. If one 'moves for good or ill', then the location chart, in conjunction with other subsidiary charts, can be of assistance in deciding the suitability of a particular area.

Lord: The planet which rules a sign; e.g. Mars, lord of Aries; Sun, lord of Leo. In the case of the Moon or Venus, the term 'lady' is used. These terms are now falling into disuse.

Malefic: Saturn and Mars, and in modern times Uranus, Neptune and Pluto, are thought to be associated with malevolence. The doctrine of 'good or bad' planets is untenable and is not supported by evidence. It is true that the expression of planetary principles can be challenging and in some cases destructive, but this will depend on many factors, and the chart as a whole must be assessed.

Masculine planets/signs: Traditionally, the masculine planets were the Sun, Mars, Jupiter and Saturn, to which have been added Uranus and Pluto. Aries, Gemini, Leo, Libra, Sagittarius and Aquarius (Fire and Air triplicities) were classified as masculine signs. The even-numbered signs (Earth and Water triplicities) were considered feminine. The masculine signs and planets are associated with self-expression, initiative and extroversion. (See Feminine signs.)

Mercury: (See Natal astrology.)

Moon: (See Natal astrology.)

Movable signs: The Cardinal signs — Aries, Cancer, Libra and Capricorn. Not to be confused with the Mutable signs.

Mutual aspect: An aspect between two transiting bodies.

Mutual reception: An interchange between two planets each of which occupies a sign 'ruled' by the other; e.g. Mercury in Aries, Mars in Virgo.

Natal chart; Natus; Nativity: A birth chart cast for the time and place of birth.

Negative signs: The signs of the Earth and Water triplicities (Taurus, Cancer, Virgo, Scorpio, Capricorn and Pisces).

Neptune: (See Natal astrology.)

Opposition: A major aspect (q.v.) of 180°.

Orb: The distance from a partile or exact aspect (q.v.) at which a planet is said to 'operate'; in a broad sense, a planet's sphere of influence'.

Outer planets: Uranus, Neptune and Pluto.

Part of Fortune: See *Arabian Parts.*

Peregrine: Term mostly used in horary astrology to describe a planet posited in a sign where it has no essential dignity (q.v.) or debility (q.v.).

Pisces: The twelfth sign of the Zodiac. It is a Mutable, Water, Negative sign, ruled by Neptune and Jupiter.

Platic: Wide. An aspect that is not exact, but within orbs.

Pluto: (See Natal astrology.)

Polarity: Signs are classified as either Positive or Negative, masculine or feminine, fortunate or unfortunate. Some of this terminology is archaic, and although some signs are associated with extroversion and others with introversion, this kind of classification is too simplistic — astrology is far more complex and does not permit rule-of-thumb categories. Signs and houses do have a polarity, a type of mutual interaction whereby the qualities and actions associated with a particular sign or house may be expressed by its opposite.

Positive signs: The signs of the Fire and Air triplicities (Aries, Gemini, Leo, Libra, Sagittarius and Aquarius).

Promittor: Term found in old texts relating to a planet that 'promises' good or ill according to its condition by sign, house or aspect. This particularly, when 'excited' by progressions, directions or transits. In horary astrology (q.v.), the planet signifying the event is the promittor. (See also *Significator.*)

Quadrate/Quartile: The square aspect of 90°.

Quadruplicity: A group of four signs classified in three groups (Cardinal, Fixed and Mutable).

Querent: Term used in horary astrology (q.v.). The person who enquires.

Quesited: The person or thing enquired about.

Quincunx: A minor aspect of 150°. Evidence seems to suggest that this aspect, when involving the major planets, denotes stress and the need for readjustment.

Quintile: A minor aspect of 72°.

Return: The completion of a planet's cycle; the time taken to make one complete circuit of the Zodiac. (See Solar and Lunar Returns page 226.)

Revolution: A cycle of phenomena or time. Solar returns are sometimes referred to as Solar Revolutions.

Rulers: Each sign of the zodiac is said to be 'ruled' by one of the planets — Sun and Moon being considered as planets. The concept of planetary rulers which is based on traditional teaching dating from the time of Ptolemy and even earlier, has not been accepted unreservedly, and has been criticized as being arbitrary and irrelevant. The traditional allocation is as follows:

Sign	*Ruler*	*Sign*	*Ruler*
Aries	Mars	Libra	Venus
Taurus	Venus	Scorpio	Mars/Pluto
Gemini	Mercury	Sagittarius	Jupiter
Cancer	Moon	Capricorn	Saturn
Leo	Sun	Aquarius	Uranus/Saturn
Virgo	Mercury	Pisces	Neptune/Jupiter

The three 'modern' planets, Uranus, Neptune and Pluto have been allocated as part rulers of Aquarius, Pisces and Scorpio respectively. Although the correspondence of Pluto with Scorpio seems well established, the relationship of the other two planets and the signs allocated to them is not so well defined, although both signs do exhibit some of the qualities associated with these planets. Some 'tradition-bound' astrologers appear to resent the growing practice of assigning the modern planets full rulership over the signs allocated to them (Aquarius, Pisces and Scorpio), and wish to see them merely as part rulers. If the zodiac of antiquity was the sidereal zodiac — and there is considerable evidence to support this — then the whole question of rulerships, as applied to the tropical zodiac, is in need of review.

Sagittarius: The ninth sign of the zodiac. It is a Mutable, Fire, Positive sign, ruled by Jupiter.

Satellitium: A grouping of several planets in the same sign or house. It is an important configuration in any chart, and depending on the planets involved, will show a major emphasis on matters connected with the sign and house in which the grouping occurs.

Saturn: (See Natal astrology.)

Scorpio: The eighth sign of the zodiac. It is a Fixed, Water, Negative sign, ruled by Mars and Pluto.

Seasonal Year: Otherwise known as the Tropical or Equinoctial Year, which is the interval between two successive passages of the Sun through the Vernal Equinox (First Point of Aries — See Chapter 1 Definitions). The period of revolution of the Earth with respect to the Vernal Equinox. Other terms for the Seasonal Year are the Astronomical Year or the Natural Year.

Semi-decile: A minor aspect of 18°.

Semi-sextile: A minor aspect of 30°.

Semi-square: An aspect of 45° considered to be like the square (90°) — challenging and stressful, only less so.

Separation: When an aspect is past, the planets are said to be separating from that aspect. The 'passing away' after having reached exactitude. (See also *Application/Applying.)*

Sesquiquadrate: A minor aspect of 135°.

Sextile: A major aspect of 60°.

Significator: The planet which represents or 'signifies' the matters connected with the house it rules or occupies; e.g. the planet 'ruling' the seventh house is the significator of the partner or other matters related to the seventh house. The term is also used in Primary Directions and horary astrology (q.v.).

Signs of the zodiac: The twelve equal divisions into which the 360° circle of the Ecliptic (see Chapter 1 Definitions) is divided. The twelve signs bear the names of the constellations that are located along the Zodiac, but due to Precession (see Chapter 1 Definitions), the signs and constellations no longer coincide.

Sinister/Dexter: Terms found in old texts relating to aspects. Aspects cast to the left and right respectively, according to the order of the signs. Thus, a slow planet in Aries will cast a sinister sextile to a more rapid planet in Gemini, while the latter casts a dexter aspect to the former.

Solar Return/Revolution: A yearly return based on the Sun's natal longitude. (See Solar and Lunar Returns, page 226.)

Square: A major aspect (q.v.) of 90°.

Sun: (See Natal astrology.)

Taurus: The second sign of the zodiac. It is a Fixed, Earth, Negative sign, ruled by Venus.

Translation of Light: Conveying the 'influence' of one planet to another by the means of a third planet which separates from the first and applies to the second; e.g. Saturn 10° Libra, Jupiter 5° Libra, Mars 7° Libra. Mars is separating from a conjunction with Jupiter and 'translates' the light and nature of Jupiter to Saturn, to whom he next applies.

Trigon (Triplicity): The division of the Zodiac into four groups of signs; each group corresponding with one of the four elements (Fire, Earth, Air and Water).

Trine: A major aspect (q.v.) of 120°.

Tropical signs: The signs Cancer and Capricorn, which the Sun enters at or about 23 June and 21 December respectively. (See *Solstices,* Chapter 1 Definitions.)

T-Square: A major configuration or pattern in which two planets are in opposition to each other, with a third planet at their mid-point, forming a square to both.

Uranus: (See Natal astrology.)

Venus: (See Natal astrology.)

Virgo: The sixth sign of the zodiac. It is a Mutable, Earth, Negative sign, ruled by Mercury.

Yod: A major configuration or pattern in which two or more planets are in sextile to each other, while both quincunx a third planet forming a large 'Y' pattern across the chart.

Zones of High Intensity: A term used by M. Gauquelin to denote significant zones or sectors in relation to the circle of the daily movement of the planets.

4.

COUNSELLING, SYNASTRY AND PSYCHOLOGY

Counselling

The last couple of decades have seen a complete reappraisal of astrology and its techniques. The banality of stereotyped meanings and delineations, which in the past characterized so much of astrology, has been replaced by a more direct approach to chart analysis in which psychology and therapy play an ever-increasing role.

Although 'kindergarten' astrology has its uses for the astrological beginner, in that he learns the basics by using hard-and-fast formulae and terms, the ultimate objective has to be an understanding and appreciation of the richer and deeper meanings of applied astrology. Elsewhere in this work, comment has been made concerning the fallacious statements relating to 'good and bad' aspects. This teaching, which is not supported by experience, coupled with the dogmatism concerning the significance of planets, signs and houses, is gradually being replaced by the realization that astrology, far from being a static, rigid or fatalistic doctrine, which amateurish treatises often imply, does in fact represent the basic principles of life-processes. Heaven and earth are interrelated. Our responses, both inner and outer, reflect this correspondence, and we are at all times reacting to the planetary interplay which is unique to each of us. Our birth chart is special to us and us alone, indicating as it does, our potentialities, energies and drives, as signified symbolically by the planets and signs. How and where these drives will be expressed depends upon the planet, sign, aspects and the house position: planet and sign showing *how;* houses showing *where.* Our birth chart is the basic frame of reference indicating what we are 'born with', and this chart with all its interrelated factors, symbolizes the unique 'I'.

Consultation

Astrology, like many other disciplines has various features and specialities. Not all astrologers work as consultants; some are more interested in research and development — the technicians working behind the scenes like boffins — who occasionally contribute something of astrological value. Others, trained in psychology and allied subjects, do practise as consultants and it is these astrologers to whom people resort when in need of advice, consolation or support.

The consultant astrologer has great responsibilities. Consultancy has to be conducted on a 'one-to-one basis', with the client and the consultant engaging in frank and confidential exchanges. Confidentiality and professionalism must be maintained at all times, with the consultant presenting his opinions and findings with care and reserve. Obviously, the consultant must before arranging an interview, study the client's relevant charts — natal and progressed — and have some knowledge of why a consultation has been requested. The charts and the information obtained from the client will enable the consultant to decide what approach should be taken in endeavouring to help the client overcome his difficulties. People who consult astrologers should be aware that 'guessing games' are out. No reputable astrologer would attempt to advise a client without some background information, and he would certainly not indulge in facile forecasting of precise events or conditions. One does not consult a physician and say '*guess* what's wrong with me.' Questions, answers and examination are required. The same applies to astrological consultancy.

In all counselling, the consultant and the client must 'work together', with the client being aware beforehand of what can or cannot be achieved through astrological analysis. The consultant has to proceed along well-defined patterns of work, but these must be flexible in order to accommodate the wishes of the client. Invariably, supplementary issues will arise, and these have to be dealt with before returning to pick up the main threads of the consultation. The requirements of the client, the nature of the problem(s) and how these may be resolved or alleviated, will decide how many interviews or sessions are necessary.

Often the consultant has no need for absolute precision concerning chart factors, but can almost instinctively 'sense or feel' the implications of the current patterns operating in a client's chart. At other times, much effort and detailed analysis coupled with extensive discussions with the client are necessary before any useful advice can be given.

Every case is individual and has to be treated as such. Counselling is, however, one of the most satisfying expressions of astrology, particularly when one is able to assist and guide others towards an understanding of human complexities.

One of the most important aspects of consultancy work is the relationship between consultant and client. Prior to agreeing to an interview, the consultant has to satisfy himself concerning the degree of rapport existing between himself and the client. This, of course, can be obtained from a comparison of charts. An easy 'interlocking' between the consultant's and client's charts will indicate a smooth relationship with the promise that progress is possible, whereas charts which have conflicting indications or appear 'uneasy', may indicate that sustained efforts on the part of the consultant and client are necessary in order for the consultation to have value and prove beneficial.

A comparison of natal charts will show how each relates to one another, but the progressed charts will provide further indications of rapport or lack of it. The question of compatibility between consultant and client could be extended by considering the chart for the time that the first contact was made, either arranging the interview, or the first meeting. Whatever comparisons are thought necessary, the natal chart and its progressions should take priority.

The Planets in Counselling

The planets (Sun and Moon being classified as planets in astrology) represent the drives, impulses and motivations which are common to all. We seek to express these in various ways and, although all the planets and the signs they occupy are significant, their expression is governed by the chart as a whole. No sign is better or worse than any other sign; they are merely different. Astrological consultancy demands a wide experience of human nature and a sympathetic approach concerning clients and their problems. Each consultant has his own individual approach to astrological concepts, and these concepts will, most likely, include some of the traditional teachings in combination with the newer techniques of astrological assessment.

Sun and Moon

Although all the planets are significant, it is through the Sun and its condition (sign, aspects and house position) that we seek to understand our essential identity. Our sense of purpose comes from identifying with our Sun and all it symbolizes. With some, this is achieved simply and directly; others have to strive — within narrow confines — to express what they are 'at heart'. As the Moon, in her monthly phases, reflects the light of the Sun, so also does it show in the natal chart, the rhythms, responses, feelings and emotional reactions of the person. Our habitual feelings, how we feel about things — our capacity to control instinctive fears; our urge to seek the familiar and safe when danger, either physical or psychological, threatens; our sense of emotional security — are all manifestations of the lunar principles.

The Sun and Moon must be studied together, for it is with these two bodies and their conditioning in a chart, that the source of conflict may be discerned. A strong Sun seeking 'identity' may 'eclipse' a weak Moon, with the result that the lunar qualities are not expressed to their full capacity. Conversely, a strong Moon may, to a certain extent, overcome a weak Sun, and swamp it with over-emotionalism and vague fears, so that the solar expression is in part curtailed. Our prejudices, feelings, habits and desire for safety, 'obscure' the Sun — our achievements do not match our expectations. A well-integrated Sun and Moon taken in relation to the whole chart — and it is the whole chart that must be assessed — will enable a person to function with the minimum of conflict.

Mercury

This planet symbolizes understanding, perception and all forms of communication. Its position by sign, house and aspect shows how we experience and react to both inner and outer influences. It is the 'connecting' factor and shows the manner in which we express our understanding and awareness.

Venus

Equilibrium and balance; that which we appreciate and value; our need for co-operation and unity are all representations of the Venusian principles. It indicates that which makes us 'feel good'. Our likes and dislikes; pleasures; affections; sense of approbation; our need for appreciation and love; the feeling of being 'at one' with all those things that we value are denoted by Venus and its condition. Most importantly, it shows the capacity for being able to 'forget self' and to direct our energies, for and on behalf of others, in mutually satisfying relationships.

Mars

Life demands that we face challenges and take action. Mars symbolizes the energy needed, not only for confronting danger and those things inimical to our well-being, but also how we direct this energy in relation to achieving 'our will'. We may struggle mentally or physically to deal with problems, situations or conditions, but our approach will be a reflection of the sign occupied by Mars, the aspects and the house position. An Aries Mars will forcefully initiate a new project, but if it cannot be accomplished quickly, abandon it due to impatience. A Taurus Mars will be persistent and is unlikely to be deterred by setbacks and will 'plod on' remorselessly. Mars indicates action, enterprise and endurance and is associated with moral courage, nerve and assertiveness. How these qualities will be displayed depends on the condition of Mars and the chart as a whole.

Jupiter

This planet is the largest in the Solar system and its enormity is symbolized astrologically by the desire to 'be larger than'. Whereas Mercury denotes perception, understanding and the desire to know, Jupiter is associated with the expansion of consciousness — the far horizons of the mind and of the physical world. It signifies how we endeavour to gain depth and breadth from experiences which can enlarge and expand our knowledge. Our faith, hope, visions, growth and development are Jupiterean expressions. How and in what manner and with what result we 'expand', depends on Jupiter's condition by sign, house and aspects. Well-placed, this planet promotes confidence, preserves us from injury and assists in the realization of aims and objectives. Uncontrolled, it can, like a balloon, over-expand and burst, leaving tattered remnants of 'what might have been'.

Saturn

Jupiter and expansiveness needs control, and it is Saturn which provides the limits. Unlimited freedom can lead to excesses. Saturn, despite its association with negativeness, fear, inadequacy and restriction, is essential if we are to develop. The throwing up of barriers, either physical or psychological, are forms of protection with which we seek to prevent the intrusion of those things which frighten us or are liable to reveal our weaknesses or fears. If the placement of Saturn indicates where and how we exhibit negative attitudes, or feel inferior, then we can — by facing up to them — acquire greater strength and learn that by coming to terms with our limitation we achieve a more structured existence.

We learn through experience and, however difficult or painful the process may be, the results usually justify the efforts. Venus enables us to 'forget self' usually voluntarily, but Saturn forces us to conform and accept reality through personal sacrifice.

Uranus

Self-discovery is an essential feature of this planet. Our sense of originality and uniqueness impels us to experiment with 'the new'. In doing so, we have to change and adapt many of our preconceived ideas and haul ourselves out of comfortable ruts. Uranus enables us to reject the old in favour of the new and this, although often accompanied by much 'heart-searching', is commendable provided that the change is not undertaken merely in order to feel or appear differently. This planet represents the rebellious and independent factor by which we seek to be ourselves, untrammelled by convention or rigid lines of demarcation. Hence its action correlates with a sudden shattering of established foundations, the demolition of barriers and the rejection of restrictive conditions. The results may be either catastrophic, or they may be a prelude to establishing the 'new man or new world'.

Neptune

The harsh realities of existence become bearable when we indulge ourselves in Neptunian escapism. This planet prompts our yearning for the ideal existence where everything is as we imagine it to be, or would like it to be, not as it actually is at present. In our flight from reality, or from mundane existence, we retreat to the world of fantasy and embrace those things and conditions which enable us to be 'out of this world'. Religion, music, art, acting or disguises of one kind or another, permit us to renounce the commonplace and to experience a make-believe world, safely cocooned in the webs of our own fancies. In our dreamworld, we pose and posture and, in our imaginings, seek compensation for what we lack. We strive for perfection either in ourselves or others, and when this does not materialize, we experience feelings of guilt, and seek absolution through atonement.

As a safety valve, the Neptunian principles are essential, for without them our creativity, idealism and ability for self-sacrifice would be curtailed. Neptune assists in releasing the bonds of reality. It is only when we cannot differentiate between fact and fiction, that our lives becomes chaotic and confused. This planet can be either subtle and insidious, like a creeping paralysis which immobilizes and destroys, or it can be the magic of existence transforming the dross to gold.

Pluto

This, the outermost planet of the solar system yet discovered, is the planet of finality. Symbolically, it denotes the transformation of life patterns, the termination of existing structures, ways of thought, beliefs, relationships and established conditions. It acts like a cleansing agent removing that which is obsolete, outmoded or obstructive, preparatory to establishing new foundations. Natally, it represents those things which we prefer to hide, forget or ignore. Due to its slow motion, it remains in a sign for many years, and although it has become fashionable to talk of its 'generation influence', the fact is that it is a highly individual planet and its mundane position and aspects are extremely important in every chart.

In our efforts to hide or ignore that which we find uncongenial, frightening or unacceptable, we fail to realize that, sooner or later, nemesis will overtake us — forcing us to face reality. As the 'face of the forgotten past', Pluto periodically brings into sharp focus the memories, fears and guilt of things long past. The surfacing of Plutonian action, painful though it may be, forces us to re-examine our values and beliefs. In the upheavals which accompany this action, we become aware of the issues which are important to us as an individual. We are ready to reject the insignificant, the unimportant and respond to the regenerative influence and we become, in a sense, transformed or 're-born'.

The Houses in Counselling

From a counselling viewpoint, the houses are a major factor, because it is within their framework that the planets — via the signs — will be expressed. As fields of action, houses show how we relate to our environment, but the correspondence is far more subtle and meaningful than the prosaic definitions usually associated with the houses.

First House (Ascendant)

Our self-image; how we relate to our environment. How we appear to others (although the seventh house may have some influence on how we project our image). The 'filter' of the whole chart.

Second House
Our values and all kinds of assets both physical and psychological.

Third House
The faculties of communication and how we relate to our immediate environment. Perception and learning skills.

Fourth House
Our concepts of security and protection. Home, family and familiar surroundings. Those persons or matters which assist in giving us emotional security.

Fifth House
Our creative needs. That which gives us pleasure. Our approach towards projecting ourselves and our abilities. Attitudes concerning risk-taking and speculation. Our 'innermost' desires and sense of self-esteem.

Sixth House
Our ability to discriminate, compare and analyse. The sense of personal efficiency and what we expect from others. The desire to achieve satisfaction and a feeling of 'goodness' from rendering services or displaying skills. Our approach to routine work, health and hygiene.

Seventh House
Human relations. The need for co-operative efforts, alliances and mutual aid. The expression of the affectional nature through personal relationships. Those things and persons which we feel will enable us to acquire an 'even balance'.

Eighth House
Our approach to the mysteries of life — birth, sex and death. Our inner strength and capacity that enables us to delve below the surface in search of the unknown, either physical or psychological. The assets and resources of others and our involvement with them.

Ninth House
The 'natural' religious nature. Our attitudes concerning philosophy, justice and higher learning. The far horizons of the mind and our capacity for visualizing and speculating concerning the meaning of

life. Those persons and matters that allow us to reach far beyond our immediate environment thereby assisting in the acquisition of knowledge and the appreciation of higher values.

Tenth House
The summit of achievement — the ultimate goal, whatever that may be. The constructive responsible attitudes adopted in order that one's aims or objectives can be realized. Our desire for recognition and a sense of worth. Our public image, reputation and credit. The tenth house indicates what one 'aspires to' and this can be one or several of many things. Work, career or ambition is a too limited description of this house.

Eleventh House
Our progressive attitudes and the capacity to embrace the new. Hopes, wishes and expectations often realized through being socially adaptive. Our approach to, and how we interact with, society at large. Our social conscience.

Twelfth House
The capacity for self-sacrifice, renunciation and withdrawal. Our concern for humanity and where the personal interests are sublimated for the benefit of others. The illusory world of fantasy where one can retreat and indulge in make-believe.

Progressions and Transits
The birth chart indicates through the inter-relatedness of its various factors — planets, signs, houses and aspects — the initial energies, drives and potentialities of the individual.

The progressions and transits which occur subsequent to birth, or if using converse motion, prior to birth, display their own patterns. These patterns taken singularly as a group and also in relation to the birth chart, will at any given time, show the attitudes, circumstances and conditions likely to be encountered by the person. The peaks and troughs of life are experienced in conformity with the various progressions, transits and cycles. Many progressed contacts do not appear to correlate with definite events. Often there are subtle undertones which cannot be pinpointed, but which when considered in retrospect, can be identified with changing attitudes, different approaches and awareness.

The challenges of life often correspond with prominent

progressions, which for want of a better term, are described as adverse. Likewise, beneficial conditions are associated with favourable aspects. Identifying concord and conflict in this manner often conceals more than it reveals. All progressions operate according to the nature of the bodies in aspect, and these configurations, when compared with the birth chart, will signify how they may be experienced. Sun square Saturn may manifest in despondent conditions, losses, damage, injury or hurt, but these could well be psychological as well as physical. Alternatively, this Sun/Saturn contact could symbolize a more structured approach to life with the acceptance of responsibilities and obligations, all of which would be conducive to the growth and development of the person.

No hard-and-fast rules are available as to how an aspect, progression or contact will manifest. The intrinsic nature of the planets, signs and houses and their various interactions have to be related to each individual chart. If we can 'work' with our charts, then all progressions, transits and the like will, in varying degrees, offer scope for self-fulfilment. 'Working with our charts' is not easy, and we have to accept that freedom of action is more apparent than real; we respond and react within the narrow confines of our charts. The borderline between fate and free will is extremely thin and however much we may speculate concerning our freedom of choice, we do act in accordance with our own individual 'patterns'. 'The wheel spins and we spin with it'.

Synastry

> 'Oh happy they, the happiest of their kind,
> Whom gentler stars unite.' — Thomson

The consultant astrologer is frequently requested to compare the charts of people who are related or who intend forming some relationship or alliance. Relationships and associations cover a wide field and range from the more personal ties of marriage to the impersonal associations of business and professional partnerships.

Many relationships have an element of 'fate', in that we have little or no say regarding them. Family relationships and those concerning co-workers are instances of these. We have to accept them and, if need be, adapt to them. Love, marriage and friendship offer freedom of choice. We can choose our partners and our friends and if, in the course of time, the relationship turns 'sour', we can if we wish, terminate the association. However, unless there is complete intransigence, a relationship can be saved if the parties concerned really want it to continue. Some relationships are always difficult and appear to survive by a 'mere thread'. Others are strongly bonded and long-lasting and, despite the vagaries of fortune and adversity, flourish and prosper.

Often, on first acquaintance, we instinctively 'sense' a liking or dislike, and this sympathy or antipathy, has a correspondence with the respective natal charts, and most probably with the current progressions. Concord and discord are by no means the only features of comparison astrology.

The appropriate charts of parents and children, partner or business associate will indicate whether there exist sympathy and compatibility, and how this may be expressed for mutual benefit. In the charts of mother and child, the natal positions of the child are, of course, the transits in the mother's chart on the date of the child's birth. The mother-and-child relationship is discussed under 'Solar Returns', page 226.

The comparison of two charts will show the basic affinities existing, or the lack of rapport. In addition to the natal charts and the current progressions, additional insight may be gained from supplementary charts such as the parents' marriage chart or the company's foundation chart. In all comparisons, the intrinsic nature of the planets has to be considered and related by sign, house and aspects according to the nature of the relationship. Love and marriage, on the one hand, and a business venture comparison, on the other, would obviously be dealt with differently.

The Planets in Synastry

Sun
The masculine principle. Vitality. Motivations. The dominant urge and the will to power. Creativity.

Moon
The feminine principle. Habits, feelings, moods and intuition. Maternal instincts. The nurturing and sustaining urge.

Mercury
The mental approach. Ideas, interests and self-expression through understanding and perception.

Venus
The affectionate nature and its expression. Attitudes and responses regarding values, love, romance, sex. The principle of harmony and unity. Mutual dependence and co-operation.

Mars
Active, assertive attitudes. The type of energy expressed. Will, desire and initiative — how they are used to promote or defend interests.

Jupiter
Enhancement, growth and expansion. The degree of confidence, faith and benevolence. The moral attitudes.

Saturn
The conservative and consolidating principles. The sense of duty and the manner in which responsibility is exercised or accepted.

Uranus
Unconventional and casual attitudes. Modernity and experimentation. Personal freedom and individualism. Magnetic attraction.

Neptune
Idealism, compassion, atonement and escapism. The degree of self-sacrifice bestowed or demanded.

Pluto
Compulsion. Obsession. Power complexes. The regenerative and transforming influence. The need and the ability to discover new depths of experience through the removal of obstacles, either physical or psychological.

The Houses and Aspects in Synastry
Many textbooks designed for beginners list various combinations of planets, signs and houses with their suggested meanings. This is probably acceptable for initial studies, but with the more advanced techniques of synastry and comparison the interrelationship between the charts must be related to the individuals and their case histories. Different types of comparison require distinctive approaches, depending upon the reasons and purposes of the comparison.

The houses usually associated with personal relationships are the first (self), seventh (others), fifth (love, children, creative enterprises), eleventh (friends and associates) and the third and ninth (local and distant contacts). This classification is true up to a point, but it is the nature of the relationship which is important, and therefore the appropriate houses need to be considered. Apart from the houses usually associated with relationships, the chart as a whole has to be compared, because planets in one chart will 'fall' somewhere in the houses of the other chart, and these positions show the mutual responses and the area of expression. The interaction of the planets, angles and their aspects in one chart with that of another show whether there is any 'basic' compatibility or antipathy. Often a cursory examination of two charts will show whether there exists a firm foundation for a relationship, or whether close contacts should be avoided, lest disillusionment, sorrow or even enmity result. Some comparisons require more detailed analysis than others, because the indications are often mixed, showing both harmony and friction.

The planets denote drives or energies and these are expressed through the signs and houses. *How* they are expressed is governed by their aspects; *where* they are expressed is governed by the houses. The challenging or difficult aspects may prove detrimental — depending upon the planets in aspect — or they may denote that a relationship has much to gain if the individuals concerned can appreciate each other's differences. Alternatively, too many easy contacts between charts may inhibit a relationship, in that one partner may become over-dependent on the other, or seek to over-compromise. Vacillation, procrastination and the avoidance of responsibility are not conducive for a well-balanced relationship.

The strongest contacts between charts are the conjunctions, particularly those of the Sun and Moon. Aspects involving the angles are always important as are groupings falling in a particular house. As with all aspects, the orb allowed should be small and any significant mid-point contacts should also be considered. When considering aspects and houses, the nature of the relationship is important. With a business comparison, the appropriate houses to note would be the first, second, sixth and tenth, as these houses are traditionally associated with self, assets, work and public activities. In the case of more personal relationships such as partnership or marriage, the first, fifth, and seventh houses would be important. In addition to the planets, signs and aspects involving these houses, the natural rulers of the houses and their condition have to be noted.

Progressions and Transits in Synastry

The comparison of the natal charts will show the 'fundamental basics' existing between two people, but the development of any relationship rests, not only on basic correspondences, but also on the progressions of the two charts. A person may be attracted to another as the result of responding to a progression, say, Sun contacting Uranus (magnetic attraction), or Venus contacting Neptune (illusion and glamour). If the natal charts indicate the likelihood of firm bonds, all well and good, but if there are no firm foundations, then the progression or transit (which is transitory) will merely show a temporary attraction which passes with the progression or transit. The ardour cools and the interest wanes.

So in all comparisons, we need to know the nature of the relationship; to analyse the birth charts relative to it; assess the current progressions, and those due subsequently, of both persons — individually and in connection with each other. Also, as in counselling, we require some 'personal history' in order that our assessments, observations and deductions have some relevance. Whether those 'in love' take the advice is sometimes debatable!.

The Marriage Chart

The time that a couple were officially pronounced 'man and wife' marks the commencement of the marriage. Although the date and time of the marriage ceremony can often be chosen, there often appears to be some 'cosmic law' which dictates that the marriage will take place at a date and time in accordance with the couple's progressions, transits or returns. Astrologers are aware of the importance of choosing favourable times for action and will 'elect' a time which promises success.

An election chart for marriage should, so far as is possible, have the appropriate planets well configurated and also in strong aspect with the couple's natal charts. Also important is how the planets in the marriage chart form aspects or come to angles, on the days (years) subsequent to the marriage date. The marriage chart is in effect, a natal chart of the partnership, and its progressions after the date of marriage (birthday) will show the fortunes of the marriage. If the planets associated with domestic felicity (Moon and Jupiter) and physical responses (Mars and Venus) are favourably placed or aspected in the marriage chart, and if the seventh house and Libra feature well in the chart (e.g. Sun in the seventh house, or Venus in Libra), then the possibility of an enduring marriage is greatly increased. Alternatively, Mars or Saturn (strife) badly placed, or adverse aspects from Neptune (deceit) or Uranus (discontent) will not make for a happy and enduring relationship. Sun, Moon, Venus and Jupiter normally give harmony and concord, while Saturn, Uranus, Neptune and Pluto often indicate difficulties, the more so if they arrive by progression at or aspect positions in the marriage chart. In comparisons such as these, the detailed 'groundwork' has to be done, and the various natal and subsidiary charts assessed carefully.

Synastry and counselling are two of the most useful methods by which astrology can be of practical use in understanding the development of human relationships. Each birth chart is unique, and although the astrological factors symbolize the drives and energies common to all, the expression of these depends upon the individual and his own behaviour patterns as signified by his natal chart.

Case History (See Figs. 26-30).

First meetings:	6.45 a.m. G.M.T. 28.7.1947, London.
Marriage:	1.30 p.m. G.M.T. 1.9.1951, London.
1st son:	9.31 p.m. G.M.T. 18.11.1954, London.
2nd son:	9.19 p.m. G.M.T. 15.5.1957, London.
Natal (His):	11.40 a.m. G.M.T. 28.10.1921, London.
Natal (Hers):	9.08 a.m. G.M.T. 28.6.1925, Lat. 51°10′ N; Long. 7°04′ E.

In the comparison of charts of those born 'close together', that is within a few years of each other, the aspects between the slow-moving planets are not always of importance; what is important is where the planets are located (house position). In the example comparison, apart from the very significant aspects between the two natal charts, her satellitium in Cancer falls in his natal seventh house, a sure sign of a 'strong bonding influence'. His Virgo, Libra, Scorpio positions fall in her first, second and third houses and, although some of the contacts are challenging, these positions are indicative of mutual supportive attitudes. Few relationships are all 'wine and roses', and although this example has disruptive contacts, the combination of Air (Libra and its need to relate) with Water (Cancer and its need to care) is significant.

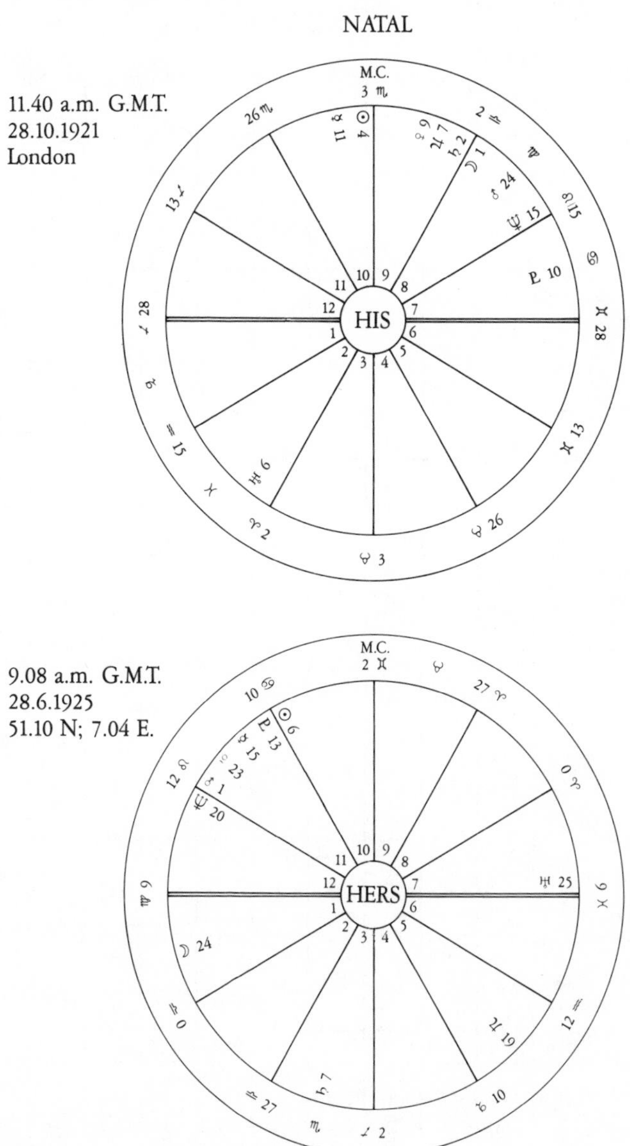

Figure 26

HERS

HIS		Sun	Moon	Mercury	Venus	Mars	Jupiter	Saturn	Uranus	Neptune	Pluto	Asc.	M.C.
		6 ♋	24 ♍	15 ♋	23 ♋	1 ♌	19 ♑	7 ♏	25 ♓	20 ♌	13 ♋	9 ♍	2 ♊
Sun	4 ♏	△				□		☌				✱	
Moon	1 ♎	□	☌			✱			☍				△
Mercury	11 ♏	△		△				☌			△	✱	
Venus	9 ♎	□		□							□		△
Mars	24 ♍		☌		✱		△		☍				
Jupiter	7 ♎	□				✱					□		△
Saturn	2 ♎	□	☌			✱							△
Uranus	6 ♓	△						△			△	☍	□
Neptune	16 ♌									☌			
Pluto	10 ♋	☌		☌				△			☌	✱	
Asc.	28 ♐		□						□	△			
M.C.	3 ♏	△				□		☌				✱	

Figure 27. Synastry (Chart Comparison).

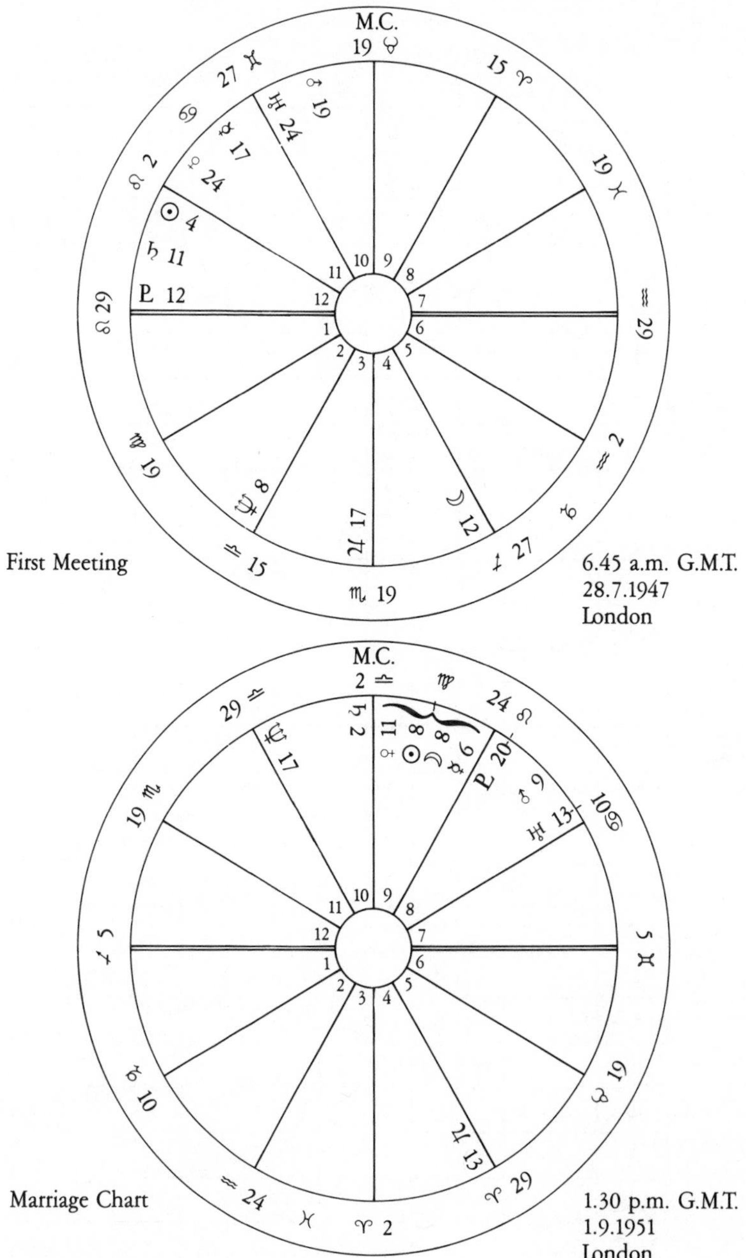

First Meeting

6.45 a.m. G.M.T.
28.7.1947
London

Marriage Chart

1.30 p.m. G.M.T.
1.9.1951
London

Figure 28

First Meeting

His Natal

	☉	☽	☿	♀	♂	♃	♄	♅	♆	♇	Asc.	M.C.
☉	□						□			□		
☽	*								☌			
☿	□		Δ			☌	□			□		☍
♀	*	*					*		☌	*		
♂				*	□			□				Δ
♃	*	*					*		☌	*		
♄	*								☌			
♅		□										
♆		Δ			*	□	☌			☌		□
♇			☌			Δ			□			
Asc.								☍			Δ	
M.C.	□											

Her Natal

	☉	☽	☿	♀	♂	♃	♄	♅	♆	♇	Asc.	M.C.
☉									□			
☽				*	□			□				Δ
☿			☌			Δ						
♀			☌	☌		Δ						
♂	☌								*			
♃			☍	☍		*						Δ
♄	□						□			□		
♅				Δ	□	Δ		□				*
♆					*	□		*			☌	□
♇			☌			Δ			□			
Asc.		□										
M.C.	*								Δ			

Figure 29 First Meeting: Comparison with Natal Positions

Marriage Chart

His Natal

	☉	☽	☿	♀	♂	♃	♄	♅	♆	♇	Asc.	M.C.
☉	*	*	*	*	□							
☽							☌				*	☌
☿	*	*	*	*	□			Δ				
♀					*	☍	☌	□			*	☌
♂												
♃					*	☍	☌	□			*	☌
♄							☌				*	☌
♅	☍	☍	☍	☍							□	
♆						Δ				☌		
♇	*	*	*	*		□		☌				
Asc.												
M.C.	*	*	*		□							

Her Natal

	☉	☽	☿	♀	♂	♃	♄	♅	♆	♇	Asc.	M.C.
☉	*	*	*	*		□	□	☌				□
☽												
☿				*		□		☌	□			
♀									□			
♂					☌		*				Δ	*
♃				Δ		□		☍	□			
♄	*	*	*	*	□			Δ				
♅												
♆						Δ			☌			
♇	*	*	*	*		□		☌	□			
Asc.	☌	☌	☌	☌				*			□	
M.C.	□	□	□	□			Δ				☍	Δ

Figure 30 Marriage Chart: Comparison with Natal Positions

♈-♎	♉-♏	♊-♐	♋-♑	♌-♒	♍-♓
♆ 6 ♈ ☉ 25 ♈ ♄ 14 ♎	☿ 6 ♉ ♇ 11 ♉ MC 25 ♉ ♃ 26 ♏	♅ 22 ♊		☽ 1 ♌ ♂ 27 ♒	Asc 4 ♍ ♀ 29 ♓
1 14.4.1864					
♆ 18 ♈	♃ 5 ♉ ♇ 16 ♉ ☉ 28 ♉	♀ 1 ♊ ♄ 15 ♐ ☿ 18 ♊	♅ 15 ♋	♂ 29 ♌	☽ 6 ♍
2 19.5.1869					
♂ 28 ♈	♄ 12 ♏ ♅ 20 ♏	Å 12 ♊ ☿ 17 ♊ ♆ 18 ♊	☉ 7 ♋ ♀ 4 ♋	♃ 10 ♌ ☽ 16 ♒	
3 28.6.1896					
♂ 6 ♎ ♃ 20 ♎ ♆ 28 ♈	☉ 21 ♏ ☿ 24 ♏ ♇ 21 ♉	♀ 24 ♐	☽ 8 ♑	♄ 8 ♒ ♅ 15 ♌	
4 13.11.1874					
☉ 12 ♈ ☿ 19 ♈ ♆ 25 ♈	♇ 19 ♉ ♀ 20 ♉ ♂ 14 ♏	☽ 3 ♊		♄ 1 ♒ ♅ 2 ♌ ♃ 21 ♌	
5 1.4.1873					
☉ 2 ♈ ☿ 21 ♈	♃ 9 ♏ Asc 10 ♉	♇ 13 ♊ ♆ 22 ♊ ♅ 8 ♐ ♄ 23 ♐	♂ 22 ♋ M.C.17 ♑	☽ 17 ♌ ♀ 19 ♒	
6 23.3.1899					
	♄ 7 ♏	M.C. 2 ♊	☉ 6 ♋ ♇ 13 ♋ ☿ 16 ♋ ♀ 23 ♋ ♃ 19 ♑	♂ 1 ♌ ♆ 20 ♌	Asc. 9 ♍ ☽ 24 ♍ ♅ 25 ♓
7 28.6.1925					

1. Great Grandfather 2. Great Grandmother 3. Their son
4. Father 5. Mother 6. Wife of 3
7. Elder daughter of 3 and 6

♈-♎	♉-♏	♊-♐	♋-♑	♌-♒	♍-♓
M.C.21 ♈ ♆ 26 ♎	☿ 7 ♏ ♄ 13 ♏ ♀ 20 ♏ ☉ 26 ♏		♅ 27 ♋ ♃ 29 ♋	Asc 11 ♌ ♂ 19 ♒ ♇ 26 ♌	☽ 13 ♍
9 18.11.1954					
M.C.14 ♎	♆ 0 ♏ ☿ 10 ♉ ☉ 24 ♉	♀ 3 ♊ ♄ 12 ♐ Asc 13 ♐ ☽ 18 ♐	♂ 7 ♋	♅ 3 ♌ ♇ 27 ♌	♃ 22 ♍
10 15.5.1957					
♅ 6 ♈	♃ 10 ♉ Asc 23 ♏	♂ 12 ♊ ♄ 12 ♐	♇ 18 ♋	☽ 15 ♒ ♆ 29 ♌	☉ 6 ♍ M.C.12 ♍ ☿ 18 ♍ ♀ 22 ♍
8 29.8.1928					
M.C. 4 ♈ ♀ 15 ♈ ♆ 21 ♎ ♄ 22 ♎ ☽ 26 ♈	☿ 5 ♉ ☉ 20 ♉	♃ 0 ♊ ♂ 7 ♊	♅ 15 ♋ Asc 29 ♋	♇ 20 ♌	
11 11.5.1953					
♀ 26 ♈	♆ 0 ♏ Asc 12 ♏	♄ 2 ♐ ☽ 19 ♐	♂ 3 ♑ ♅ 28 ♋	☿ 20 ♒ ♃ 24 ♌ ♇ 26 ♌ M.C.28 ♌	☉ 14 ♓
12 4.3.1956					
Asc 10 ♎	♆ 15 ♏	☽ 6 ♐	M.C.13 ♋	♂ 5 ♌ ♀ 14 ♒ ♄ 18 ♒	♅ 2 ♍ ♇ 10 ♍ ☿ 12 ♓ ☉ 25 ♓ ♃ 25 ♓
13 16.3.1963					

8. Younger daughter of 3 and 6
9. Elder son of 7
10. Younger son of 7
11/12/13. Daughters of 8

Figure 31 Family Relationships

At the First Meeting, the planetary positions, which are the transits on that day (28.7.47), show strong solar aspects (his), and prominent Jupiter contacts (hers). At the date of marriage, the Moon in the Meeting chart (12° Sagittarius) was close to the Marriage Ascendant and Neptune was close to the Marriage midheaven. In the Marriage chart, one of the most outstanding features is the satellitium in Virgo 'hugging' her natal Ascendant coupled with his natal Saturn astride the Marriage Midheaven. At the birth of the first son (18.11.54), the Marriage Mars (9° Leo) was precisely conjunct the son's Leo Ascendant, to which we can also relate the Leo planets in the Meeting chart. At the birth of the second son (15.5.57), the Moon in the Meeting chart was conjunction the son's Ascendant and Saturn, with the marriage Jupiter (13° Aries) exactly opposition the son's Midheaven.

Other significant contacts exist between the children's charts and the Meeting and Marriage charts. This interrelationship between charts has important implications in that not only can the basic foundations concerning relationships be discerned, but also the trends, progress and development of the relationship can be determined. Regarding Marriage charts these, if studied in enough detail, should provide information concerning the fortunes of the marriage. That the Moon is intimately related to sex and birth appears to have some foundation, thus confirming the 'old wives' tales.

Family Relationships

Families and blood relationships often exhibit common factors regarding planetary positions and/or certain degree areas. The link between partners and their children and the partners themselves can be extended to include grandparents on both sides. Provided the birth dates are available, there is no limit to this kind of comparison.

The comparison schedules show how there is a repeated emphasis on certain signs and degree areas which, from generation to generation, appear regularly. In these listings, the Ascendant and Midheaven are included when the birth time is known; where it is unknown, the positions are for noon on the birth date. In the case of parents and children, the natal positions in a child's chart are, of course, the transits in the parent's charts. These often prove very interesting, especially those involving mother and child. In the following examples (see Fig. 31) a cursory examination shows the relationship of No. 8 (mother) with daughter (No.13) with the prominence of Virgo/Pisces. Likewise, No. 8 has her Moon conjunct her father's Moon (No. 3), while his other daughter (No. 7) has her Sun conjunct his Sun, having been born on his birthday.

No. 1 (great grandfather) married No. 2 (great grandmother) and their son (No. 3) married the daughter (No. 6) of No. 4 (father) and No. 5 (mother).

No. 7 is the elder daughter of No. 3 and No. 6. No. 9 is the elder son of No. 7. No. 10 is the younger son of No. 7.

No. 8 is younger daughter of No. 3 and No. 6, and she has the three daughters: Nos. 11, 12 and 13.

In a study such as this, comparisons can be made, not only with parents/grandparents, but also between sisters and cousins. Sympathy and antipathy may rest in ourselves, but the 'stars' do have some effect, as the study of comparison astrology shows.

Psychology

If astrology is to be a guide for living, growth and development, then its rich symbolism has to be interpreted on many levels. In our attempts to understand the motivations, behaviour and life experiences, we have to combine within the astrological framework the ancient traditions and experiences of mankind. In seeking to identify the meanings and significance concealed within the mythologies and legends common to all mankind, we discover many universal truths, of which astrological symbolism is a paramount example.

The psychology of Jung, which has attracted some attention from astrologers, deals with the concepts of a collective unconscious and its material — archetypes. By this, Jung was referring to psychic contents common to all (collective) and the psychological counterpart of instinct (archetype). Jung considered that myths are an expression of how man experiences not only physical processes, but also their emotional content. Arising as an expression of the collective unconscious, myths are found in similar form among all races and in all ages. The application of psychology to astrology — which need not be the psychology of Jung — has proved to be of immeasurable value in the analysis and assessments of charts. Jung, of course, introduced a wide terminology into his work and although much of it is complex or obscure or both, some of it embodies the universal truths long known to astrologers.

The consultant astrologer is normally aware that astrology has its limitations, and that not all problems or difficulties can be resolved solely by astrological consultation. A deep-rooted condition may require a specialist's attention and in such cases, the astrologer will refer his client to a psychologist or psychotherapist. Even so, the astrologer still has an important role, in that his initial findings can be conveyed to the specialist, thereby reducing the time and labour required by the specialist in assessing the client's difficulties. Information will, of course, only be exchanged with the client's permission.

The development of psychology during this century has enabled astrologers to concentrate on the more fundamental principles of astrology in relation to the person and his motivations, attitudes and responses. Three of the most notable figures in psychology and psychiatry during the last hundred years, and whose work is relevant to astrology, are Freud, Jung and Adler. Of the three, it is the work of Jung, and his interest in astrology and allied matters, that has attracted the attention of astrologers. Whether Jung's theories have the importance that some astrologers attach to them is a matter of opinion. However, his approach and theories appear to have value for some consultants. But there are several theories of psychotherapy which combine the ancient knowledge of antiquity with human behaviour and experience, and these too deserve to be considered in relation to astrology.

The founding of psychoanalysis by Freud, and his work on dreams and the theory of sexuality, has contributed immensely towards an understanding of the complexities of the human mind. Adler's theory, 'the urge to power', is similar to the wish fulfilment theory which underlines Freud's concepts concerning dreams. The wish for power and superiority as a compensation for a feeling of inferiority is the essence of Adler's psychology. Although the psychologies of Jung, Freud and Adler often differ widely, there would appear that, so far as astrology is concerned, each has much to offer: Jung and his Analytical Psychology; Freud and his Psychoanalysis; Adler and his Individual Psychology. Although it may seem a simplistic view, the mention of Adler and his 'urge to power' has connotations with the Sun and Leo — the heart of an individual. Likewise, Freud and his theorem of sexuality call to mind Mars, Pluto and Scorpio.

The various techniques of psychology used in the study of human behaviour are often of a bewildering variety. Many other disciplines have influenced the development of psychology and, although astrology is gradually emerging from its former insular position, it still has much to learn from the other sciences. This is not to say that astrology must become a rigid, mechanistic 'science' — it can never be that, but that it must align itself with the findings of science, particularly those concerned with human behaviour and development. The forward-looking astrological consultant is aware of this and will seek to encourage this approach. The consultant using psychological techniques can, after having established a rapport with his client, endeavour to show him how the complexes and conflicts, as indicated in the natal chart, may be accepted or outgrown. The progressions and transits always need consideration, because they often show whether a problem or difficulty is likely to be long-standing or short-lived. Today's problems often have their origins in the past, and it is by reference to previous years (progressions) that the nature of a conflict can be determined. Again, by studying the years ahead, indications may be obtained of future developments. It is only by accepting one's individual 'pattern' that progress is possible.

The duty of a consultant is to help his client to discover things about himself. Sometimes the process is relatively easy; the client is understanding and co-operative and is prepared to 'un-layer' himself in response to the consultant's promptings. Sometimes it is more difficult and much patience is required. At any rate, all astrological consultations must be on a one-to-one basis, with the client being 'drawn out' if need be, so that by talking he discovers things of which he was previously unaware. The consultant will, by listening to his client, be able to say the right thing at the right time, thereby assisting his client in understanding himself and his problems.

5.
FUTURE TRENDS

Progressions and Directions: the Astronomical Basis

In a study of progressions and directions, we need to differentiate between the two systems because the terminology is often confused. *Progressions,* usually referred to as *secondary progressions,* are based on the theory that one day = one year, by which the positions of the Sun, Moon and planets on the day after birth are taken to relate to the conditions during the year after birth. If, for example, we require the progressions for the twentieth year of life, we study the positions on the twentieth day after the birth. The revolutions of the Earth, Moon and planets in their orbits result in changes in the positions of the heavenly bodies in that they change signs and houses, and form different aspects between each other. By progression, all bodies move at their own rates in their orbits, the Moon round the Earth, and the Earth and planets round the Sun. This motion may be direct or retrograde (apparent backward movement).

Directions are formed by the axial rotation of the Earth, whereby all the heavenly bodies are made to rise, culminate and set. These directions, usually referred to as *Primary,* are all formed within a few hours after birth, and the passage of each degree of right ascension (or each four minutes of sidereal time, which is the same thing) across the meridian is equivalent to one year of life. All primary directions in the life of a person aged 90 years are formed within six hours of birth.

Secondary progressions, at the rate of one day for each year of life take longer to complete than the corresponding primary directions, hence the term. With the primary system, a direction which operates at, say ninety years will have been formed six hours after birth, whereas in the secondary system, the direction that operates at the age of 90 will have been formed ninety days after birth or at about 3 months.

Primary directions are all formed by the rotation of the Earth on its axis and, as a result of the axial rotation, the heavenly bodies appear to rise and set, passing through the mundane houses. These types of directions relate to the zodiacal and mundane positions of the

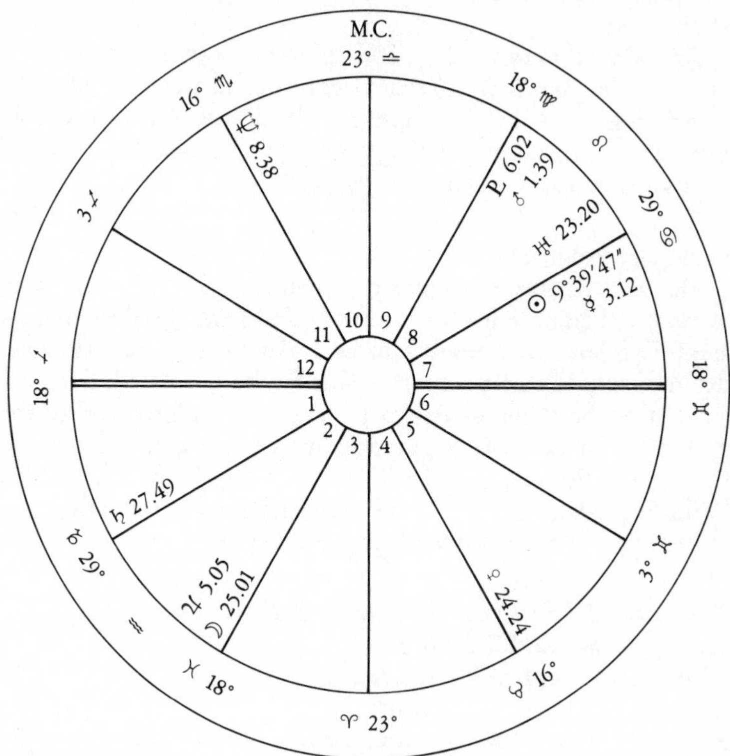

Birth date: 1.7.1961, 6.45 p.m. G.M.T.
Sandringham, 52°51′ N, 0° 30′ E.

	Hours	*Mins.*	*Secs.*	
S.T. at noon 1.7.61	6	37	12	
Interval from noon	6	45	00	+
Mean time correction	0	01	06	+
Long. Equiv. East	0	02	00	+
S.T. at birth (R.A.M.C.)	13	25	18	
Mean Sun	6	38	18	
Apparent Sun	6	42	03	

Figure 32 H.R.H. The Princess of Wales, Natal Chart.

heavenly bodies at the time of birth and with the changes afterwards caused in these positions by the Earth's axial rotation. Primary directions were the vogue during the nineteenth century, but their calculation was tedious and required a certain amount of arithmetical ability.

Secondary progressions depend upon the movement of the Sun, Moon and planets in the Zodiac after birth and are the easiest type of progression to list, as there is little calculation involved; an inspection of the appropriate Ephemeris being all that is required plus some simple counting.

Secondary Progressions

As this work has been designed principally to assist those who wish to expand their knowledge of astrology and astrological techniques and principles, it may be advisable to deal with progressions in some detail. Obviously, before progressions can be calculated, the natal chart must be available (see page 84). As an illustration of the procedure for calculating progressions, we will take the chart of H.R.H. The Princess of Wales (Diana) (see Fig. 32) and progress it by the Secondary measure for the year of her marriage and the birth of her first child (Prince William) (See Fig. 33).

Birth data: 1 July 1961, 6.45 p.m. G.M.T.,
Sandringham, 52°51′ N; 0°30′ E.
Progressions required for 1981/82:
Age — 1 July 1981 = 20 years:
Progressed date = 20 days after birth = 21 July 1961
Noon date (see p. 214) = 20 March
The positions at noon in the ephemeris 21.7.61 correspond to 20 March 1981. The method of calculating the progressed Ascendant/M.C. and the cusps of the houses is the same as for a natal chart.

	Hours	*Mins.*	*Secs.*	
S.T. at noon 21.7.61	7	56	03	
Interval from noon (p.m.)	6	45	00	+
Mean time correction 9.86 secs.	0	01	06	+
	14	42	09	
Long. Equiv. (0°30′) East	00	02	00	+
	14	44	09	

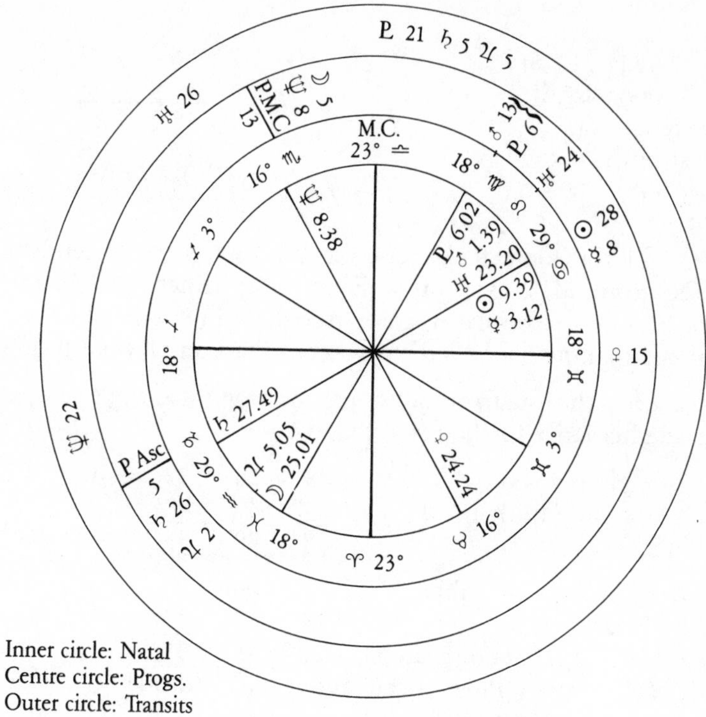

Inner circle: Natal
Centre circle: Progs.
Outer circle: Transits

Secondary Progressions 1981/82

	Hours	Mins.	Secs.	
S.T. at noon 21.7.61	7	56	03	
S.T. at noon 1.7.61	6	37	12	–
Difference	1	18	51	
S.T. at birth	13	25	18	+
S.T. Prog.	14	44	09	

Noon Date

	D.	M.	Y.
Noon Positions on	21	7	1961
Correspond to	20	3	1981
House System: PLACIDUS			

Figure 33 H.R.H. The Princess of Wales, Progression.

or

S.T. at noon 21.7.61	7	56	03
S.T. at noon 1.7.61	6	37	12
Difference	1	18	51
S.T. at birth	13	25	18
Prog. S.T.	14	44	09

From Tables of Houses for latitude 52°51′ N (or nearest): Ascendant 5° Capricorn; M.C. 13° Scorpio. From the ephemeris 21.7.61, the noon positions of the planets are extracted and inserted in the chart in the normal manner. (See Progressions chart on previous page.)

The above is the usual way for finding the progressed angles/cusps, but an alternative method is as follows:

Sun's longitude Noon 21.7.61	28°	28′	22″	Cancer
Sun's longitude Birth 1.7.61	9°	39′	47″	
Difference	18°	48′	35″	
Natal Midheaven 23° Libra	23°	00′	00″	
Add solar arc	18°	48′	35″	
Prog. M.C. 12° Scorpio (nearest)	11°	48′	35″	

= 4° Capricorn = Prog. Ascendant at birth latitude.

The method, using the sidereal time and the time of birth, is based on the motion of the Mean Sun (first column of a noon ephemeris), whereas the solar arc method uses the true motion of the Sun, hence the difference which can occur. The solar arc is probably the correct method. The practice of taking the planets at noon but calculating the progressed Ascendant and Midheaven according to the birth time interval, is not strictly correct. As with many things astrological, theories, methods and practices become established routines even though some of them are contradictory.

The planets at Noon method (noon-date — not essential unless absolute precision required) can have the cusps for the noon-date, as the following calculation shows:

	Hours	*Mins.*	*Secs.*
S.T. of progressed chart as previously found	14	44	09
Less mean time correction (noon-date earlier) (6.45×9.86 secs.)	00	01	06
S.T. corresponding to noon-date =	14	43	03

Note that with an a.m. birth, the correction is added.

Having calculated the progressed chart, the aspects or configurations are listed according to the following classification:

1. Solar progressions to natal or progressed positions.
2. Mutual progressions — that is, from one planet to another including those to the natal Moon.
3. Lunar progressions (see example).
4. Progressions to the angles (Ascendant/M.C.) including the natal or progressed Asc./M.C.

The easiest method of listing progressions (solar and mutual) is to refer to the ephemeris and note the day (year) when an aspect is formed. Solar progressions operate over a period of approximately three years — the year before exactitude, the year of exactitude and the following year as the influence begins to wane. All progressions can be related to the natal chart, but the time of their operation can be accelerated or retarded by other factors such as New Moons, eclipses, or planets becoming stationary or retrograde on critical points in the natal chart. The Secondary method of progression gives a broad outline of 'planetary patterns' but for rigorous timing, the solar and lunar returns often prove superior.

The progression of the angles (Ascendant and its opposite and the Midheaven and its opposite), and their aspects are very important and often denote events and conditions of major importance. The progressed Moon often acts as a 'timer' in that it stimulates or excites into action progressions in the process of formation.

The lunar progressions are calculated as follows:

Age — 1 July 1981 = 20 years
Progressed date = July 21 1961
Noon date = March 20 1981 = 21.7.61
1981 Moon's Longitude
20 March July 21 1961 = 4°45′05″ Scorpio
1982
20 March July 22 1961 = 17°48′35″ Scorpio
Therefore Moon's motion in one day (year) =

	17° 48′ 35″
less	4° 45′ 05″
=	13° 03′ 30″

13°03′30″ divided by 12 = motion per month = 1°05′17″ which, added successively to March 1981 (21.7.61), gives the Moon's longitude at the 20th of each month = Moon's progressed position.

1981	*Moon's Long.*	*1981*	*Moon's Long.*
March	4° 45′ Scorpio	Oct.	12° 21′
April	5° 50′	Nov.	13° 27′
May	6° 55′	Dec.	14° 32′
June	8° 01′	Jan. 1982	15° 37′
July (marriage)	9° 06′	Feb. 1982	16° 42′
Aug.	10° 11′	March	17° 48′
Sept.	11° 16′		

A cursory examination shows the progressed Moon conjunction the natal Neptune during the 'marriage month' July, and although there are other factors prominent during this period, such as the transiting Pluto hovering on the Midheaven, the progressed Moon with Neptune shows the flurry and excitement that normally attend events such as weddings and the like. This event is further discussed, when we look at the Princess's returns for 1981/82, which cover not only her marriage, but also the birth of her first child (Prince William).

The secondary progressions for 1982/83 commence from 20 March 1982 (noon-date), the progressed date being 22 July 1961, which corresponds to age 21 on the 1 July 1982. As Prince William was born on 21.6.82, the Princess's progressions need to be studied from March 1982/83, the method of calculation being the same as already outlined.

Progressions required for 1982/1983:
Age — 1 July 1982 = 21 years:
Progressed date = 21 days after birth = 22 July 1961
Noon date = 20 March
The noon positions in the 1961 ephemeris (22.7.61) correspond to 20 March 1982.

		H M S
S.T. at noon 22.7.61.		8 00 00
Interval from noon (p.m.)	add	6 45 00
Mean time correction	add	0 01 06
		14 46 06
Long. Equiv. (0.30′) E.	add	00 02 00
Prog. S.T.		14 48 06

which, from Tables of Houses for the latitude of birth, gives 6°

Capricorn Ascendant: 14° Scorpio Midheaven. The planets at noon on 22 July 1961 are listed and inserted in the chart, and these are the progressed positions covering the period March 1982/83 corresponding to the 21st birthday (1 July 1982).

The Progressed Moon's position is:

23.7.61 Long.	1° 18′ 57″ Sagittarius	
22.7.61 Long.	17° 48′ 35″ Scorpio	
Motion 1 day (year) =	13° 30′ 22″ over 12 =	1°07′32″

= Moon's monthly motion:

1982	*Moon's Long.*	*1982*	*Moon's Long.*
March	17° 48′ Scorpio	Oct.	25° 39′
April	18° 55′	Nov.	26° 48′
May	20° 03′	Dec.	27° 55′
June (birth of son)	21° 10′	Jan. (1983)	29° 02′
July	22° 18′	Feb.	00° 10′ Sagitt.
Aug.	23° 25′	Mar.	01° 19′
Sept.	24° 32′		

Other Kinds of Progressions and Directions

The Secondary system of progressions, as already stated, gives a broad indication of current trends, and is the method most frequently used in assessing a particular period of the life. Primary directions, which require a reasonable proficiency in handling figures, lost their appeal partly because of their time-consuming nature concerning the calculations, although this no longer applies with the availability of computers. Other systems have been suggested from time to time, all of which have their ardent adherents. Symbolic Directions, which consist of a fixed increment rate such as one degree or some other fractional method, all have their supporters, as have many other methods of progressions or directions. However, many of these systems do not stand critical analysis for the simple reason that they do not satisfy two important criteria, namely, that the event or condition should reflect the nature of the bodies in contact, and that the 'expression' of this contact should act closely in time. Unless a system complies with these two factors, it has little to commend it; a system that only sometimes works is worse than no system at all!

As with so much in astrology, only empirical observations, using well-attested data will confirm whether a particular forecasting technique merits consideration. In recent years several methods of progressions or directions have been proposed and, of these, the following have attracted some attention.

The Solar Arc in Longitude

This consists of measuring the distance (arc) that the Sun has moved from its radical (natal) position to its progressed position. If, for example, we require the arc for 20 years, then the Sun's position 20 days after birth or 20 days before birth, less its radical position, will give the direct or converse arc. It may seem strange that converse positions have validity, but they do have value and significance. If the solar arc is direct, it is added to every planet in the chart and the Moon and Midheaven, and conversely the arc is deducted from the radical positions. This arc is used to direct the Midheaven and for ascertaining the progressed Ascendant from the 'directed' Midheaven, using the appropriate tables of houses. The solar arc should not be used to direct the Ascendant. The Ascendant is directed using the Ascendant arc, which is found by taking the difference between the Ascendant as found by the directed Midheaven and the radical Ascendant, and this arc is used in the same manner as the solar arc.

An example of this measure, using the Princess of Wales' chart, is as follows:

Solar arc: Birth data: 1.7.61, 6.45 p.m. G.M.T.

20th year = 20 days = 21.7.61 = 1.7.81 = 20.3.81 Noondate

Sun's long.	21.7.61 (noon)	28° 28′ 21″	Cancer
Sun's long.	1.7.61 (noon)	9° 23′ 41″	Cancer
Solar arc		19° 04′ 40″	

or

Sun's long.	21.7.61 (6.45 p.m.)	28° 44′ 27″	Cancer
Sun's long.	1.7.61 (6.45 p.m.)	9° 39′ 47″	Cancer
Solar arc		19° 04′ 40″	

Natal Midheaven	=	23°	00′	Libra
Add		19°	—	(nearest)
Prog. M.C.	=	12°	—	Scorpio

From Tables of houses for latitude of birth 52°51′ N, Ascendant = 4° Capricorn:

Ascendant Arc

Prog. Ascendant	4°	Capricorn
Natal Ascendant	18°	Sagittarius
Difference	16°	Ascendant Arc

The Midheaven is always directed by the solar arc, never by the Ascendant arc. Likewise, the Ascendant cannot be directed by the solar arc.

Having calculated the appropriate arcs, all that remains to be done is to add each arc independently to the natal positions and note the aspects. In the chart under review, the solar arc brings the natal Sun to a 'separating' opposition of natal Saturn (9° Cancer plus 19° arc), which is quite compatible with marriage and the acceptance of responsibilities. The Ascendant arc gives an opposition from Neptune to natal Venus, which is also applicable for marriage.

The converse arc is obtained by deducting the difference between the natal and converse Sun:

Natal Sun: noon 1.7.61	9° 23′ 41″	Cancer
Converse Sun: noon 11.6.61 (20 days)	20° 18′ 34″	Gemini
Solar Converse Arc	19° 05′ 07″	

Note that the Converse Noon-date is the same interval from the birthdate but in the opposite direction; i.e. an a.m. birth has a noon-date prior to the birthday, a p.m. birthday, subsequent to the birthday.

The Converse arc, deducted from the natal Midheaven, gives 4° Libra as the converse M.C., and the Ascendant extracted from the Tables of Houses as 5° Sagittarius, gives an Ascendant Arc of 13° (18 – 5).

The easiest way to work with converse directions is to use the 360° circle:

Aries	0°	Libra	180°
Taurus	30°	Scorpio	210°
Gemini	60°	Sagittarius	240°
Cancer	90°	Capricorn	270°
Leo	120°	Aquarius	300°
Virgo	150°	Pisces	330°

The natal chart under review has Sun 9° Cancer = 99° less converse arc (solar) 19° = 80° = 20° Gemini = Sun's converse position. The same arc for the natal Moon gives 325° (25° Aquarius) less 19° = 306° = 6° Aquarius. The Ascendant arc (13), when applied to Neptune, has 218° (8° Scorpio) less 13° = 205° = 25° Libra, which gives converse Neptune conjunct natal Midheaven. This is a wide orb and would appear to suggest that the birth time is a little later than recorded, particularly as the converse Sun (20° Gemini) would then be brought to the seventh cusp. However, it is unwise to tamper with birth times in order to prove that a system is valid, particularly with royal births which are normally recorded accurately.

It would appear that the Solar Arc Measure has great potential as its advocates assert and that, used in conjunction with the usual secondary progressions, it is a valuable adjunct for assessing future trends.

Solar Arc in Right Ascension

This method entails converting natal longitudes into right ascension. The Sun and Midheaven have no latitude, so the conversion is simple, using either tables or a simple formula. The Moon and planets, however, usually have celestial latitude and to convert their longitudes in right ascension, the latitude, longitude and declination of the body must be known. Aspects to, or by, the Midheaven are based on the True Solar arc in right ascension. A body that becomes conjunct the Midheaven by right ascension is *bodily* on the meridian plane, which is not always the case of conjunction in longitude (unless it has no celestial latitude).

Tertiary Progressions

Edward Troinski, a German astrologer, introduced this system of progressions which is based on the lunar period of 27.32 days. If one day in the ephemeris is equal to one year of life, then one lunar month corresponds with one year of life. In other words, 27.32 days = 365.25 days. The underlying principle is that one tropical lunar month after birth is equal to one day's progression in the birth chart. Thus, for every lunar month, add one day to the birth date and calculate the chart for that day. As there are approximately 13 lunar months in a year, the chart will progress by about 13 days each year.

Calculation of Tertiary Progressions

Birth data: 1.7.1961, 6.45 p.m. G.M.T.
Progressions required for age 20:
From Table, 20 years = 268 tropical months plus 18 days. This means that approximately 18 days after the 20th birthday (years), 268 lunar revolutions have elapsed.

The progressed day is found thus:

Day of year (1 July)	182
Add one day for each lunar month	268
	450th day of 1961

450 less 365 = 85th day of year = 26 March = progressed date corresponding to about 18 days after the 20th birthday. The tertiary progressed date is 26 March 1962 at 6.45 p.m., which equates with 19 July 1981. Reference to the ephemeris (19 July) shows the natal position of the Moon (25° Aquarius). The tertiary progressed date for any month during the year can be found by adding one day every time the Moon transits it natal longitude. For example:

26 March 1962 at 6.45 p.m.	=	19 July 1981
27 March 1962 at 6.45 p.m.	=	15 Aug. 1981
28 March 1962 at 6.45 p.m.	=	12 Sept. 1981

The object of using progressions and directions of one kind or another, is to attempt to discern the 'life pattern' of an individual at any given time. The various methods all have their ardent supporters who defend their particular system(s), but the fact remains that, unless the system produces results which accord with life experiences both in time and in nature, it has little to commend it. The Primary system went out of favour because of its intricate calculations and the time needed to perform them. But this in no way excuses the neglect of their use; just because a thing is difficult, there is no reason for rejecting it.

Many of the methods which are proposed from time to time achieve a brief popularity, due principally to the enthusiasm of their innovators, and then like a periodic comet, they fade away into oblivion. A perusal of astrological journals published during this century will confirm the variety of new systems, (which, in many cases, are not new at all, but only a variation on an old theme), that have appeared but have not measured up to the claims of their initiators. Naturally, we should strive to improve our directional techniques, but this can only be attained by adopting a realistic approach and awareness that most systems are part of a greater whole; circles within circles. Even though the technical basis of a system may be sound, the system must be capable of indicating the time, to within reasonable limits, when a particular direction is likely to operate. It would seem that most systems are subject to subsidiary factors and that, although the 'stage is set', action only occurs when the chief significators are excited by other forces such as transits, eclipses or some form of celestial phenomena.

If, for example, we were considering a review of the current year, then the secondary progressions, coupled with the solar and lunar returns, should be studied. These, in conjunction with any transits which are close to critical points in the natal chart or which are likely to be significant in the return charts, will indicate the broad pattern of the year in question. Other phenomena which correlate with the natal and progressed charts, should also be noted. Precision timing may be achieved if one is prepared to utilize faster measures in conjunction with the usual secondary system. The ideal system is one that is simple to use and which produces reliable results in conformity with the factors involved. Such a system may always be elusive, for life is a complex business and astrology reflects this complexity.

Table 1 Tertiary Progressions

Jan.	1-31	Apr.	91-120	July	182-212	Oct.	274-304
Feb.	32-59	May	121-151	Aug.	213-243	Nov.	305-334
Mar.	60-90	June	152-181	Sept.	244-273	Dec.	335-365

Age (Years)	Days	Trop. Months	Age (Years)	Days	Trop. Months	Age (Years)	Days	Trop. Months
1	18	14	16	3	214	31	16	415
2	8	27	17	20	228	32	6	428
3	25	41	18	11	241	33	23	442
4	15	54	19	0	254	34	13	455
5	5	67	20	18	268	35	3	468
6	22	81	21	8	281	36	20	482
7	11	94	22	26	295	37	11	495
8	1	107	23	14	308	38	1	508
9	19	121	24	4	321	39	18	522
10	9	134	25	22	335	40	8	535
11	26	148	26	12	348	41	25	549
12	16	161	27	1	361	42	15	562
13	6	174	28	19	375	43	4	575
14	24	188	29	9	388	44	21	589
15	13	201	30	0	401	45	12	602

Age (Years)	Days	Trop. Months	Age (Years)	Days	Trop. Months	Age (Years)	Days	Trop. Months
46	2	615	61	15	816	76	1	1016
47	19	629	62	6	829	77	18	1030
48	9	642	63	22	843	78	8	1043
49	26	656	64	13	856	79	25	1057
50	16	669	65	3	869	80	15	1070
51	6	682	66	21	883	81	6	1083
52	24	696	67	10	896	82	23	1097
53	14	709	68	0	909	83	12	1110
54	4	722	69	17	923	84	2	1123
55	21	736	70	7	936	85	20	1137
56	12	749	71	24	950	86	10	1150
57	1	762	72	14	963	87	26	1164
58	19	776	73	4	976	88	16	1177
59	8	789	74	22	990	89	20	1190
60	25	803	75	11	1003	90	25	1204

91-100		
91	14	1217
92	4	1230
93	22	1244
94	12	1257
95	0	1270
96	18	1284
97	8	1297
98	26	1311
99	15	1324
100	5	1337

Table 2 Adjusted Calculation Date (Noon-date)

$\frac{365.25 \text{ days}}{24 \text{ hours}}$ 1 hour = 15.218 days

Hours	=	*Days*
1		15.2
2		30.4
3		45.7
4		60.9
5		76.1
6		91.3
7		106.5
8		121.7
9		137.0
10		152.2
11		167.4

$\frac{15.218 \text{ days}}{60 \text{ mins.}}$ 1 min. = 0.25 days

Mins	*=Days*	*Mins*	*= Days*	*Mins*	*= Days*	*Mins*	*= Days*	*Mins*	*= Days*
1	0.3	13	3.3	25	6.3	37	9.4	49	12.4
2	0.5	14	3.6	26	6.6	38	9.6	50	12.7
3	0.8	15	3.8	27	6.8	39	9.9	51	12.9
4	1.0	16	4.0	28	7.1	40	10.1	52	13.2
5	1.3	17	4.3	29	7.4	41	10.4	53	13.4
6	1.5	18	4.6	30	7.6	42	10.6	54	13.7
7	1.8	19	4.8	31	7.9	43	10.9	55	13.9
8	2.0	20	5.1	32	8.1	44	11.2	56	14.2
9	2.3	21	5.3	33	8.4	45	11.4	57	14.4
10	2.5	22	5.6	34	8.6	46	11.7	58	14.7
11	2.8	23	5.8	35	8.9	47	11.9	59	14.9
12	3.0	24	6.1	36	9.1	48	12.2		

Table 3 Day of the Year

	Jan.	*Feb.*	*Mar.*	*Apr.*	*May*	*June*
1	1	32	60	91	121	152
2	2	33	61	92	122	153
3	3	34	62	93	123	154
4	4	35	63	94	124	155
5	5	36	64	95	125	156
6	6	37	65	96	126	157
7	7	38	66	97	127	158
8	8	39	67	98	128	159
9	9	40	68	99	129	160
10	10	41	69	100	130	161
11	11	42	70	101	131	162
12	12	43	71	102	132	163
13	13	44	72	103	133	164
14	14	45	73	104	134	165
15	15	46	74	105	135	166
16	16	47	75	106	136	167
17	17	48	76	107	137	168
18	18	49	77	108	138	169
19	19	50	78	109	139	170
20	20	51	79	110	140	171
21	21	52	80	111	141	172
22	22	53	81	112	142	173
23	23	54	82	113	143	174
24	24	55	83	114	144	175
25	25	56	84	115	145	176
26	26	57	85	116	146	177
27	27	58	86	117	147	178
28	28	59	87	118	148	179
29	29	—*	88	119	149	180
30	30	—	89	120	150	181
31	31	—	90	—	151	—

* *Leap Year:* If the calculation for the noon-date crosses 29 February in a leap year, *deduct* one day from the equivalent number of days found.

	July	*Aug.*	*Sept.*	*Oct.*	*Nov.*	*Dec.*
1	182	213	244	274	305	335
2	183	214	245	275	306	336
3	184	215	246	276	307	337
4	185	216	247	277	308	338
5	186	217	248	278	309	339
6	187	218	249	279	310	340
7	188	219	250	280	311	341
8	189	220	251	281	312	342
9	190	221	252	282	313	343
10	191	222	253	283	314	344
11	192	223	254	284	315	345
12	193	224	255	285	316	346
13	194	225	256	286	317	347
14	195	226	257	287	318	348
15	196	227	258	288	319	349
16	197	228	259	289	320	350
17	198	229	260	290	321	351
18	199	230	261	291	322	352
19	200	231	262	292	323	353
20	201	232	263	293	324	354
21	202	233	264	294	325	355
22	203	234	265	295	326	356
23	204	235	266	296	327	357
24	205	236	267	297	328	358
25	206	237	268	298	329	359
26	207	238	269	299	330	360
27	208	239	270	300	331	361
28	209	240	271	301	332	362
29	210	241	272	302	333	363
30	211	242	273	303	334	364
31	212	243	—	304	—	365

The Adjusted Calculation Date

The noon-date, otherwise known as the 'Adjusted Calculation Date' or 'Planets at Noon Method', is simply a fixed date in the year which is used in order to dispense with the necessity of re-calculating the planetary positions for any year of life for the progressed chart.

The Secondary system of progressions is based on the theory that each day following the day of birth corresponds to one year of life. Therefore, if one day (24 hours) corresponds to one year (365 days), then any proportion of a day will have this relationship with a year; e.g. 6 hours = a quarter of a day = a quarter of a year = 3 months.

To find the progressed positions for a particular year, we count forward in the ephemeris one day for each year and call the result the *Progressed Date.* However, unless the birth was at *Greenwich Noon*, the positions shown for that date will not correspond to the birthday, but to another in the year, either earlier or later depending on the time of birth. Once we have found the day to which they do correspond, we can copy the positions as for noon. In other words, the noon-date is that day in the year when the positions given for noon become exact for a certain birth time. It is called 'Perpetual Noon-date', remaining constant for that birth.

It should be noted that, having found the progressed date, the Ascendant and Midheaven will have to be calculated exactly as for the natal chart, and that *Conversion of Birth time to Greenwich Mean Time* must be completed for all charts at home and abroad before the noon-date is found, since it is the interval of time in hours and minutes between the birth time at Greenwich and Greenwich noon on which the noon-date is based. This is necessary if a Greenwich-based ephemeris, such as Raphael's, is used. (See also Progressions, page 202, concerning noon-date cusps.)

All birth times *prior* to noon will have a noon-date *later* in the year than the birthday, because at the time of birth the noon positions will not have been reached; and all birth times *after* noon will have a noon-date *earlier* in the year than the birthday, because at the time of birth the positions for noon will have been passed. This will become clear from the following examples, but it is a useful factor to remember.

The Progressed Date in the ephemeris equals the Progressed Year (i.e. the age of the person at any particular period), but the year will commence from the date of the noon-date, which, in the majority of cases, will not be the date of the birthday. Only if birth occurred at Greenwich noon will the noon-date and the birth date coincide. Tables to facilitate finding the noon-date are available, but the easiest method is to note the difference in sidereal time between noon and the birth time.

Two methods of calculating the noon-date are shown: Method 1, which is usually taught, requires the use of a noon-date table. Method 2, which has much to commend it, is based on the interval of time between noon and the birth time.

Summary of Procedure of Method 1

1. Convert the time of birth to the equivalent Greenwich Time.
2. Find the interval of time between noon G.M.T. and the birth time expressed in G.M.T.
3. Convert the interval of time into the equivalent number of days, using the noon-date table.
4. *Add* this number of days to the birthdate for an *a.m. birth*, and *subtract* for a *p.m. birth*. (Any fraction of a day less than a half can be disregarded.)
5. The result will be the required noon-date.

Example No. 1
Birth data: 10 May 1985 — 6.15 a.m. G.M.T.

Calculation:		Hours	Mins.		
		12	00		
Interval to noon (a.m.)	–	6	15		
	=	5	45		
From noon-date table		5	00	=	76.1 days
		0	45	=	11.4 days
		5	45	=	87.5 days
			say		88 days.

Birthday — 10 May	=	130th day of year
Add for *a.m.* birth		88 days
		218th day of year

218th day of year = *6 August* = *noon-date.*

Progressions required for 2000:
Age: 15 years on 10 May 2000
Progressed Day = 25 May 1985 . . . . . 10 May + 15 = 25
Planets at noon on 25 May 1985 correspond to (i.e. become exact on) 6 August 2000 *noon-date.*

Method No. 1
Example No. 2
Birth data: 4 July 1985 — 11.10 p.m. G.M.T.

Calculation:	Hours	Mins.		
Interval from noon (p.m.)	11	10		
From noon-date tables	11	00	=	167.4 days
	0	10	=	2.5 days
	11	10	=	169.9 days
		say		170 days.

Birthday — 4 July = 185th day of year
Deduct for *p.m.* birth 170 days
15th day of year
15th day of year = *15 January* = *noon-date.*

Progressions required for 2000
Age: 15 years on 4 July 2000
Progressed Day = 19 July 1985 . . . . . . 4 July + 15 = 19th
Planets at noon on 19 July 1985 correspond to (i.e. become exact on) 15 January 2000 *noon-date.*

Noon-date Falling in Different Years
So far, the examples given have resulted in the noon-date falling in the same year as the birthday, but it frequently happens that it will fall either in the year before or the year after the birthday.

Example No. 3
Birth data: 1 January 1985 — 5.30 p.m. G.M.T.

Calculation:	*Hours*	*Mins.*		
Interval from noon (p.m.)	5	30		
From noon-date table	5	00	=	76.1 days
	0	30	=	7.6 days
	5	30	=	83.7 days
			say	84 days.

Birthday — 1 January (366 for ease of subtraction) 366th day of year
Deduct for *p.m. birth* *84*
282nd day of year
282nd day of year = 9 October 1984 = noon-date in year preceding birthday.

Progressions required for 2000
Note that care must be taken when finding the progressed date.

Age: 15 years on 1 January 2000
Progressed day = 16 January 1985 if positions during 2000 are required, which will be exact on 9 October 1999.
Progressed day = 17 January 1985 if positions are required from October 2000 onwards.

Example No. 4
Birth data: 25 December 1985 — 9.15 a.m. G.M.T.

Calculation:	*Hours*	*Mins.*		
	12	00		
Interval to noon (a.m.) –	9	15		
	2	45		
From noon-date table	2	00	=	30.4 days
	0	45	=	11.4 days
	2	45	=	41.8 days
			say	42 days

Birthday 25 December	=	359th day of year
Add for *a.m. birth*		42
		401st day of year

401st day of year = *5 February 1986* = *noon-date.* (401 – 365 = 36)
Note that an a.m. birth towards the end of the year will usually result in the noon-date falling in the following year.

Leap Year Adjustment
When the birthdate falls in a Leap Year, you will notice that the calculation for the noon-date sometimes crosses 29 February, which does not exist in the tables. To be accurate, a minor correction can be made so that you can use the table in the usual way. When you have found the equivalent number of days to the interval of time and *before you add or subtract from the birthdate, DEDUCT 1 (one day).* This compensates for crossing an extra day, in either direction, and you will arrive at the correct noon-date.

Example No. 5
Birth data: 1 March 1984 Leap Year — 2 p.m. G.M.T.
A p.m. birth will have a noon-date prior to the birthday, so will cross 29 February.

Calculation:	*Hours*	*Mins.*	
Interval from noon	2	00	= 30.4 days
			say 30 days.
30 days less 1 day (Leap year adjustment)			= 29 days
Birthday 1 March			= 60th day of year
Deduct for *p.m. birth*			29 days
			31st day of year

31st day of year = *31 January 1984* = *noon-date.*

Method No. 2. Sidereal Time Variation

As sidereal time increases by approximately four minutes per day, the sidereal time at noon on the noon-date can be found by taking the difference between the birth time interval and the sidereal time at noon on the birthday. Using the data in method 1, example No. 1, we have :

Example No. 1

Birth data: 10 May — 6.15 a.m. G.M.T.

Calculation:	*H M S*	
S.T. at noon G.M.T.	3 12 55	
Less correction (5.45×9.86)	0 00 57	
	3 11 58	
Add Interval	5 45 00	
S.T. at noon on noon-date	8 56 58	= 6 Aug. (nearest).

Example No. 2

Birth data: 4 July 1985 — 11.10 p.m. G.M.T.

Calculation:	*H M S*	
S.T. at noon G.M.T.	6 49 46	
Add correction (11.10×9.86)	0 01 50	
	6 51 36	
Less interval	11 10 00	
S.T. at noon on noon-date	19 41 36	= 15 Jan. (nearest).

Example No. 3

Birth data — 1 January 1985 — 5.30 p.m. G.M.T.

Calculation:	*H M S*	
S.T. at noon G.M.T.	18 44 19	
Add correction (5.30×9.86)	0 00 54	
	18 45 13	
Less Interval	5 30 00	
S.T. at noon on noon-date	13 15 13	= 9 Oct. (nearest).

A p.m. birth will always have a noon-date earlier than the birthday; in this particular example the noon-date is 9 October prior to the birthday. For an *a.m. birth* the noon-date will fall later than the birthday. Both these methods of computing the noon-date are simple to use; the important fact to remember is that the Progressed Year commences from the noon-date. We can, of course, dispense with the noon-date and commence the progressed year from the birthdate, but this entails calculating the planetary positions for the birth time (see Progressions).

Summary of Procedure for Method No. 2.

1. List the S.T. (sidereal time) at noon G.M.T. on the birthdate.
2. Apply the correction of 9.86 seconds per hour to the interval of time between Noon and the birth time; for an *a.m.* interval *deduct*, and for a *p.m.* interval *add*.
3. To the sidereal time from 1 and 2 (which is in fact the Right Ascension of the Mean Sun) *add* the birth time interval for an *a.m. birth* but *deduct* the interval for a *p.m. birth.*
4. The S.T. found from 3 is the sidereal time at noon on the noon-date.

Using a Midnight Ephemeris
Birth data: 10 May 1985 — 8 p.m. G.M.T.

	H	*M*
Interval from midnight 9/10 May =	20	00

From Tables 20 hours = 304 days:
Birthday — 10 May = 130th day of year
As the time (8 p.m.) occurred subsequent to midnight we have to go 'back' to obtain the midnight date:

130 + 365 for ease of subtraction =	495
less	304
	191

191st day of year = 10 July = Midnight Date, prior to birthdate.

Check using sidereal times:	*H M S*	
S.T. at 0 hours 9/10 May	15 10 57	
Interval from 0 hours	20 00 00	–
Mean time correction	00 03 17	+
S.T. at midnight date	19 14 14	
= 10 July		

The midnight date is an adjusted calculation date in the same way as the usual noon-date. An additional check can be made by considering the time interval from midnight as a proportion of a day/year. In the example using 8 p.m., this is 20/24ths of a day = 10/12ths of a year, so the required date will be the previous July.

If the birth time was 6 a.m. 10 May, then the proportion is 6/24ths = 3/12ths of a year which, subtracted from the birthdate, gives February as the required month when using a midnight ephemeris.

From Tables: 6 hours = 91 days
10 May = 130th day of year
91 less
39th day of year

= 8 February, which agrees with our approximate estimate (3/12ths of a year).

The sidereal time method gives:	*H M S*	
S.T. at 0 hours 9/10 May	15 10 57	
Interval from 0 hours	6 00 00	–
Mean time correction	0 01 00	+
S.T. at midnight date	9 11 57	
= 8 February		

The accuracy of any noon-date calculation can be checked by the position of the progressed Moon. The progressed Moon's position, as at noon on the progressed day, will correspond to the noon-date month, and also, if the Moon's position is calculated for the birth time, its position will correspond with the birth month.

Example No. 1
Birth Data: 1 July 1961 — 6.45 p.m. G.M.T.
Age — 1 July 1981 = 20 years.
Progressed date = 21st July 1961
Noon-date = 20 March 1981 = 21.7.61
Moon's progressed long. 21.7.61 = 20.3.81 4° 45′ Scorpio
Moon's progressed long. 22.7.61 = 20.3.82 17° 48′ Scorpio
Motion in 24 hours (1 day/year) = 13° 03′
13°03′ divided by 12 = 1°05′ = monthly motion.

1981	*Prog. Day*	*Moon's Long.*	
March 20th =	21.7.61	4° 45′	Scorpio
April		5° 50′	
May		6° 55′	
June		8° 01′	
July birth month		9° 06′	

The birth time is 6.45 p.m. G.M.T. and, if we calculate the Moon's position for this time on the progressed day (21.7.61), it is in 8°

Scorpio. The tabulation shows that the progressed Moon has this longitude in June/July, thereby proving that the noon-date, as already calculated, is correct. An additional check is the midnight position, as listed in the ephemeris, which should correspond to September 1981 (six months later than March — the noon-date).

1981	*Prog. Day*	*Moon's Long.*	
Aug.	21.7.61	10° 11′	Scorpio
Sept. (midnight)		11° 16′	Scorpio

The midnight position (21.7.61) = 11°13′, which equates with September 1981, six months later than the noon-date.

Each two hours of the progressed day will give the average motion of the progressed Moon during each month. If, for example, we take August which is five months subsequent to the noon-date, we have 5×2=10 hours, and as the motion in 24 hours = 13°03′, the longitude of the Moon during August should be 10×13.05 (13°03′) over 24=5°26′, which, added to the March longitude, gives 4°45′ plus 5°26′=10°11′ as tabulated.

Example No. 2 (Noon Ephemeris)
Birth data: 10 May 1985 — 6.15 a.m. G.M.T.
Age — 10 May 2000 = 15 years
Progressed Date = 25 May 1985
Noon-date = 6 Aug 2000 = 25.5.1985

Moon's progressed position 25.5.85 = 6.8.2000	8° 45′	Leo
Moon's progressed position 26.5.85 = 6.8.2001	22° 03′	Leo
Motion in 24 hours (1 day/year) =	13° 18′	

13°18′ divided by 12 = 1°06′30″ = monthly motion.

2000	*Prog. Day*	*Moon's Long.*
Aug. 6th	25 May 1985	8° 45′ Leo
Sept.		9° 51′
Oct.		10° 58′
Nov.		12° 04′
Dec.		13° 10′
Jan. 2001		14° 17′
Feb.		15° 23′
Mar.		16° 30′
Apr.		17° 36′
May birth month		18° 43′
June		19° 49′
July		20° 56′
Aug	26 May 1985	22° 03′

Check using birth time: 6.15 a.m. 26 May 1985:
Moon's longtitude in 24 hours (1 day) 26.5.85 = 22° 03′ Leo
less 25.5.85 = 8° 45′ Leo
13° 18′

Birth time = 5 hours 45 mins. before noon, therefore

$$\frac{5.45 \times 13°18'}{24}$$

3°11′ deducted from noon position on the 26.5.85 = 22°03′ = 18°52′ Leo, which corresponds to the longitude as tabulated for May 2001.

Example No. 3 (Midnight Ephemeris)
Birth data: 10 May 1985 — 6.15 a.m. G.M.T.
Age — 10.5.2000 = 15 years
Progressed date = 25 May 1985
Midnight date = 4th February 2000 = 25.5.85
Moon's progressed position = 24/25th May midnight 2°13′ Leo
25/26th May midnight 15°22′ Leo
Motion in 24 hours (1 day/year) 13°09′
13°09′ divided by 12 = 1°06′ = monthly motion.

2000	*Prog. Day*	*Moon's Long.*
Feb. 4th	25 May 1985	2° 13′ Leo
Mar.		3° 19′
Apr.		4° 25′
May birth month		5° 31′
June		6° 36′
July		7° 41′
Aug.		8° 46′
Sept.		9° 51′
Oct.		10° 56′
Nov.		12° 02′
Dec.		13° 07′
Jan. 2001		14° 13′
Feb.	26 May 1985	15° 22′

Check, using birth time: 6.15 a.m. 25 May 1985: Moon' longitude at 6.15 a.m. G.M.T. 25 May 1985 =

$$\frac{6.15 \times 13°09'}{24}$$

3°25′ which, added to the midnight position (2°13′) gives 5°38′ Leo, which confirms the Moon's progressed longitude during May 2000 as tabulated.

Although the term twentieth year or sixtieth year is often used, it is misleading when dealing with noon-date and progressions, because errors can arise if the noon-date falls in the year either prior or subsequent to the year of birth. For example, an a.m. birth late in the year will have a noon-date in the following year. Conversely, a p.m. birth early in the year will have a noon-date in the year prior to birth. In dealing with progressions, the commencing year is always counted from the noon-date. So, although a person will attain a certain age on their birthday, their progressed year can commence on a very different date, depending upon the date and time of birth. Once the natal chart is calculated, the noon-date can be obtained and then all future progressions can be derived from that date.

Maturation

In the study of progressions, it is sometimes useful to know when a progressed aspect becomes exact, and this can be found by various methods. Whichever method is used, two factors are required: (a) the daily motion, (b) the distance to the exact aspect. The daily motion is the motion of the progressed body when considered in relation to a natal position. If dealing with progressed to progressed, both daily motions must be used. The distance to an exact aspect is the amount that a progressed position moves to reach, either a natal position, or another progressed position.

Example No. 1

Progressed date: 21.7.61: Birth Data 1.7.61:
When will progressed Moon reach exact conjunction natal Neptune in 8°38′ Scorpio?

Noon 21.7.61 = noon-date 20.3.81 =	Moon position	4° 45′ 05″
Noon 22.7.61	Moon position	17° 48′ 35″
Daily motion 21/22 July		13° 03′ 30″

Distance of Moon from Neptune	= 8° 38′
Less	4° 45′
Distance to go	= 3° 53′

Therefore $\frac{(3°53')}{(13°03')}\ \frac{3.883 \times 24}{13.058} = 7$ hours 08 mins.

Convert 7 hours 08 mins into proportion of 24 hours (365 days) =

$$\frac{7.133 \times 365}{24}$$

108 days after 20.3.81 = 6 July 1981

Example No. 2. (same data)
When will progressed Mercury reach the exact trine of the progressed Neptune?

Noon 21.7.61 — Mercury	8° 24′	Cancer
Noon 22.7.61 — Mercury	9° 33′	Cancer
Daily motion	1° 09′	
Neptune stationary 21/22 July	8° 33′	Scorpio
Mercury's position 21.7.61	8° 24′	Cancer
Distance to go	0° 09′	

Therefore $\frac{(0.09')}{(1.09')} \frac{0.15 \times 24}{1.15} = 3$ hours 07 mins.

Convert 3 hours 07 mins. into proportion of 24 hours (3.07′)
$= \frac{3.116 \times 365}{24} = 47$ days after 20.3.81.
= 6 May 1981.

Example No. 3
When will progressed Moon reach the exact trine of progressed Mercury?

Moon's daily motion 21.7.61	13° 03′ 30″	(Long. 4° 45′)
Mercury's daily motion 21.7.61	1° 09′ 00″	(Long. 8° 24′)
Difference	11° 54′ 30″	3° 39′

$\frac{(3° 39')}{(11° 54')} \frac{3.65 \times 24}{11.908} = 7$ hours 21 mins.
Conversion: $\frac{7.35 \times 365}{24} = 112$ days after 20.3.81
= 10 July 1981.

An easier way to find the date of maturation is to work with the Mean Sun (first column S.T. of the ephemeris).

Raphael's Ephemeris has an Aspectarian table which gives the time of exactitude of all aspects. Referring to example No. 2, (prog. Mercury trine prog. Neptune) the aspectarian lists the time of exactitude as 3.01 p.m. on 21 July 1961.

Working:

		H M S	
Time as listed (3.01 p.m.)		15 01 00	U.T.
Birth time (6.45 p.m.)	–	18 45 00	
Difference		20 16 00	
Mean time correction	+	00 3 20	
Mean Sun (Natal)	+	06 38 17	
Mean Sun of Maturation		02 57 37	

which corresponds with the 6 May.

Solar and Lunar Returns (Tropical)

Solar Return

The Solar Return is a 'revolution' chart cast for the exact time that the Sun, in its yearly progress, returns to the longitude that it held at birth. This occurs each year on or about the birthday. It is a personal chart as distinct from other types of return charts, such as the Ingress, Solstice or New Moon charts, which are mundane figures cast for the commencment of a new cycle.

This return chart denotes the 'pattern of the year' and indicates the events which are likely to occur, or the conditions and circumstances which will be experienced during the year in which the return is operative — the year, of course, commencing from the date of the solar return. In discussing events, circumstances and conditions, we should note that it is the intrinsic nature of the planet(s) and their mutual configurations with each other, coupled with their mundane positions, that determines how a particular event or condition may materialize. The traditional teaching concerning 'good and bad aspects' is sadly in need of review, as the study of solar returns will amply confirm.

The usual method of calculating these returns is to ascertain the exact time when the Sun returns to the same longitude that it held at birth. As the Sun moves one minute of arc in about 24 minutes of time, it is esential that its place is calculated accurately. Any uncertainty concerning the birth time will result in a corresponding error in the time of the Sun's return, and this will cause the cusps of the return chart to be inaccurate, particularly if a sign of short ascension is rising. In determining the Sun's exact longitude, several methods of calculation are available, but it should be noted that the four-figure logarithms usually given in ephemerides are not sufficiently accurate for this purpose. If logarithms are used, then

Ternary proportional in conjunction with Diurnal logarithms are required. The simplest method is to use a calculator which incorporates a sexagesimal function (one that can count in sixties).

The solar return chart operates from birth to death; as one return ends, another commences. This continuous cycle indicates the potentialities which may be expressed, or the events likely to be experienced during the 'return year'. But the indications contained in the return chart will only be activated when the planets are brought into major aspect with the natal, solar (planets in the return chart) or transiting planets.

The key to the solar return and its indications lies in its progressions, and the maximum effect is when one or more planets, natal, solar or transiting, are conjunct either the angles of the progressed return or the angles of the natal chart or the return chart.

Traditional astrology has never accorded the solar return the credit due to it, principally because it was regarded as a static instrument. It is only when the return is progressed, i.e. becomes kinetic, that its true value becomes apparent. Another factor which was not conducive to a proper evalution of the solar return was the belief that all 'good aspects' such as the trine and sextiles were beneficial, irrespective of the bodies forming the contact. Likewise, all oppositions and squares were deemed to be 'bad', particularly if the angles were involved. This teaching is not supported by the study of solar return charts, using well-attested data for accurately timed events. Planets operate according to their intrinsic natures and, although the type of aspect formed will be significant, it is the planets in the various signs and houses and particularly the angles, which are all-important.

The solar return is in a perpetual state of fluctuation, and many aspects and configurations are formed during the course of the year. Obviously, not every contact will correlate with a major event or condition, for it is the nature of the contact and its closeness to an angle which will determine its operation. Again, the condition and circumstances of the person concerned will play an important role. Similar contacts or progressions in the chart of a child and a mature person will act according to the nature of the planets involved and the ability of the person to respond to them. If, for example, both had Venus conjunct an angle, the mature person may experience tokens of friendship and affection, perhaps even form an alliance, whereas the child may also receive some form of affection, presents, or be involved in social events, but would not form a bond such as marriage or some other similar alliance. And so, in judging the effects of the return and its progressions, we need to know something of the person's temperament, environment and general approach to life, for without this information, we cannot really obtain an accurate assessment of how the contact will be experienced or indeed, what the person's reaction will be.

With the solar return, it seems as though the solar planets (the planets in the return chart) correlate with actions which are initiated by the person, whereas the transiting planets (those positions on the day under review) relate to events and conditions which stem from the action of self and others combined. The solar planets appears to indicate independent action, in contrast to the transiting planets, which show reactions associated with or initiated by others. Each chart is individual to that person, and all factors in the return chart and its progressions must be related to the natal chart and to the person as such, in order to arrive at a realistic analysis.

Calculation of the Solar Return

(A) Finding the Sun's natal longitude

Example No. 1
Find the Sun's longitude at 11.50 a.m. G.M.T.
29 August 1928
Working: using a Calculator

		Deg.	*Mins.*	*Sec.*	
Sun's long. noon 29.8.28	=	5	52	34	Virgo
Sun's long. noon 28.8.28	=	4	54	36	
Motion in 24 hours	=	0	57	58	
Birth time interval to noon	=	0	10	00	

Therefore (10 mins.) $\frac{0.1666 \times 0.9661}{24}$ (57 mins. 58 secs.)

= 24 seconds, which deducted from the noon position on 29 August = 5°52′10″ Virgo = Sun's natal position at 11.50 a.m. G.M.T. as required.

The time when the Sun reaches this position each year will be the commencement of the solar return year.

Working: using logarithms

	Deg.	Min.	Sec.		
Sun's motion in 24 hours	00	57	58	Ternary log.	0.49209
Interval to noon	00	10	00	Diurnal log.	0.38021 +
Motion during interval	00	00	24	Ternary log.	0.87230
Sun's noon position 29.8.28	5	52	34		
Less	0	00	24		
Sun's natal position	5	52	10	Virgo	

Example No. 2
Find the Sun's longitude at 9.08 a.m. G.M.T. 28 June 1925

Working: Using a Calculator

		Deg.	Min.	Sec.	
Sun's long. noon 28.6.25	=	6	14	49	Cancer
Sun's long. noon 27.6.25	=	5	17	36	
Motion in 24 hours	=	0	57	13	

	H.	Min.
Birth time interval to noon =	2	52

Therefore (57′13″) $\frac{0.9536 \times 2.866}{24}$ (2 hours 52 mins.)

= 6 mins. 50 secs., which, deducted from the noon position

		Deg.	Min.	Sec.
28 June	=	6	14	49
Less		0	06	50
Sun's natal position at 9.08 a.m. G.M.T. as required.		6	07	59

Working: using logarithms

	Deg.	Min.	Sec.		
Sun's motion in 24 hours	0	57	13	Ternary log.	0.49775
Interval to noon (hours)	2	52	00	Diurnal log.	0.92284 +
Motion during interval	0	06	50	Ternary log.	1.42059

Sun's noon position 28.6.25	6	14	49	
Less	0	06	50	
Sun's natal position	6	07	59	Cancer

Example No. 3
Find the Sun's Longitude at 06.45 a.m. G.M.T. 23 March 1899

Working: using a calculator

		Deg.	*Min.*	*Sec.*	
Sun's long. noon 23.3.1899	=	2	39	15	Aries
Sun's long. noon 22.3.1899	=	1	39	47	
Motion in 24 hours	=	0	59	28	

	H.	Mins.
Birth time interval to noon =	5	15

Therefore (59′28″) $\frac{0.9911 \times 5.25}{24}$ (5 hours 15 mins.)

= 13 mins. 00 secs., which, deducted from the noon position

23 March	=	2	39	15
Less		0	13	00
Sun's natal position at 06.45 a.m. G.M.T. as required		2	26	15

Working: using logarithms

	Deg.	*Min.*	*Sec.*		
Sun's motion in 24 hours	0	59	28	Ternary log.	0.48100
Interval to noon (hours)	5	15	00	Diurnal log.	0.66005 +
Motion during interval	0	13	00	Ternary log.	1.14105
Sun's noon position 23.3.1899	2	39	15		
Less	0	13	00		
Sun's natal position	2	26	15	Aries	

(B) Finding the date and time of the solar return

Examples No. 1 and 2 are the daughters of example No. 3. The year 1979 was a tragic time, because all three were involved in a car accident and, although the two daughters escaped with minor injuries, the mother died shortly afterwards from the injuries she received. If the solar return has any value, we should be able to see whether the return and its progressions for that year throw any light on the event that occurred.

Exampe No. 1
Find the date and time of the solar return for 1979/80
Working:

From the 1979 ephemeris:	*Deg.*	*Min.*	*Sec.*
Sun's long. 30.8.79	6	31	33
Sun's long. 29.8.79	5	33	33
Sun's motion in 24 hours	0	58	00
Sun's natal long.	5	52	10
Sun's long. at noon 29.8.79	5	33	33
Difference	0	18	37

Therefore if 58′ = 24 hours, 18′37″ = ?

(18′37″) $\frac{0.3102 \times 24}{0.9666}$ (58′00″) = 7 hours 42 minutes after noon on 29 August.

The solar return occurred at 7.42 p.m. G.M.T. 29 August 1979.

Working: using logarithms

	Deg.	*Min.*	*Sec.*	*Ternary log.*
Sun's motion 29/30 August 1979	0	58	00	0.49184
Difference	0	18	37	0.98537

Then log. of difference	0.98537	Ternary log.
less log. of motion	0.49184	Ternary log.
= Time of Return	0.49353	Diurnal log.

= *7.42 p.m. G.M.T. 29.8.79*

Example No. 2
Find the date and time of the solar return for 1979/80

Working:

From the 1979 ephemeris	*Deg.*	*Min.*	*Sec.*	
Sun's long. 28.6.79	6	12	17	Cancer
Sun's long. 27.6.79	5	15	03	
Sun's motion in 24 hours	0	57	14	
Sun's natal long.	6	07	59	
Sun's long. at noon 28.6.79	6	12	17	
Difference	0	04	18	

Therefore if 57′14″ = 24 hours, 4′18″ = ?

(4′ 18″) $\frac{0.0716 \times 24}{0.9538}$ (57′ 14″) = 1 hour 48 mins. *before* noon = 10.12 a.m. G.M.T. *The solar return occurred at 10.12 a.m. G.M.T. 28 June 1979.*

Working: using logarithms

	Deg.	Min.	Sec.	Ternary log.
Sun's motion 27/28 June 1979	0	57	14	0.49762
Difference	0	04	18	1.62180

Then log. of difference 1.62180 Ternary log.
less log. of motion 0.49762 Ternary log.
= Time of Return 1.12418 Diurnal log.
= 1 hour 48 mins. before noon = *10.12 a.m. G.M.T. 28 June 1979.*

Example No. 3
Find the date and time of the solar return for 1979/80

Working:

From the 1979 ephemeris	Deg.	Min.	Sec.	
Sun's long. 24.3.79	3	15	06	Aries
Sun's long. 23.3.79	2	15	35	
Sun's motion in 24 hours	0	59	31	
Sun's natal long.	2	26	15	
Sun's long. at noon 23.3.79	2	15	35	
Difference	0	10	40	

Therefore if 59′31″ = 24 hours, 10′40″ = ?
(10′40″) 0.1777 × 24
(59′31″) 0.99194 = 4 hours 18 mins. after noon 23 March 1979
The solar return occurred at 4.18 p.m. G.M.T. 23 March 1979.

Working: using logarithms

	Min.	Sec.	Ternary log.
Sun's motion 23/24 March 1979	59	31	0.48063
Difference	10	40	1.22724

Then log. of difference 1.22724 Ternary log.
less log. of motion 0.48063 Ternary log.
= Time of Return 0.74661 Diurnal log.
= 4.18 after noon = *4.18 p.m. G.M.T. 23 March 1979.*

Having found the date and time of the solar return, the chart can be calculated as follows:

Example No. 1 (see chart No. 1)
Solar return data: 7.42 p.m. G.M.T. 29 August 1979

	H.	M.	S.	
S.T. at noon 29.8.79	10	28	24	
Interval of time (p.m.)	7	42	00	Add
Mean time correction 9.86 secs. per hour	0	1	16	Add
S.T. at Greenwich	18	11	40	
Long. equivalent	—	—	—	
Local S.T. (R.A.M.C.) of return	18	11	40	

Example No. 2 (see Chart No. 2)
Solar return data: 10.12 a.m. G.M.T. 28 June 1979

	H.	M.	S.	
S.T. at noon 28.6.79	6	23	57	
Interval of time (a.m.)	1	48	00	Deduct
	4	35	57	
Mean time correction	0	00	18	Deduct
S.T. at Greenwich	4	35	39	
Long. equivalent	—	—	—	
Local S.T. (R.A.M.C.) of return	4	35	39	

Example No. 3 (see Chart No. 3)
Solar return data: 4.18 p.m. G.M.T. 23 March 1979

	H.	M.	S.	
S.T. at noon 23.3.79	0	01	32	
Interval of time (p.m.)	4	18	00	Add
Mean time correction	0	00	42	Add
S.T. at Greenwich	4	20	14	
Long. equivalent	—	—	—	
Local S.T. (R.A.M.C.) of return	4	20	14	

It is the accepted practice to cast the solar return chart for the place of residence at the date of the return, and this is probably correct. The above examples are for the place of residence at the time of the return (London), although all three were born abroad. The charting of the solar return is exactly the same as for a natal chart (see page 84).

The above procedure enables the return chart to be calculated, but the real value of all solar return charts is in the progressions, and these are dependent upon an important factor, namely the *Right Ascension of the Apparent Sun. (R.A.A.S.)*

The Apparent Sun is the *True Sun* which moves along the Ecliptic at a varying rate, whereas the *Mean Sun* (first column of a noon ephemeris) moves along the Celestial Equator at a mean or average rate. The Mean Sun's motion is the average rate throughout the year, and the difference between this motion and that of the Apparent Sun is known as the *Equation of Time,* which varies throughout the year. As the progression of the solar return is not strictly a mean rate matter, we use the Right Ascension of the Apparent Sun. If the Mean Sun was taken, we would need to correct for the Equation of Time, and this would require additions and subtractions according to the time of the year. The following examples show the methods for finding the R.A. of the Apparent Sun.

Example No. 1
Sun's longitude 5°52′10″ Virgo
Working:

From any Tables of Houses 10th cusp:	*H.*	*M.*	*S.*	
6° Virgo	10	31	08	
5° Virgo	10	27	22	
1° (60 mins.)	0	03	46	Difference

Calculator

$$(52'10'')\ \frac{52.16 \times 3.76}{60}\ (3'46'') = 3.27 = 3'16''$$

	H.	*M.*	*S.*
which added to (5° Virgo) S.T.	10	27	22
	0	03	16
Right Ascension of Apparent Sun =	10	30	38

Example No. 2
Sun's longitude 6°07′59″ Cancer
Working:

From any Tables of Houses 10th cusp:	*H.*	*M.*	*S.*	
7° Cancer	6	30	30	
6° Cancer	6	26	09	
1° (60 mins.)	0	04	21	Difference

Calculator

$$(7'59'')\ \frac{7.9833 \times 4.35}{60}\ (4'21'') = 0.5788 = 34''$$

	H.	*M.*	*S.*
which added to (6° Cancer) S.T.	6	26	09
	0	00	34
Right Ascension of Apparent Sun =	6	26	43

Example No. 3
Sun's longitude 2°26'15" Aries
Working:

From any Tables of Houses 10th cusp:	*H.*	*M.*	*S.*	
3° Aries	0	11	00	
2° Aries	0	07	20	
1° (60 mins.)	0	03	40	Difference

Calculator

(26'15") $\frac{26.25 \times 3.66}{60}$ (3'40") = 1.60 = 1'36"

	H.	*M.*	*S.*
which added to (2° Aries) S.T.	0	07	20
	0	01	36
Right Ascension of Apparent Sun =	0	08	56

An alternative method for finding the Sun's R.A. is to use the trigonometric formula:

Tan. A = Cos. E. Tan. L.
where A = the required Right Ascension, E, the Obliquity of the Ecliptic (23°27'), and L, the Sun's longitude.

Example No. 1 has the Sun's longitude as 5°52'10" Virgo. Measuring from 0° Cancer to Virgo = 65°52'10".

Deg.	*Min.*	*Secs.*	
65	52	10	= Tan. 2.232333
23	27	00	= Cos. 0.917407 (E) Obliquity of Ecliptic
			= Tan. 2.433305
			= 67.65912
			+ 90.
			157.65912 divided by 15

= 10.5106 = *10. 30. 38 Sidereal time = R.A. of Apparent Sun as required.*

Example No. 2
Sun's longitude 6°07′59″ Cancer.

Deg.	*Min.*	*Sec.*	
6	07	59	= Tan. 0.10745
23	27	00	= Cos. 0.91740
			= Tan. 0.11712
			= 6.68041
			+ 90.
			96.68041 divided by 15

= 6.44536 = *6. 26. 43 Sidereal time = R.A. of Apparent Sun as required.*

Example No. 3
Sun's longitude 2°26′15″ Aries.

Deg.	*Min.*	*Sec.*	
2	26	15	= Tan. 0.042568
23	27		= Cos. 0.917407
			= Tan. 0.039052
			= 2.2363 divided by 15

= 0.14909 = *0. 08. 56 Sidereal time = R.A. of Apparent Sun as required.*

The calculation of the R.A. of the Apparent Sun at the date under review, is found in the same manner as that at the time of the Return. For ordinary purposes, the above procedure is accurate enough, but for a rigorously timed return and its progressions, a schedule showing the times when a planet bodily crosses an angle should be prepared. This entails calculating its right ascension and its Ascensional Difference (A.D.).

Due to planets normally having latitude (being either above or below the Ecliptic), their times of rising and setting will not coincide with their Ecliptic degrees. The actual time that a planet with latitude rises and sets is easily found by noting its R.A., declination and the latitude of the place. Its time of culmination is, of course, the time which corresponds to its R.A. However, to avoid introducing complexities into what is intended to be an introductory exposition of solar returns and their progressions, we will be content with accuracy as opposed to precision.

(C) Calculation of the progressed solar return

The progression of the solar return chart is based on the *Right* Ascension of the Apparent Sun (R.A.A.S.). As the ending of one return marks the commencement of the next return, it follows that any method of progression must incorporate the total period for which a particular return is valid, which in the case of solar returns, is approximately 365¼ days.

The formula for progressing the solar return consists in determining the R.A. of the Midheaven (R.A.M.C.) at the time of the solar return and at the succeeding return. The difference between the times of the two returns, plus 24 hours and divided by 24 hours 0 minutes 3.5 seconds, will give the *'year constant'*. By multiplying the difference between the Sun's R.A. at the date under review and its R.A. at the time of the return by this constant, we obtain the *sidereal time increment* which — added to the R.A.M.C. of the solar return — gives the R.A.M.C. of the progressed return. This procedure expressed as a formula becomes:

(a) S 1:R.A.M.C. (sidereal time) Succeeding Solar Return
less S 2:R.A.M.C. (sidereal time) Preceeding Solar Return
= Difference + 24 hours and divided by 24 hours 0 min. 3.5 sec.
= 'Y' = *Year constant*

(b) R 1: Sun's right ascension at date and time required
less R 2: Sun's right ascension Preceeding Solar Return
= *Difference* × *'Y'* = *Increment of sidereal time (I)*

(c) R.A.M.C. (S 2) of Preceeding Solar Return
+ Increment (I) = *R.A.M.C. of the Progressed return*

This procedure entails calculating the returns for two years in order to arrive at the difference between the two returns, but the results justify these extra efforts as a study of case histories will show.

If we refer to our three examples and progress their returns for the date and time of the accident, we should (if the solar return techniques are valid) find indications of the tragic event which occurred on 31.12.79.

Example No. 1
Birth data: 29.8.28. 11.50 a.m. G.M.T.
Solar return 1979/80 7.42 p.m. G.M.T. 29.8.79 (Chart No. 1)
Event: Accident 0.25 a.m. G.M.T. 31 December 1979, London.

Progressed Return

		H.	*M.*	*S.*
(A)	R.A.M.C. 1980 return 1.42 a.m. G.M.T. 29.8.80	00	11	41
	R.A.M.C. 1979 return 7.42 p.m. G.M.T. 29.8.79	18	11	40
	Difference	6	00	01
	Add	24	00	00
		30	00	01

H. M. S.
30 00 01
÷ 24 00 03.5 = *1.249960* = *Constant*

		H.	*M.*	*S.*
(B)	Sun's R.A. 31.12.79 0.25 a.m. G.M.T.	18	37	56
	Sun's R.A. 29.8.79 7.42 p.m. G.M.T.	10	30	38
	Difference	8	07	18
	8.07.18×1.249960 = Increment =	10	09	06
(C)	R.A.M.C. Solar Return add	18	11	40
	R.A.M.C. Progressed Solar Return 31.12.79	4	20	46

(see Figs. 34 and 35.)

Example No. 2
Birth data: 28.6.25. 9.08 a.m. G.M.T.
Solar return 1979/80 10.12 a.m. G.M.T. 28.6.79 (Chart No. 2)
Event: Accident 0.25 a.m. G.M.T. 31 December 1979, London.

Progressed Return

		H.	*M.*	*S.*
(A)	R.A.M.C. 1980 return 4.09 p.m. G.M.T. 27.6.80	10	32	41
	R.A.M.C. 1979 return 10.12 a.m. G.M.T. 28.6.79	4	35	39
	Difference	5	57	02
	Add	24	00	00
		29	57	02

H. M. S.
29 57 02
÷ 24 00 03.5 = *1.247889* = *Constant*

	H.	M.	S.
(B) Sun's R.A. 31.12.79 0.25 a.m. G.M.T.	18	37	56
Sun's R.A. 28.6.79 10.12 a.m. G.M.T.	6	26	43
Difference	12	11	13
12. 11. 13 × 1.247889 =	15	12	28
(C) R.A.M.C. solar return add	4	35	39
R.A.M.C. progressed solar return 31 December 1979	19	48	07

(see Figs. 36 and 37.)

Example No. 3
Birth data: 23.3.1899. 06.45 a.m. G.M.T
Solar return 1979/80 4.18 p.m. G.M.T. 23.3.79 (Chart No. 3)
Event: Accident 0.25 a.m. G.M.T. 31 December 1979

Progressed Return

	H.	M.	S.
(A) R.A.M.C. 1980 return 10.06 p.m. G.M.T. 22.3.80	10	08	13
R.A.M.C. 1979 return 4.18 p.m. G.M.T. 23.3.79	4	20	14
Difference	5	47	59
Add	24	00	00
	29	47	59

H. M. S.
29 47 59
÷ 24 00 03.5 = *1.241604* = *Constant*

	H.	M.	S.
(B) Sun's R.A. 31.12.79 0.25 a.m. G.M.T.	18	37	56
Sun's R.A. 23.3.79 4.18 p.m. G.M.T.	0	08	56
Difference	18	29	00
18. 29. 00. × 1.241604 =	22	56	56
(C) R.A.M.C. solar return add	4	20	14
R.A.M.C. progressed solar return 31 December 1979	3	17	10

(see Figs. 38 and 39.)

In all the progressed Solar Return charts listed, the Ascendant, Midheaven and cusps are shown for the progressed time and date. The inner circle shows the natal positions, the centre circle has the solar return positions and the outer circle (transits) has the positions on the date under review. This format is useful in that the pattern of natal, solar and transiting planets can be studied together and

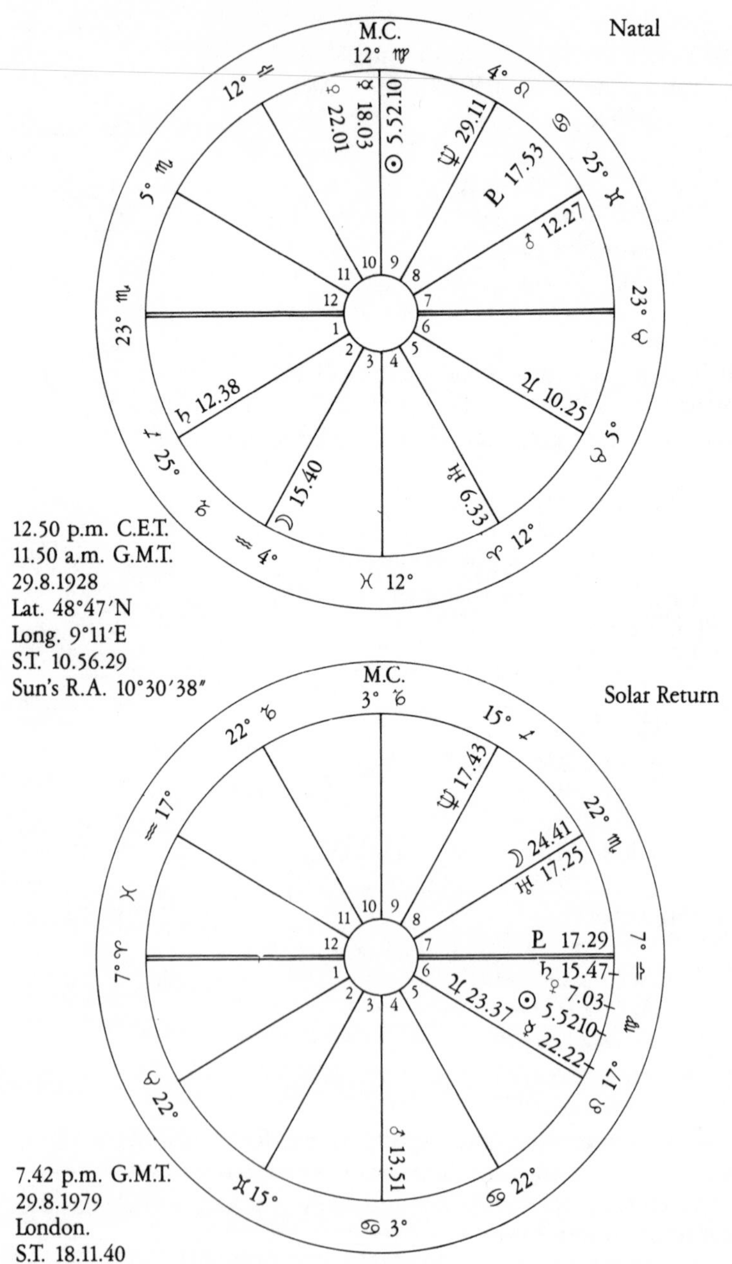
Natal
M.C.
12° ♍
4° ♌
♋
25° ♊
23° ♉
♉ 5°
♈ 12°
♓ 12°
♒ 4°
♑
♐ 25°
23° ♏
5° ♏
12° ♎
☉ 5.52.10
☿ 18.03
♀ 22.01
♆ 29.11
♇ 17.53
♂ 12.27
♃ 10.25
♅ 6.33
☽ 15.40
♄ 12.38
12.50 p.m. C.E.T.
11.50 a.m. G.M.T.
29.8.1928
Lat. 48°47′N
Long. 9°11′E
S.T. 10.56.29
Sun's R.A. 10°30′38″
Solar Return
M.C.
3° ♑
15° ♐
22° ♏
7° ♎
♍
♌ 17°
♋ 22°
♋ 3°
♊ 15°
♉ 22°
7° ♈
♓
♒ 17°
22° ♑
♆ 17.43
☽ 24.41
♅ 17.25
♇ 17.29
♄ 15.47
♀ 7.03
☉ 5.5210
☿ 22.22
♃ 23.37
♂ 13.51
7.42 p.m. G.M.T.
29.8.1979
London.
S.T. 18.11.40

Figure 34

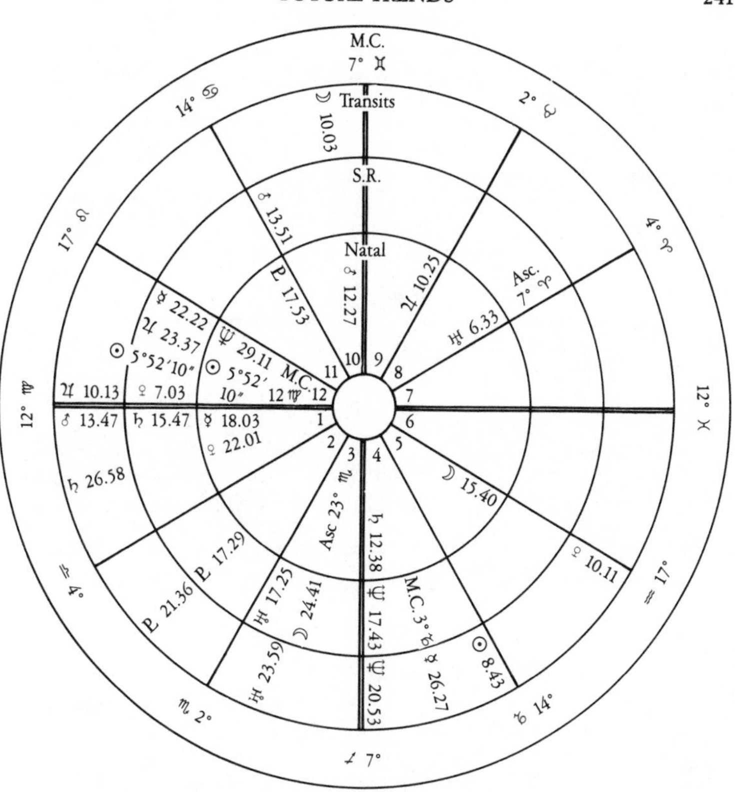

SOLAR RETURN			
Date: 29.8.79 Time: 19.42			
	H	M	S
R.A. Sun	10	30	38
R.A.M.C.	18	11	40
Constant 1.24996			

PROGRESSED RETURN			
Date: 31.12.79 Time: 0.25			
	H	M	S
R.A. Sun P.S.R.	18	37	56
R.A. Sun S.R. minus	10	30	38
= Difference	8	07	18
× Constant =	10	09	06
R.A.M.C. S.R. add	18	11	40
= R.A.M.C. P.S.R.	4	20	46

Figure 35 Progressed Solar Return.

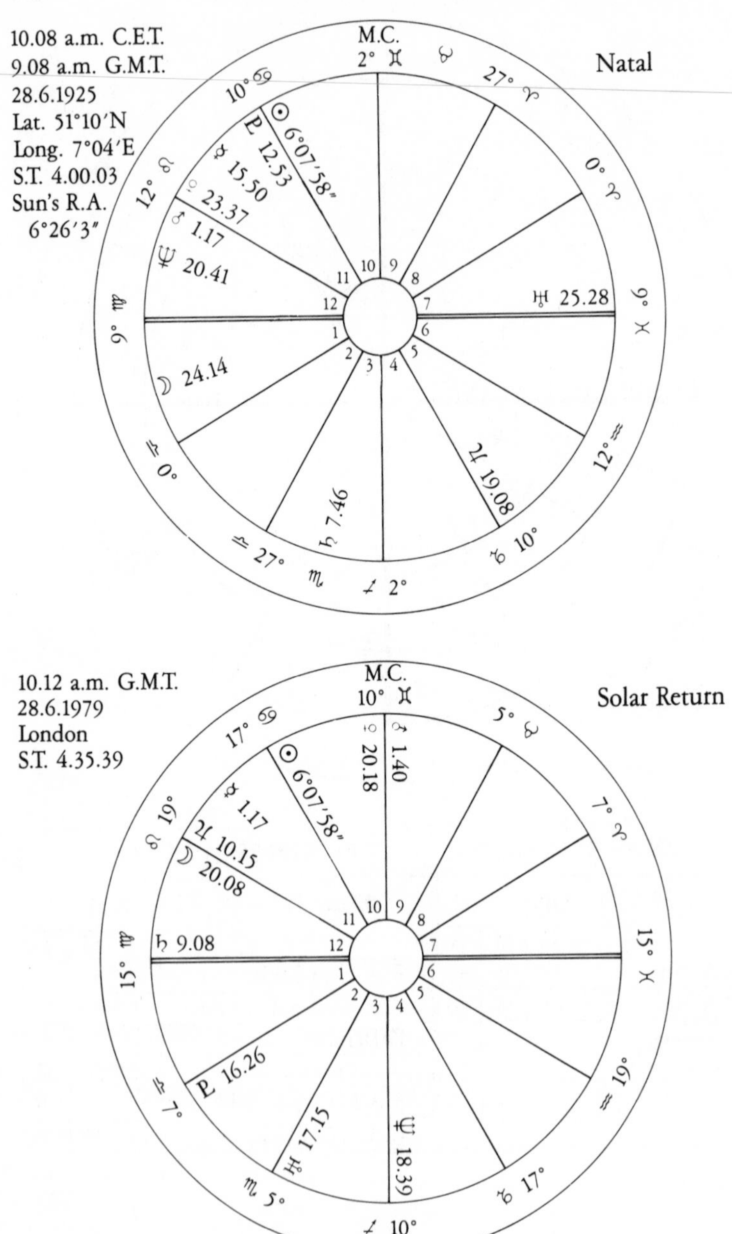
10.08 a.m. C.E.T.
9.08 a.m. G.M.T.
28.6.1925
Lat. 51°10′N
Long. 7°04′E
S.T. 4.00.03
Sun's R.A.
6°26′3″
Natal
M.C.
2° ♊
27° ♈
0° ♉
9° ♓
12° ♒
♑ 10°
♐ 2°
♎ 27°
♎ 0°
9° ♍
12° ♌
10° ♋
☉ 6°07′58″
♇ 12.53
☿ 15.50
♀ 23.37
♂ 1.17
♆ 20.41
☽ 24.14
♄ 7.46
♃ 19.08
♅ 25.28
10.12 a.m. G.M.T.
28.6.1979
London
S.T. 4.35.39
Solar Return
M.C.
10° ♊
5° ♉
7° ♈
15° ♓
19° ♒
♑ 17°
♐ 10°
♏ 5°
♎ 7°
15° ♍
♌ 19°
17° ♋
♀ 20.18
♂ 1.40
☉ 6°07′58″
☿ 1.17
♃ 10.15
☽ 20.08
♄ 9.08
♇ 16.26
♅ 17.15
♆ 18.39

Figure 36.

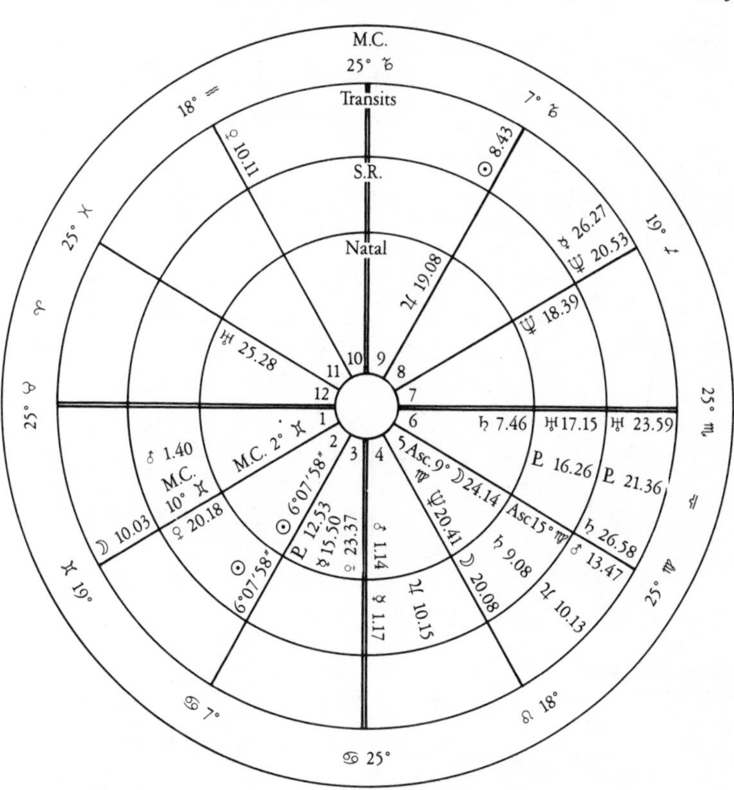

SOLAR RETURN			
Date: 28.6.79 Time: 10.12			
	H	M	S
R.A. Sun	6	26	43
R.A.M.C.	4	35	39
Constant 1.24789			

PROGRESSED RETURN			
Date: 31.12.79 Time: 0.25			
	H	M	S
R.A. Sun P.S.R.	18	37	56
R.A. Sun S.R. minus	6	26	43
= Difference	12	11	13
× Constant =	15	12	28
R.A.M.C. S.R. add	4	35	39
= R.A.M.C. P.S.R.	19	48	07

Figure 37 Progressed Solar Return

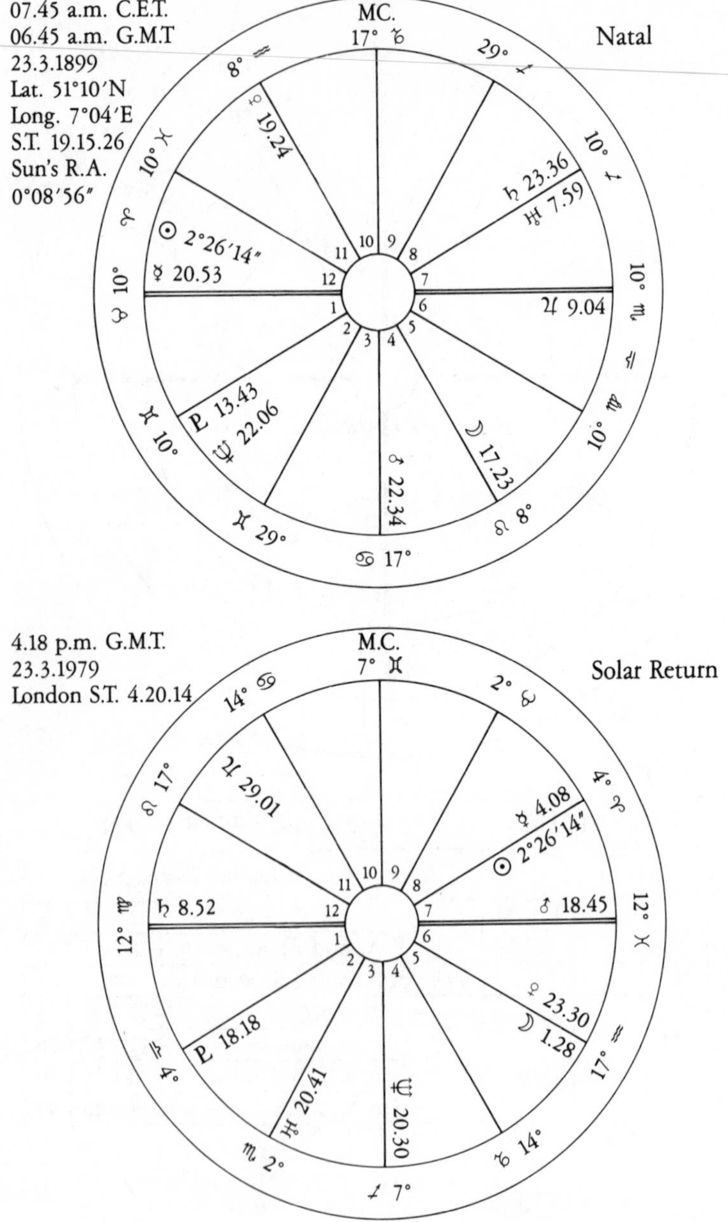
07.45 a.m. C.E.T.
06.45 a.m. G.M.T
23.3.1899
Lat. 51°10′N
Long. 7°04′E
S.T. 19.15.26
Sun's R.A.
0°08′56″
Natal
MC.
17° ♑
29° ♐
10° ♐
10° ♏
♎
10° ♍
♌ 8°
♋ 17°
♊ 29°
♊ 10°
♉ 10°
♈
10° ♓
8° ♒
♀ 19.24
♄ 23.36
♅ 7.59
☉ 2°26′14″
☿ 20.53
♃ 9.04
♇ 13.43
♆ 22.06
☽ 17.23
♂ 22.34
4.18 p.m. G.M.T.
23.3.1979
London S.T. 4.20.14
Solar Return
M.C.
7° ♊
2° ♉
4° ♈
12° ♓
17° ♒
♑ 14°
♐ 7°
♏ 2°
♎ 4°
12° ♍
♌ 17°
14° ♋
♃ 29.01
☿ 4.08
☉ 2°26′14″
♄ 8.52
♂ 18.45
♀ 23.30
☽ 1.28
♇ 18.18
♅ 20.41
♆ 20.30

Figure 38

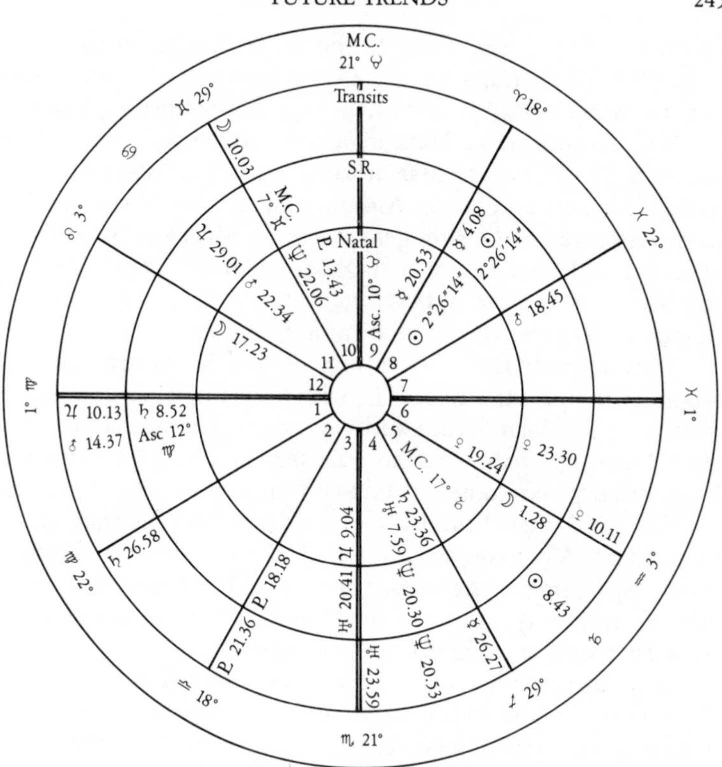

SOLAR RETURN			
Date: 23.3.79 Time: 16.18			
	H	M	S
R.A. Sun	0	08	56
R.A.M.C.	4	20	14
Constant 1.24160			

PROGRESSED RETURN			
Date: 31.12.79 Time: 0.25			
	H	M	S
R.A. Sun P.S.R.	18	37	56
R.A. Sun S.R. minus	0	08	56
= Difference	18	29	00
× Constant =	22	56	56
R.A.M.C. S.R. add	4	20	14
= R.A.M.C. P.S.R.	3	17	10

Figure 39 Progressed Solar Return.

also their relationship, if any, to the angles can be noted.

In P.S.R. *No. 1* (Figs. 34 and 35) we have several contacts such as natal Mars and Saturn astride the meridian: transiting Moon on the M.C. conjunct natal Mars, in opposition to natal Saturn. Solar Saturn and and transiting Mars are conjoined on the Ascendant close to natal Mercury and Venus. Although Jupiter and Venus are close to the Ascendant, the stronger contacts of Mars and Saturn have operated and, as a result, a tragic accident occurred. The only consolation in this case is, that serious injury was avoided, and this we can attribute to the angular Jupiter and Venus.

When we study P.S.R. *No. 2* (Figs. 36 and 37) we see transiting Moon precisely on the Solar M.C. with transiting Mars and Jupiter contacting the solar Saturn and Ascendant. Uranus, close to the seventh cusp, probably indicates the shock element. Also notable is the Mercury-Mars contact — often prominent in cases of accidents.

P.S.R. *No. 3* (Figs. 38 and 39) who suffered from this tragedy, has the transiting Moon conjunct the solar M.C., with Saturn and Uranus closely aspecting the angles (first and fourth). All these charts have other significant contacts, but the foregoing illustrates the value of the solar return as a predictive instrument.

The pomp and circumstance of royal occasions is shown in P.S.R. *No. 4* (Figs, 40 and 41) (Princess of Wales' wedding), where the transiting Sun conjoins solar Venus, and Jupiter and Saturn are close to the M.C., the transiting Venus being conjunct the natal Mars and Pluto. The conjunction of the Sun and Moon often denotes a 'new cycle', and here we have the solar Sun and Moon together in Cancer — a most appropriate indication of the event, particularly as the solar Moon is conjuct the natal Mercury. At the birth of her first child (P.S.R. *No. 5* — Fig. 43), the natal Neptune is conjunct the solar Ascendant and the P.S.R. Midheaven, in addition to the solar and transiting Neptune close to the P.S.R. Ascendant. The flurry and excitement denoted by these Neptunian contacts is in keeping with the event which attracted great public interest, the nature of which, is aptly signified by the Cancer groupings (natal, solar and transiting) astride the seventh house.

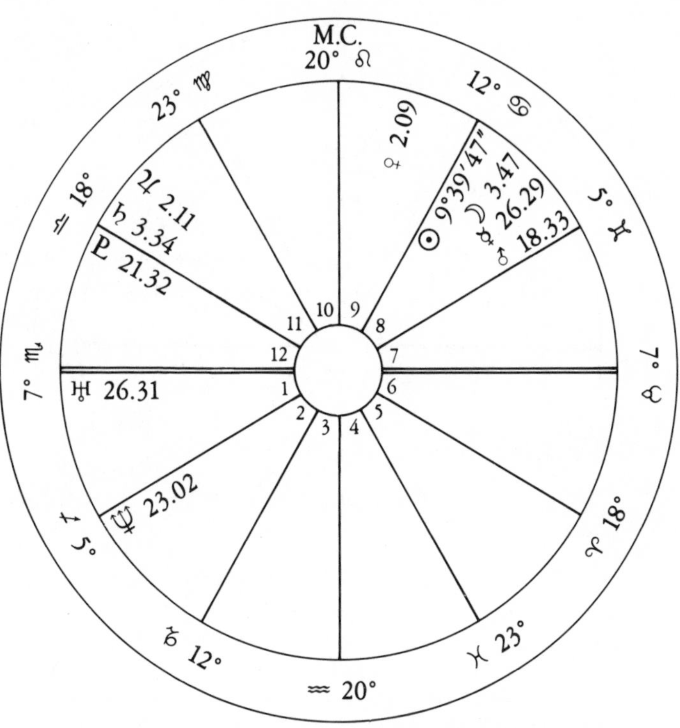

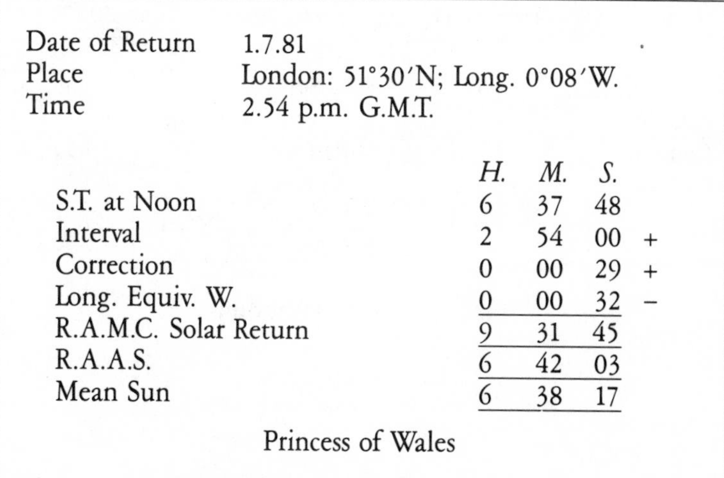

Date of Return	1.7.81
Place	London: 51°30′N; Long. 0°08′W.
Time	2.54 p.m. G.M.T.

	H.	*M.*	*S.*	
S.T. at Noon	6	37	48	
Interval	2	54	00	+
Correction	0	00	29	+
Long. Equiv. W.	0	00	32	–
R.A.M.C. Solar Return	9	31	45	
R.A.A.S.	6	42	03	
Mean Sun	6	38	17	

Princess of Wales

Figure 40 Solar Return 1981/82.

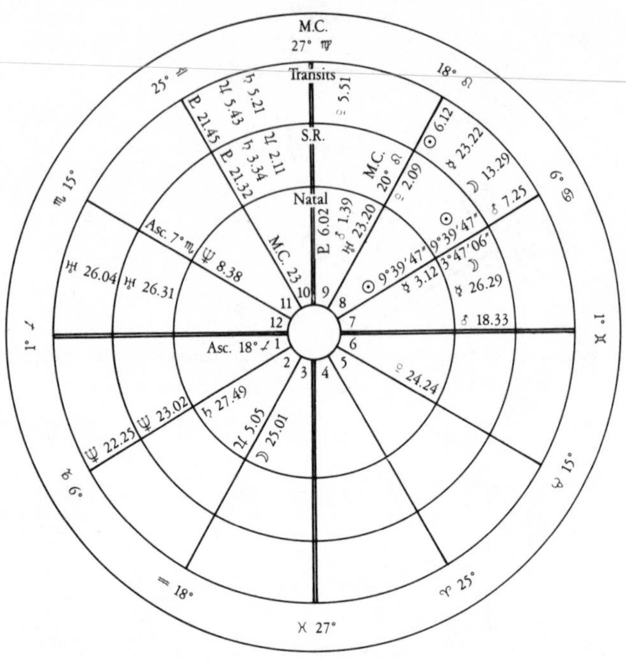

SOLAR RETURN			
Date: 1.7.81 Time: 14.54			
	H	M	S
R.A. Sun	6	42	03
R.A.M.C.	9	31	45
Constant 1.23469			

PROGRESSED RETURN			
Date: 29.7.81 Time: 10.17			
	H	M	S
R.A. Sun P.S.R.	8	34	19
R.A. Sun S.R. minus	6	42	03
= Difference	1	52	16
× Constant =	2	18	36
R.A.M.C. S.R. add	9	31	45
= R.A.M.C. P.S.R.	11	50	21

Princess of Wales (Wedding)

Figure 41 Progressed Solar Return 1981/82.

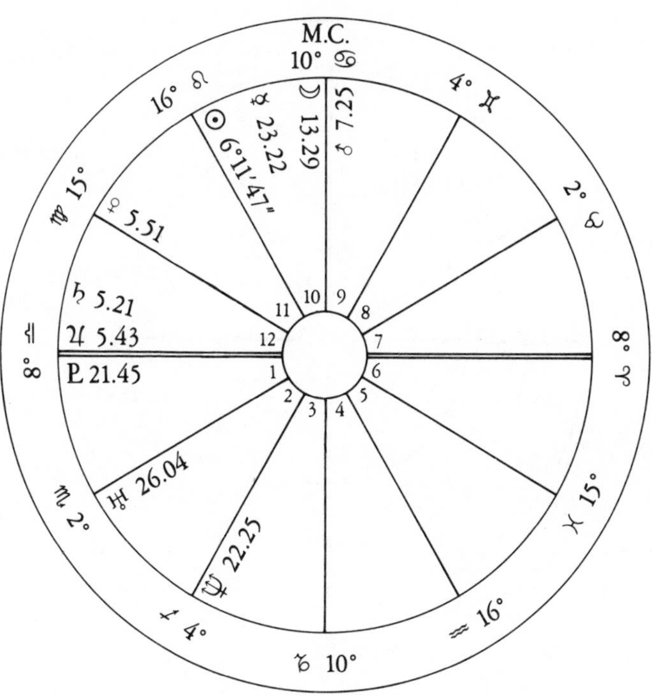

Date	29.7.81
Place	St Paul's, London: 51°31′N; 0°05′W.
Time	10.18 a.m. G.M.T.

	H.	M.	S.	
S.T. at Noon	8	28	12	
Interval	1	42	00	–
Correction	0	00	17	–
Long. Equiv. W.	0	00	20	–
R.A.M.C.	6	45	35	
R.A.A.S.	8	34	19	
Mean Sun	8	27	55	

The Prince and Princess of Wales

Figure 42 Marriage Chart

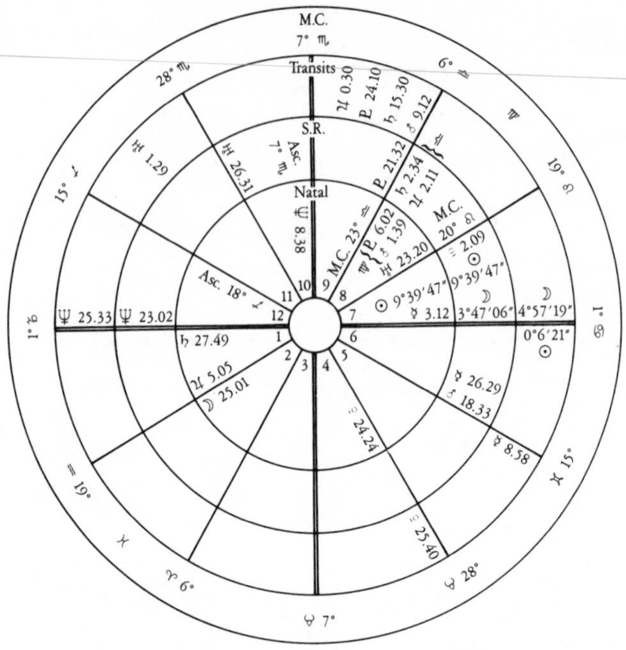

SOLAR RETURN			
Date: 1.7.81 Time: 14.54			
	H	M	S
R.A. Sun	6	42	03
R.A.M.C.	9	31	45
Constant 1.23469			

PROGRESSED RETURN			
Date: 21.6.82 Time: 20.03			
	H	M	S
R.A. Sun P.S.R.	6	00	28
R.A. Sun S.R. minus	6	42	03
= Difference	23	18	25
× Constant =	4	46	37
R.A.M.C. S.R. add	9	31	45
= R.A.M.C. P.S.R.	14	18	22

Princess of Wales (Birth of 1st Child)

Figure 43 Progressed Solar Return 1981/82.

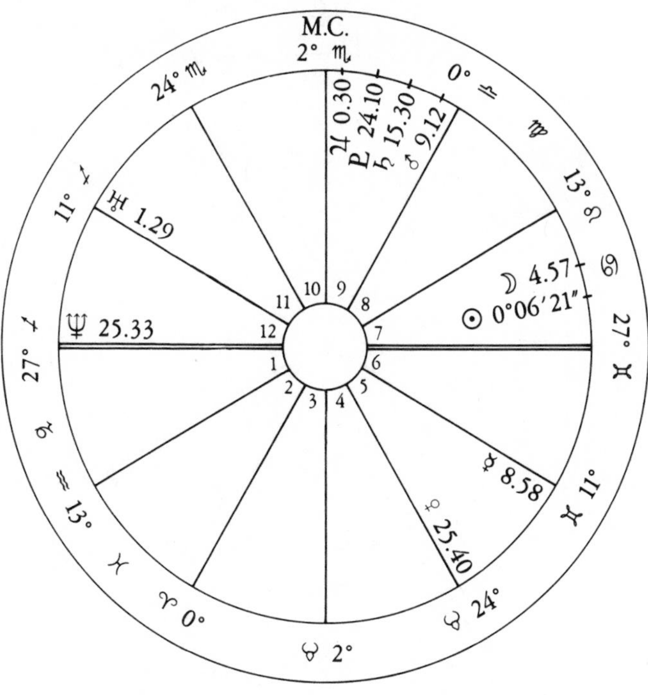

Date 21.6.82
Place Paddington: Lat. 51°32′N; Long. 0.12 W
Time 8.03 p.m. G.M.T.

	H.	*M.*	*S.*	
S.T. at Noon	5	57	25	
Interval	8	03	00	+
Correction	0	01	19	+
Long. Equiv. W.	0	00	48	–
R.A.M.C.	14	00	56	
R.A.A.S.	6	00	28	
Mean Sun	5	58	44	

Prince William

Figure 44 Natal Chart.

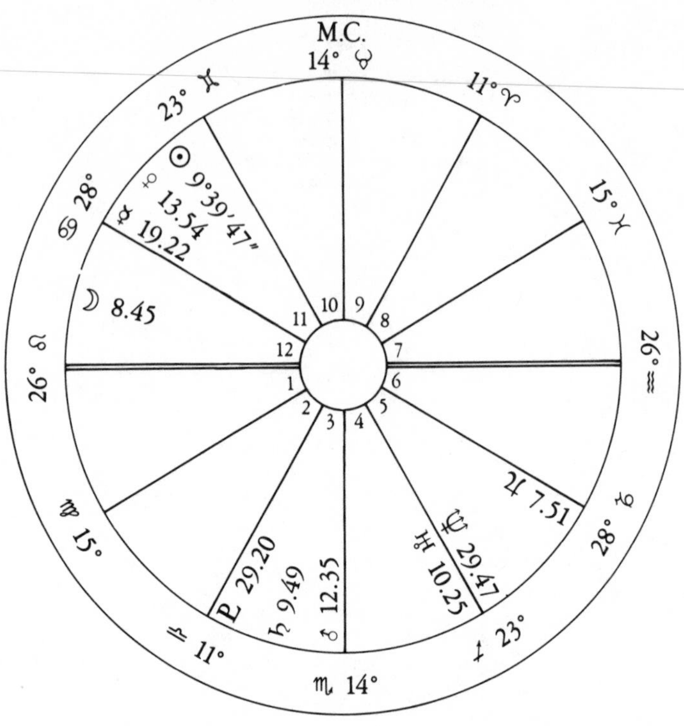

Date of Return	1.7.84
Place	London: 51°30′N; Long. 0.08 W.
Time	8.09 a.m. G.M.T.

	H.	M.	S.	
S.T. at Noon	6	38	53	
Interval	3	51	00	–
Correction	0	00	38	–
Long. Equiv. W.	0	00	32	–
R.A.M.C. Solar Return	2	46	43	
R.A.A.S.	6	42	03	
Mean Sun	6	38	15	

Princess of Wales

Figure 45 Solar Return 1984/85.

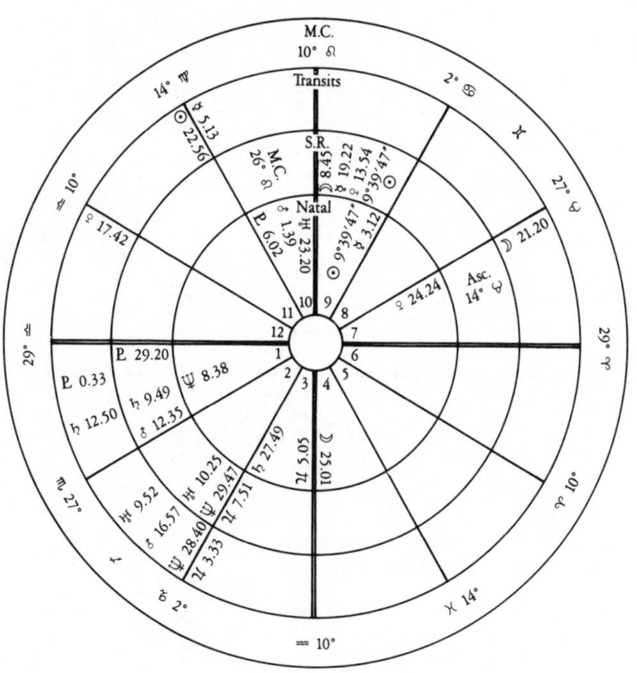

SOLAR RETURN			
Date: 1.7.84 Time: 8.09			
	H	M	S
R.A. Sun	6	42	03
R.A.M.C.	2	46	43
Constant 1.24053			

PROGRESSED RETURN			
Date: 15.9.84 Time: 15.20			
	H	M	S
R.A. Sun P.S.R.	11	34	06
R.A. Sun S.R. minus	6	42	03
= Difference	4	52	03
× Constant =	6	02	18
R.A.M.C. S.R. add	2	46	43
= R.A.M.C. P.S.R.	8	49	01

Princess of Wales (Birth of 2nd Child)

Figure 46 Progressed Solar Return 1984/85.

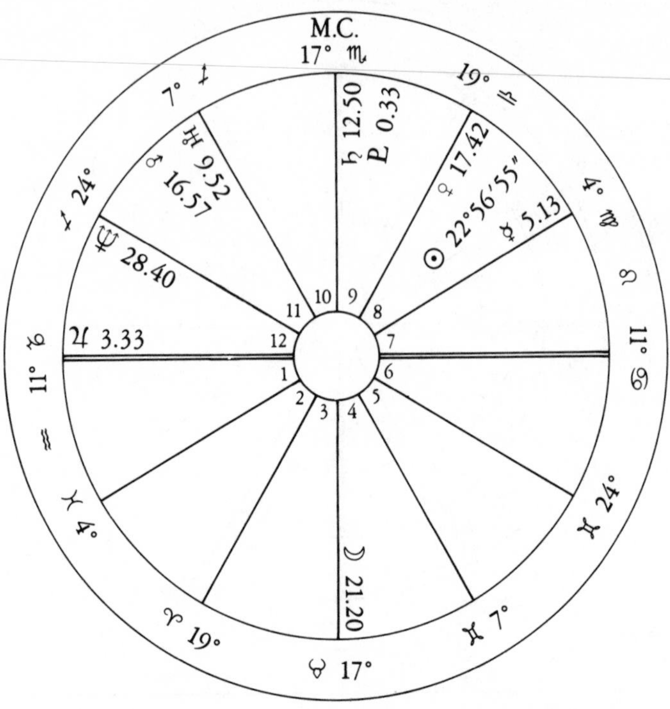

Date	15.9.84
Place	Paddington: Lat. 51°32′ N; Long. 0.12 W.
Time	3.20 p.m. G.M.T.

	H.	*M.*	*S.*	
S.T. at Noon	11	38	31	
Interval	3	20	00	+
Correction	0	00	33	+
Long. Equiv. W.	0	00	48	–
R.A.M.C.	14	58	16	
R.A.A.S.	11	34	06	
Mean Sun	11	39	04	

Prince Henry

Figure 47 Natal Chart.

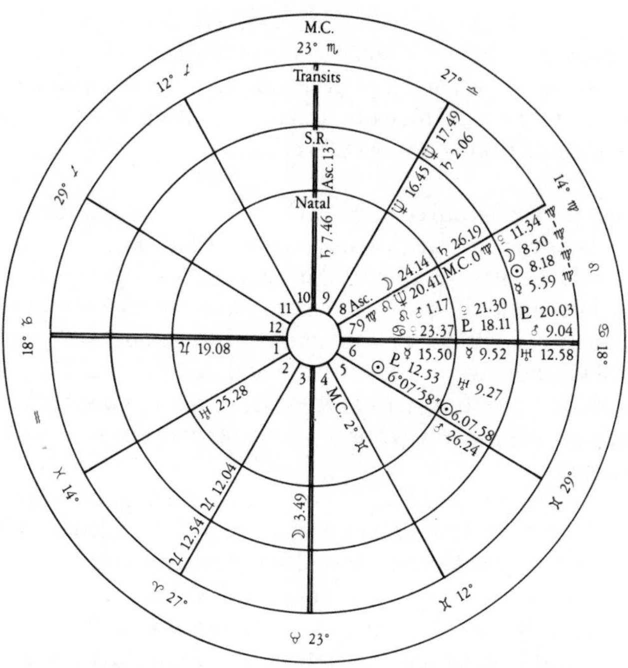

SOLAR RETURN			
Date: 28.6.51 Time: 15.45			
	H	M	S
R.A. Sun	6	26	43
R.A.M.C.	10	09	19
Constant 1.23922			

PROGRESSED RETURN			
Date: 1.9.51 Time: 13.30			
	H	M	S
R.A. Sun P.S.R.	10	39	47
R.A. Sun S.R. minus	6	26	43
= Difference	4	13	04
× Constant =	5	13	36
R.A.M.C. S.R. add	10	09	19
= R.A.M.C. P.S.R.	15	22	55

Marriage — 1.9.51 (see Case No. 2)

Figure 48 Progressed Solar Return 1951/52.

At the birth of her second child (P.S.R. *No. 6* — Figs. 45 and 46) Pluto rises and the Solar Moon is conjunct the P.S.R. Midheaven, in opposition to the natal Jupiter. In addition, the transiting Jupiter is opposed to the natal Mercury, and the transiting Moon is applying to the conjunction of the natal Venus.

Progressed Solar Return chart *No. 7* (Fig. 48) is for the date of marriage of the daughter involved in an accident (P.S.R. *No. 2* — Figs. 36 and 37). Not only does the natal Jupiter rise — opposing the natal Venus, Mercury and Pluto — but there is also a remarkable grouping of planets in the P.S.R. seventh house in contact, not only with the solar M.C., but also conjunct her natal Ascendant. This case is particularly interesting, in that the solar return has been calculated for the place of residence (London) and not for the birthplace, which was abroad.

The subject of solar and lunar returns offers great scope, and although we have dealt in broad terms with those calculated in the tropical zodiac, this does not mean that the sidereal techniques should be neglected. On the contrary, both should be considered independently and then compared, concerning their significance and how and in what way they reflect the life and circumstances of individuals.

The Lunar Return

A Lunar Return is a chart cast for the exact time when the Moon returns to the same longitude that it held at birth. This occurs every twenty-seven days or so. These returns, which are computed to the degree and minute of longitude, are cast for the place of residence, as is the solar return. It has been suggested that all returns should be related to the birthplace, which in the case of persons who have emigrated from their native land and settled elsewhere, could produce very different charts. Only research will confirm whether this is correct or not.

As the solar return covers twelve months from the time of the Sun's return, so the lunar return covers one month from the time of the Moon's return to its natal position. In all cases, the indications afforded by the lunar return should be related to the natal chart and to the current progressions in conjunction with the current solar return.

It may be that the lunar indications 'trigger off' the solar chart, particularly when the angles are involved. Again, only careful study

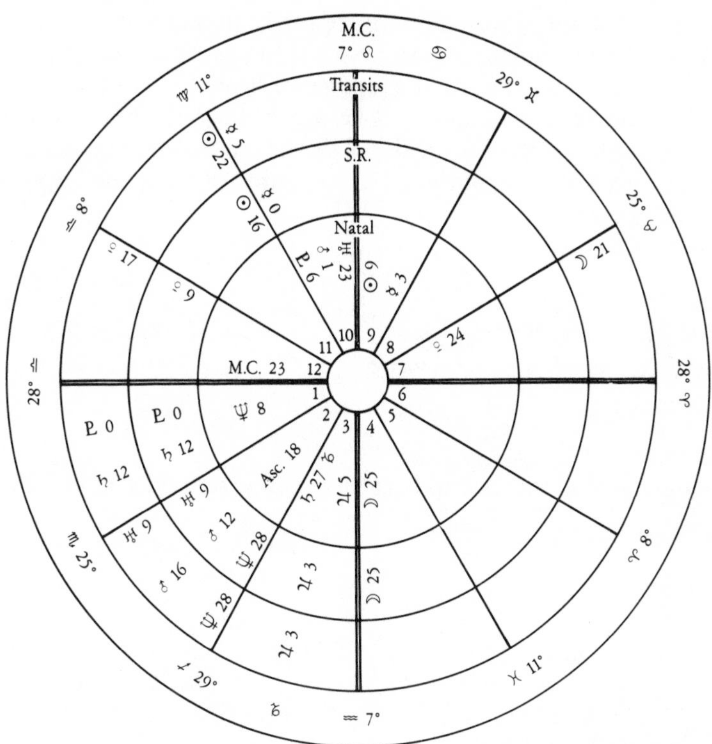

Asc. M.C. and cusps as at date and time of the Lunar Return

Lunar Return
Prior to the birth of Prince Henry 9.29 a.m. G.M.T.
8 September 1984, London. R.A.M.C. 8.39.30

Inner circle — Natal

Centre circle — Lunar

Outer circle — Transits on day (15.9.84)
= child's natal positions

Figure 49 Princess of Wales.

will confirm this assumption. The solar return indicates the 'pattern of the year', while the lunar return appears to be indicative of health and well-being, and has a more personal and psychological impact.

The method for finding the Moon's exact position and the time of the return to the longitude it held at birth, is the same as that used to determine the Sun's position. Due to the Moon's swift motion, its place need only be computed to the nearest minute; odd seconds can be ignored.

Calculation
Birth data: 1 July 1961, 6.45 p.m. G.M.T. Lat. 52°51′ N Long. 0°31′ E
Natal Moon: 25°01′ Aquarius

Example No. 1.
Required to find the time and date of the lunar return for September 1984

Working:

	Deg.	*Min.*	
(1) Moon's long. 8 Sept. 1984: Aquarius	26	17	at noon
Moon's long. 7 Sept. 1984: Aquarius	14	11	at noon
Motion in 24 hours	12	06	
(2) Moon's long. 8 Sept.	26	17	at noon
Moon's long. at birth	25	01	
Difference	1	16	

Therefore if 12°06′ = 24 hours
1°16′ = ?

Method No. 1.

Deg.	*Mins.*	*Secs.*	*Logarithms*
1	16	00	2.15261 Ternary
12	06	00	1.17249 Ternary Deduct
			0.98012 Diurnal

Diurnal Log. 0.98012 = 2 hours 31 mins. before noon on the 8 September 1984 = 9.29 a.m. G.M.T. The lunar return occurred at *9.29 a.m. G.M.T. 8 September 1984,* and a chart cast for this time for London (place of residence) is the lunar return for Sept./Oct.

Method No. 2. Calculator

Deg.	*Mins.*	*Sec.*	
1	16	00	=1.2666×24=2.5123=2 hours 31 mins.
12	06	00	=12.100

which agrees with method 1.

A chart computed as follows is the lunar return:

		H.	*M.*	*S.*
S.T. at noon G.M.T. 8.9.84		11	10	55
Interval of time (a.m.)	deduct	2	31	00
		8	39	55
Mean time correction 9.86 secs. per hour	deduct	—	—	25
		8	39	30
Long. Equivalent		—	—	—
R.A.M.C. lunar return		8	39	30

The Solar Moon Return

Among the many fine techniques introduced by Cyril Fagan more than twenty years ago, was one which he termed the 'Lunar Kinetic'. This return is a chart computed for the time that the Solar return Moon transits its progressed longitude. Although this type of return was originally introduced and used in terms of the sidereal zodiac, its technique is applicable to the Tropical returns as the following examples show.

Example No.1

Solar return 29.8.79: 7.42 p.m. G.M.T.
Moon's long. 24°41′ Scorpio.
Required, the solar Moon return for the period covering 31.12.79.

Method:

		H.	*M.*	*S.*
(A) 31.12.79 0.25 a.m. G.M.T.	Mean Sun	18	35	22
29.8.79 7.42 p.m. G.M.T.	Mean Sun	10	29	40
Difference		8	05	42
Correction 9.86 secs. per hour	minus	0	01	20
Mean solar hours		8	04	22
G.M.T. of solar return	add	7	42	00
G.M.T. of progressed solar return		15	46	22

= 3.46 a.m. 30.8.89

(B) Moon's long. at 3.46 a.m. G.M.T. 30.8.79
= *29°02′ Scorpio = Progressed Moon's Longitude*

(C) For the period covering 31 December 1979, the Moon transits 29°02′ Scorpio sometime on 17 December.

	Deg.	*Min.*	*Sec.*
Moon's long. noon 17.12.79 Sagittarius	1	51	44
Moon's long. noon 16.12.79 Scorpio	18	50	11
Motion in 24 hours	13	01	33
Moon's long. at noon 17.12.79	1	51	44
Prog. Moon's long.	29	02	00
Difference	2	49	44

$$\frac{(\ 2.49.44)}{(13.01.33)}\ \frac{2.828 \times 24}{13.0258} = \text{5 hours 12 mins. from noon}$$

= *6.48 a.m. G.M.T. 17 December 1979*
= *Solar Moon Return*

		H.	*M.*	*S.*
(D) S.T. at noon on transit date (17.12.79)		17	42	05
Interval to noon (a.m.)	minus	5	12	00
		12	30	05
Mean time correction	minus	00	00	51
R.A.M.C. Solar Moon Return		12	29	14

(E) Progress the above chart for 31.12.79 at 0.25 a.m. G.M.T.

		H.	*M.*	*S.*
31:12.79, 0.25 a.m. G.M.T.	Mean Sun	18	35	22
17.12.79 6.48 a.m. G.M.T.	Mean Sun	17	41	14
Difference		00	54	08
R.A.M.C. solar moon return	add	12	29	14
R.A.M.C. Progressed Solar Moon Return		13	23	22

The Mean Sun referred to in the calculation of the solar Moon return, is the sidereal time at noon, which increases by 9.86 seconds per hour.

Having found the R.A.M.C. (sidereal time), the solar Moon return chart is computed in the usual manner, likewise the progressed chart, and their indications studied in relation to the natal chart and the solar return chart for the particular year.

A cursory examination of the solar Moon charts for the three persons involved in an accident (charts A, B and C) show several major contacts which are appropriate to the event. These charts are listed to the nearest degree, with the cusps showing the progressed lunar return, i.e. at the time of the event.

Chart A: Pluto culminates, with the lunar and transiting Neptune conjunct the Ascendant. The natal Mars-Saturn opposition is close to the horizon, with the transiting Moon contacting both planets. At the time of the return (17.12.79), the 'lunar' Mercury was conjunct the lunar Ascendant and the natal Uranus opposed the lunar M.C.

Chart B: The transiting Sun is conjunct the seventh cusp, opposed to its natal position and the natal Pluto. The lunar Mars and Jupiter oppose the progressed M.C. and are also conjunct the natal Ascendant. Despite the transiting Venus being conjunct the lunar M.C., trine the transiting Moon, little good appears to have resulted from this contact. It could be said that it acted as a protective influence, and this may be its chief significance. Each year, of course, the Sun will at some time aspect the natal positions, but action stemming from its contacts will be governed by other factors. It is possible that these returns, 'cycles within cycles', have much within them of great astrological value.

Chart C: This is the chart of the mother who subsequently died from her injuries. Here we have the solar Moon and the natal Moon on the meridian, with the transiting Moon conjunct the lunar Ascendant. The natal planets Pluto, Saturn, Neptune and Uranus, in Gemini and Sagittarius are either astride the horizon or close by. Again the transiting Venus conjunct the lunar M.C. offers little help. The symbolism of Neptune/Saturn across the horizon with the transiting Sun on the eight cusp (Placidus) is highly significant.

As has been stated previously, all forms of progressions, directions and the like must show a relationship between the time and nature of the event/condition. Solar/lunar returns, properly calculated and interpreted, have a large part to play in our endeavours to relate astrology to life.

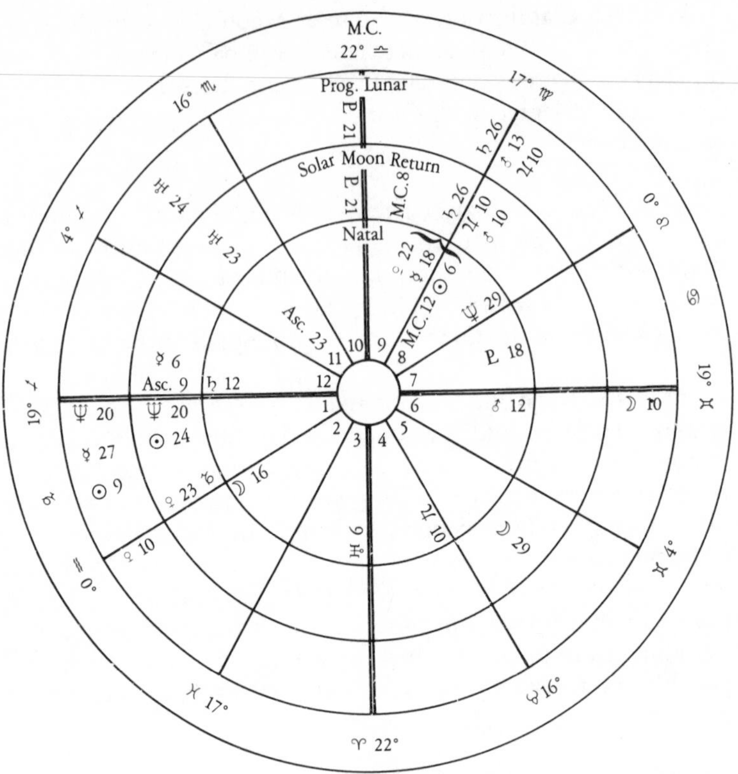

	Solar Return			Solar Moon Return			Prog. Lunar		
	D	M	Y	D	M	Y	D	M	Y
Date	29	8	79	17	12	79	31	12	79
	H	M	S	H	M	S	H	M	S
U.T.	19	42	00	06	48	00	0	25	00
R.A.M.C.	18	11	40	12	29	14	13	23	22
Mean Sun	10	29	40	17	41	14	18	35	22
Moon's Long.	24	41	♏	29	02	♏	10	♊	

Figure 50 Progressed Lunar Return Solar Moon. Chart A.

SOLAR MOON RETURN

			H.	M.	S.
(A)	Date 31.12.79 Time 0.25 Required:	Mean Sun	18	35	22
	Date 29.8.79 Time 19.42 Solar Return	Mean Sun	10	29	40
	Difference		8	05	42
	Correction for Mean Solar Time	minus	—	1	20
	Mean Solar Hours		8	04	22
	U.T. of Solar Return	Add	19	42	00
	Progressed Solar Return		3	46	22
	U.T. 03.46 Date 30.8.79				

		Sign	*Deg.*	*Mins*
(B)	Progressed Solar Return: Moon's Long.:			
	03.46 U.T.: 30.8.79 Date:	♏	29	02

		Date	*U.T.*
(C)	Moon Transits Progressed Long.: = *Solar Moon Return*	17.12.79	06.48

			H.	M.	S.
(D)	S.T. at 0 hours U.T. on Transit date	*	5	40	07
	U.T. of Moon's Return	Add	6	48	00
	Correction 9.86 secs. per hour	Add **	—	1	07
	R.A.M.C. at Greenwich		12	29	14
	Long. Equiv.	+ E: – W:	—	—	—
	R.A.M.C. Solar Moon Return		12	29	14
	Mean Sun = *+**+12 hours		17	41	14

			H.	M.	S.
(E)	*PROGRESSED SOLAR MOON RETURN*				
	Date 31.12.79 Time 0.25 Required:	Mean Sun	18	35	22
	Solar Moon Return	minus – Mean Sun	17	41	14
	Difference		—	54	08
	R.A.M.C. Solar Moon Return	Add	12	29	14
	R.A.M.C. Progressed Solar Moon Return		13	23	22

Calculations for Chart A (Fig. 50)

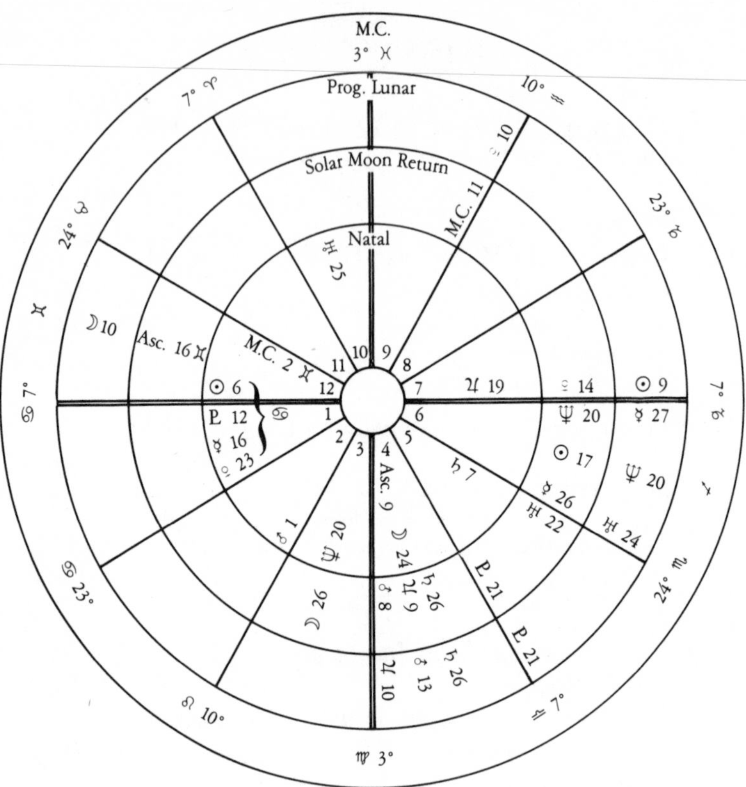

	Solar Return			Solar Moon Return			Prog. Lunar		
	D	M	Y	D	M	Y	D	M	Y
Date	28	6	79	9	12	79	31	12	79
	H	M	S	H	M	S	H	M	S
U.T.	10	12	00	15	44	00	0	25	00
R.A.M.C.	04	35	39	20	55	09	22	19	22
Mean Sun	06	23	39	17	11	09	18	35	22
Moon's Long.	20	08	♌	26	07	♌	10	♊	

Figure 51 Progressed Lunar Return Solar Moon. Chart B.

SOLAR MOON RETURN

			H.	M.	S.
(A)	Date 31.12.79 Time 0.25 Required:	Mean Sun	18	35	22
	Date 28.6.79 Time 10.12 Solar Return	Mean Sun	6	23	39
	Difference		12	11	43
	Correction for Mean Solar Time	minus	—	2	00
	Mean Solar Hours		12	09	43
	U.T. of Solar Return	Add	10	12	00
	Progressed Solar Return		22	21	43
	U.T. 22.22 Date 28.6.79				

		Sign	Deg.	Mins
(B)	Progressed Solar Return: Moon's Long.:			
	22.22 U.T.: 28.6.79 Date:	♌	26	07

		Date	U.T.
(C)	Moon Transits Progressed Long.: = *Solar Moon Return*	9.12.79	15.44

			H.	M.	S.
(D)	S.T. at 0 hours U.T. on Transit date	*	5	08	34
	U.T. of Moon's Return	Add	15	44	00
	Correction 9.86 secs. per hour	Add **	—	2	35
	R.A.M.C. at Greenwich		20	55	09
	Long. Equiv.	+ E: – W:	—	—	—
	R.A.M.C. Solar Moon Return		20	55	09
	Mean Sun = *+**+12 hours		17	11	09

(E)	*PROGRESSED SOLAR MOON RETURN*				
	Date 31.12.79 Time 0.25 Required:	Mean Sun	18	35	22
	Solar Moon Return	minus – Mean Sun	17	11	09
	Difference		1	24	13
	R.A.M.C. Solar Moon Return	Add	20	55	09
	R.A.M.C. Progressed Solar Moon Return		22	19	22

Calculations for Chart B (Fig. 51)

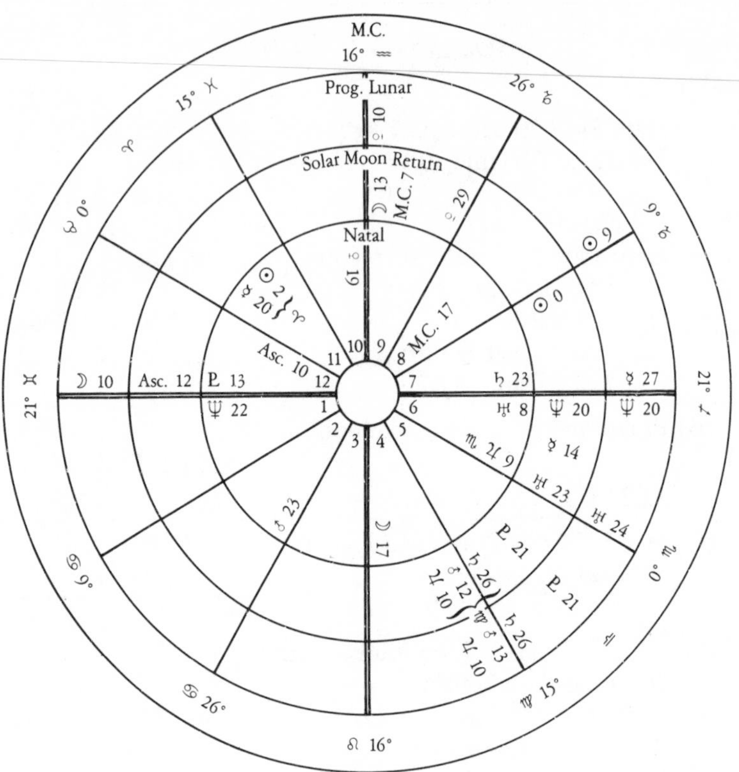

	Solar Return			Solar Moon Return			Prog. Lunar		
	D	M	Y	D	M	Y	D	M	Y
Date	23	3	79	22	12	79	31	12	79
	H	M	S	H	M	S	H	M	S
U.T.	16	18	00	14	37	00	0	25	00
R.A.M.C.	04	20	14	20	39	13	21	12	22
Mean Sun	00	02	14	18	02	13	18	35	22
Moon's Long.	1	28	♒	12	40	♒	10	♊	

Figure 52 Progressed Lunar Return Solar Moon. Chart C.

SOLAR MOON RETURN

			H. M. S.
(A)	Date 31.12.79 Time 0.25 Required:	Mean Sun	18 35 22
	Date 23.3.79 Time 16.18 Solar Return	Mean Sun	0 02 14
	Difference		18 33 08
	Correction for Mean Solar Time	minus	— 3 03
	Mean Solar Hours		18 30 05
	U.T. of Solar Return	Add	16 18 00
	Progressed Solar Return		10 48 05
	U.T. 10.48 Date 24.3.79		

		Sign	*Deg.*	*Mins*
(B)	Progressed Solar Return: Moon's Long.:			
	10.48 U.T.: 24.3.79 Date:	≈	12	40

		Date	*U.T.*
(C)	Moon Transits Progressed Long.:		
	= *Solar Moon Return*	22.12.79	14.37

			H. M. S.
(D)	S.T. at 0 hours U.T. on Transit date	*	5 59 49
	U.T. of Moon's Return	Add	14 37 00
	Correction 9.86 secs. per hour	Add **	— 2 24
	R.A.M.C. at Greenwich		20 39 13
	Long. Equiv.	+ E: – W:	— — —
	R.A.M.C. Solar Moon Return		20 39 13
	Mean Sun = *+**+12 hours		18 02 13

(E)	*PROGRESSED SOLAR MOON RETURN*		
	Date 31.12.79 Time 0.25 Required:	Mean Sun	18 35 22
	Solar Moon Return minus –	Mean Sun	18 02 13
	Difference		— 33 09
	R.A.M.C. Solar Moon Return	Add	20 39 13
	R.A.M.C. Progressed Solar Moon Return		21 12 22

Calculations for Chart C (Fig. 52)

6.
OTHER TECHNIQUES

Mid-points

A mid-point is that point which is exactly half-way between any two factors in a chart reckoned in zodiacal longitude, e.g. Mars 0° Aries — Moon 0° Cancer = 90° over 2 = 45° = 15° Taurus mid-point. The theory of mid-points is not new, and the history of their use can be traced back prior to the Middle Ages and even earlier. The resurgence of mid-points and their use is associated with the German schools of astrology: the 'Uranian' astrology of the Hamburg School as expounded by Alfred Witte, and the 'Cosmobiology' as developed by Reinhold Ebertin and his associates. Much work continues to be done on mid-points, and Dr Baldur Ebertin — the son of Reinhold Ebertin — is a notable researcher in this field. Mid-points and their application offer a rich, sophisticated method of interpretation and often highlight and clarify planetary patterns which, taken in isolation, do not always reveal their true significance.

A mid-point is by definition a point, in zodiacal longitude, that is half-way between any two points in a birth chart. This equidistant point represents a blending of two factors, either two planets, a planet and angle or some other half-way point between significant chart factors. For example, Sun 5° Scorpio, Uranus 5° Pisces gives a mid-point Sun/Uranus of 5° Capricorn. Or, Mercury 11° Scorpio, Pluto 10° Cancer gives a mid-point of Mercury/Pluto of 10½° Virgo. Normally, the sign position of the mid-point of the shorter arc is taken, but the opposite point is also a mid-point reckoned by the longer arc. In the two cases mentioned, the longer arc is 5° Cancer and 10½° Pisces. These degrees and areas now assume a Sun/Uranus or Mercury/Pluto influence, and the principles associated with the Sun and Uranus, or Mercury and Pluto will combine to produce the maximum effect. It has been suggested that a mid-point will be activated if another chart factor aspects it by conjunction or by any multiple of 45°, and that it is not activated by other aspects such as the sextile (60°), trine (120°) or quincunx (150°). It is the challenging aspects (those that are a multiple of 45°) such as the square, opposition etc., which activate mid-points and make them effective.

The Sun, Moon, planets, Moon's north node, Ascendant and Midheaven are the factors in the chart used for mid-point purposes. The number of mid-points in a chart can be derived from the formula: $(n-1)\frac{n}{2}$ where n = the number of factors used for mid-point purposes. Therefore n = 13, so $(13-1)\frac{13}{2} = 12 \times 6.5 = 78$ mid-points. With this many mid-points, the combinations are considerable, and using the formula $(n-2)(n-1)\frac{n}{2}$ where n is the number of factors used, we have n = 13, $(13-2)(13-1)\frac{13}{2} = 11 \times 12 \times 6.5 = 858$ mid-points.

The method of calculating mid-points is to find the half-sum of the two factors. This can be done either by listing all the chart factors in absolute longitude, i.e. their positions reckoned from 0° Aries, or by taking exactly half the absolute longitude. If working with half the absolute longitude, these are added to give the absolute longitude of the mid-point. For example, Sun 5° Scorpio = 215°: Uranus 5° Pisces = 335°: $\frac{215}{2}$ and $\frac{335}{2}$ = 107.5 and 167.5 which, added together, gives 275 absolute longitude = 5° Capricorn = mid-point of Sun/Uranus. Or we can say Uranus 335° less 215° = 120 divided by 2 = 60° + 215° = 275° as required. The easiest way is to work with absolute longitude using an electronic calculator. Devices such as the 90° Dial and 90° Circle are available, whereby it is possible to note all the mid-points of a particular chart factor.

As there are seventy-eight mid-points in a chart, the orb allowed needs to be small, particularly when considering progressions and directions, because the chances of any one of the thirteen chart factors arriving at a particular mid-point are very high. The transits to mid-points are extremely important as are all transits when properly related to various types of charts. Much of the work concerning mid-points is still experimental, but there is little doubt that the theory and application of mid-point techniques has great value.

Mid-point literature contains many unfamiliar terms, of which the following are a few examples:

Absolute longitude: Degrees, minutes and seconds of arc measured along the Ecliptic from 0° Aries.

Sign	*Degree*	*Absolute Longitude (Degree)*
Aries	0-29	0-29
Taurus	0-29	30-59
Gemini	0-29	60-89
Cancer	0-29	90-119
Leo	0-29	120-149
Virgo	0-29	150-179
Libra	0-29	180-209
Scorpio	0-29	210-239
Sagittarius	0-29	240-269
Capricorn	0-29	270-299
Aquarius	0-29	300-329
Pisces	0-29	330-359

Composite picture (planetary picture): The total way in which a factor is involved in a chart by mid-point and aspect, etc.
Cosi or Csi: Relates to the classic work of R. Ebertin, *The Combination of Stellar Influences,* concerning mid-points and their astrological interpretation.
Cosmobiology: An alternative description for scientific astrology.
Cosmogram: An alternative description for the birth chart or horoscope.
Dial: Device used for the examination of mid-points.
Factor: Refers to any of the thirteen commonly used elements in a chart.
Half-sum: Another term for mid-point.
Hard angle: Aspects which are derived from dividing the circle by 2 and 2 again, i.e. 2,4,8,16, etc.
Soft Angles: Multiples of 30°, 60° and 120°.

The terminology of mid-points is extensive, and a detailed study of the literature dealing with mid-points is essential for an understanding of their significance and application. (See Fig. 53.)

Harmonics

The use of harmonics as an astrological technique is basically concerned with aspects, which enable a greater insight to be obtained concerning the birth chart. The harmonic theory is not new; the principles underlying it have formed part of Hindu astrology for centuries. But although the principles are basic to astrology, it was

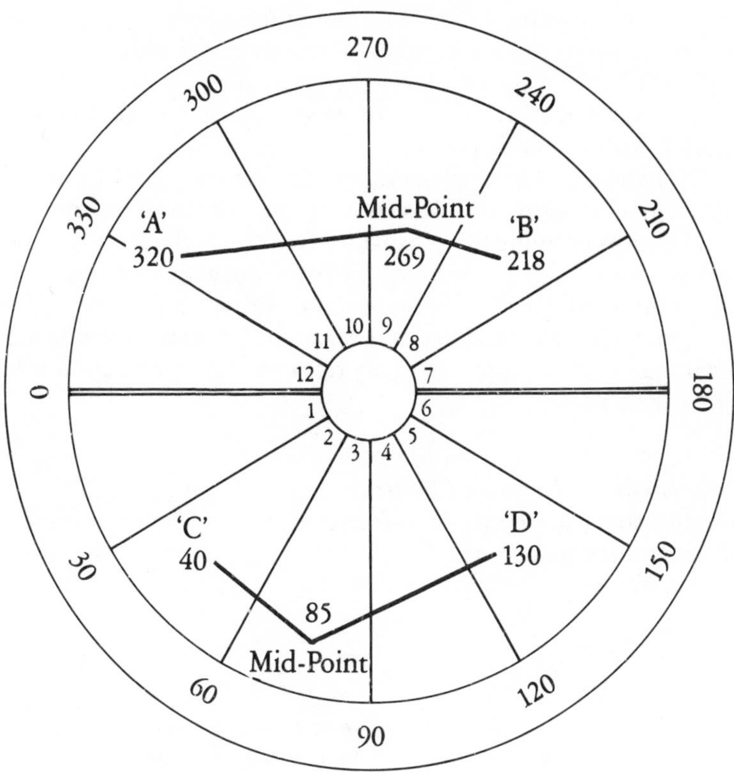

Figure 53 Mid-points.

A (320) 20° Aquarius
B (218) 8° Scorpio
538 over 2 = 269 = 29° Sagittarius = Mid-point
D (130) 10° Leo
C (40) 10° Taurus
170 over 2 = 85 = 25° Gemini = Mid-point

not until John Addey published the results of his twenty years research that harmonic analysis proved its value.

The essence of harmonics in astrology is that, when the 360° circle of the zodiac is divided by a specific number, it will reveal sub-rhythms, the nature of which, depending on the type of harmonic, will give added meaning to the natal chart. The calculation of any harmonic chart is simple; all natal positions are multiplied by the number of the harmonic and, if the result exceeds 360°, reduced to less than 360°. A harmonic chart is then erected with these new positions. Obviously, the higher the harmonic number used, the greater the need for accuracy by using several decimal places when dealing with the natal positions.

The harmonic chart does not supersede the natal chart. Although the number of harmonic charts that can be calculated for any one natal chart is unlimited, it is usually recommended that only a few are dealt with. Of these, the fourth, fifth, seventh and ninth harmonic charts are considered to be significant. Various arguments exist concerning the basic meanings of numbers but, with an experimental technique such as harmonics, only research and investigation will prove their worth.

Calculation of Harmonic Charts

The first step with these calculations is to reduce all natal positions or longitudes to absolute longitude; i.e. 360° circle: *Absolute Longitude (A/L)*

0°		°	*0°*		°
Aries	=	*0*	*Libra*	=	*180*
Taurus	=	*30*	*Scorpio*	=	*210*
Gemini	=	*60*	*Sagittarius*	=	*240*
Cancer	=	*90*	*Capricorn*	=	*270*
Leo	=	*120*	*Aquarius*	=	*300*
Virgo	=	*150*	*Pisces*	=	*330*

Thus 5° Scorpio = 210° + 5° = 215°. The quickest and easiest method is to use a calculator.

The procedure for calculation using easy steps is:

1. Convert the planet's natal longitude into absolute longitude.
2. Multiply the absolute longitude by the harmonic number.
3. Reduce the resulting figure, if greater than 360, to a figure which is less than 360.
4. Convert back into zodiacal longitude.

Example No. 1

Find the seventh harmonic position of a planet at 5°51′ Pisces:

1. 5°51′ Pisces = 335°51′ (A/L)
2. A/L 335°51′×7 = 2350.95
3. Reduce 2350.95 = $\frac{2350.95}{360}$ = 6.5304
   Deduct 6 (6 complete circles) = 0.5304
   0.5304×360 = 190.94 (190°57′)
4. 190°57′ = 10°57′ Libra = 7th harmonic position as required.

Example No. 2
Find the fifth harmonic position of a planet at 25°52′ Gemini:

1. 25°52′ = 85°52′ (A/L)
2. A/L 85°52′×5 = 429.33
3. Reduce 429.33 = $\frac{429.33}{360}$ = 1.19259
   Deduct circle = 0.19259
   0.19259×360 = 69.33 (69°20′)
4. 69°20′ = 9°20′ Gemini = 5th harmonic position as required.

If the calculations have to be done the 'hard' way by hand, then example No. 1 would be as follows:

5°51′ Pisces = 330.00+5.51	=	335°	51′	(A/L)
335°×7	=	2345.	00	
51′×7	=	5.	57	
		2350.	57	
2350°57′ divided by 360	=	2160.	00	less
(6×360 = 2160)		190.	57	
Convert to zodiacal longitude	=	10.	57	Libra.

= 7th harmonic position as required.

The harmonic theory is based on the astrological aspects, and the harmonic number is the number by which the 360° circle is divided. This division determines the length of the wave; the higher the number of the harmonic, the shorter and more numerous the waves become. For example, the fourth harmonic of a circle has four waves each 90° in length; the fifth 72°; the third 120°, and so on, depending on the harmonic number employed. Each wave is treated as being 360° in extent or one complete circle. The amount by which a wave rises and falls above or below the mean is the amplitude, and where the peak of the wave comes along its length, is expressed as the phase angle. Not only is the harmonic chart a useful adjunct to the birth chart, but its implications can be studied in relation to progressions, transits and the like. Research concerning this theory has concentrated chiefly on a few divisions of the circle, notably the fourth, fifth, seventh and ninth. Essentially what is being dealt with in harmonics is the nature of numbers in astrology, but the harmonic techniques are in no sense associated with numerology.

Aspects and Interpretation

The calculation of the aspects in a harmonic chart is by the same procedure as for a natal chart. However, it has been suggested that the orbs allowed should have relation to the type of harmonic. For example, an orb of 12° for the conjunction; for the opposition an orb of 6° ($^{12}/_{2}$) — 2nd harmonic; for the trine, the 3rd harmonic, an orb of 4° ($^{12}/_{3}$). The other aspects such as the square (90°), and the sextile (60°) would have an orb of 3° ($^{12}/_{4}$) and 2° ($^{12}/_{6}$).

The interpretation of harmonic charts is again similar to that employed with natal charts. If there is any uncertainty regarding the birth time, the Ascendant and Midheaven positions will need to be treated with caution, as considerable distortion can occur. If the traditional interpretation of aspects has value, then the appropriate harmonic chart should reflect the qualities normally associated with a particular aspect. The square aspect (90°), the opposition aspect (180°) and the semi-square aspect (45°) are indicative of challenges, tension and conflict. This being so, the harmonics associated with these divisions (2, 4, 8) may show that effort is needed to overcome difficulties. Likewise, the so-called 'good aspects' of 120° (trine) and the 60° (sextile) and their association with the third and sixth harmonics should have some relation with ease and the achievement of objectives.

The application and use of harmonic analysis is considerable, provided it is approached in a realistic manner. At no time should it be considered as a substitute or alternative for the natal chart; it is merely an additional technique which, if used correctly, will reveal the finer points of a birth chart which may not always be apparent. Much research needs to be done on harmonics, but it is possible that the system can be extended to include its use with mundane techniques, synastry and comparison astrology.

The Pre-natal Epoch

The association of the Moon with sex and birth has its origins deep in the past. But it was not until the early years of this century that two notable astrologers, Sepharial and E.H. Bailey, formalized this association astrologically by presenting details concerning the theory, laws and practical application of the pre-natal epoch.

The original theory and laws of this technique are attributed to the philosopher Hermes Trismegistus and are commonly referred to as the 'Trutine of Hermes', which states that the place of the Moon at conception is the Ascendant at birth or its opposite point. The investigations by Bailey and others appeared to confirm that there is some form of interchange between the Moon and the horizon, and that the traditional teaching was correct so far as it went. However, the original statement was only part of a series of laws, in that, while the Ascendant or Descendant was the place of the Moon at a certain epoch, the Ascendant or its opposite point at the epoch was the place of the Moon at birth.

The question of the epoch's validity and the arguments surrounding it will be discussed later, after we have considered the theory and its application in broad terms. The interchange of the Moon with the Ascendant/Descendant can be summarized initially by four defined laws:

1. *Moon increasing in light:*
   When the Moon at birth is increasing in light (i.e. going from New to Full Moon), its longitude will be the ascending degree at the epoch, and the Moon's position at the epoch will be the degree of the Ascendant at birth.
2. *Moon decreasing in light:*
   When the Moon at birth is decreasing in light (i.e. going from Full to New Moon), its longitude will be the descending degree at the epoch, and the Moon's position at the epoch will be the degree of the Descendant at birth.
3. (a) *Moon at birth increasing in light and below the Earth;*
   (b) *Moon at birth decreasing in light and above the Earth.*
   When the Moon at birth is increasing in light and below the Earth, or decreasing in light and above the Earth, the period of gestation will be longer than the norm (273 days).
4. (a) *Moon at birth increasing in light and above the Earth;*
   (b) *Moon at birth decreasing in light and below the Earth.*
   When the Moon at birth is increasing in light and above the Earth, or decreasing in light and below the Earth, the period of gestation will be less than the norm.

Summarizing these laws we have:

1.(a) When the Moon at birth is increasing and above the earth, or decreasing and below the Earth, the period of gestation is less than ten lunar revolutions (273 days) by one day for approximately every 13° of the Moon's distance from the horizon to which it next comes after birth.

(b) When the Moon at birth is increasing and below the Earth, or decreasing and above the Earth, the period of gestation is more than ten lunar revolutions, counted backwards from the day of birth.

2.(a) When the Moon at birth is increasing, its place will be the Ascendant at the epoch, and the Moon's place at the epoch will be the Ascendant at birth.

(b) When the Moon at birth is decreasing, its place will be the Descendant at the epoch, and the Moon's place at the epoch will be the Descendant at birth.

The laws of the epoch as defined govern what have been termed 'regular epochs', but there are variations to these laws resulting in 'irregular epochs'. An irregular epoch is one wherein the Moon, although increasing at birth, is found at the epoch in the descending sign, or wherein the Moon, decreasing at birth, is found at the epoch in the ascending sign. Also, the Moon's place at birth rises at the epoch, or sets, contrary to the general laws of the pre-natal epoch. Despite the variations which can occur, there appears to be a correlation existing between the epoch and birth factors which determines the time of birth, and this relationship also governs the period of gestation.

In the case of regular epochs, the period of gestation can be summarized as follows:

	Period of Gestation in days
1. Moon above and increasing —	273 less *x*
2. Moon above and decreasing —	273 plus *x*
3. Moon below and increasing —	273 plus *x*
4. Moon below and decreasing —	273 less *x*

The norm is the period of nine calendar months or ten lunar months (273 days) counted backwards from the date of birth, and it measures to within two or three days of the same day of the month as the day of birth. The Moon on that day is in the same sign and at about the same degree as it held at birth. The date, which is exactly ten revolutions of the Moon prior to the date of birth, is the *Index Date*, and all subsequent calculations commence from that particular date.

The normal period of gestation is increased or decreased in accordance with the Moon's position relative to the Ascendant or Descendant, and *x* is the number of days equal to the distance in degrees and minutes divided by 13° — the average daily motion of the Moon. If, for example, the Moon's distance is 60°, the number of days would be approximately 4½. The early researchers into the epoch suggested that, astrologically, the epoch is a moment in time, not necessarily coincident in time with the physical processes of generation, but occurring approximately at the commencement of gestation and the time of coitus.

The general law of the epoch (Moon/Horizon interchange) allows a variation of fourteen days on either side of the normal period of 273 days. Other variations do exist, whereby the period is increased or decreased by a further 14 days, giving a total variation of 28 days greater or lesser than the normal 273 days of gestation.

The value of the epoch, apart from demonstrating the cosmic influence which affects all life, is that it permits the approximate time of birth to be confirmed, and possibly has some relationship concerning the development of the embryo, abnormalities during pregnancy and other associated factors.

The early investigators of the pre-natal epoch theory stated that every epoch must conform to certain specified conditions:

1. It must confirm the time of birth to within reasonable limits.
2. It must define the sex of the subject according to the well-defined laws of sex.
3. The chart for the epoch must show general character and fortunes of the subject.
4. The chart must be capable of being directed/progressed, and these should accord with the events/conditions of life.

If any epoch does not meet these requirements, then it should be regarded as fictitious.

In so far as the sex of the subject is concerned, this is related to the *Law of Sex* based primarily on the Hindu sub-division of the zodiac into 28 mansions, each $12\frac{6}{7}$ degrees in extent. The four cardinal points are the starting points for the determination of sex and these, with their respective sex distinctions, are: Aries 0°, female; Cancer 0°, female; Libra 0°, male; Capricorn 0°, male. A further extension of this division is made by dividing the circle of the zodiac into seven equal parts $51\frac{3}{7}$ degrees, commencing at each point of the quandrant, making 28 divisions. Each point of the zodiac cut by these divisions is alternately male and female, commencing with the sex of the cardinal point from which the division is made. For example, starting from 0° Aries (female), the points of the zodiac arrived at and the sex are: Taurus 21°26′ (male); Cancer 12°51′ (female); Virgo 4°17′ (male); Libra 25°43′ (female); Sagittarius 17°09′ (male); and Aquarius 8°34′ (female). Commencing from Libra 0° (male), the points of the zodiac are the same degrees and minutes of the opposite signs as those starting with Aries with the *sex reversed*. The following table shows the complete division and illustrates that there are four sets of sex degrees, alternately male and female, which have their starting point in the four cardinal points. The difference between each point is $12\frac{6}{7}$ (12°51′) which

Degrees	*Min*	*Sign*	*Sex*	*Sign*	*Sex*
0	00	Aries	Female	Libra	Male
12	51	Aries	Male	Libra	Female
25	43	Aries	Male	Libra	Female
8	34	Taurus	Female	Scorpio	Male
21	26	Taurus	Male	Scorpio	Female
4	17	Gemini	Female	Sagittarius	Male
17	09	Gemini	Female	Sagittarius	Male
0	00	Cancer	Female	Capricorn	Male
12	51	Cancer	Female	Capricorn	Male
25	43	Cancer	Male	Capricorn	Female
8	34	Leo	Male	Aquarius	Female
21	26	Leo	Male	Aquarius	Female
4	17	Virgo	Male	Pisces	Female
17	09	Virgo	Female	Pisces	Male

approximately agrees with the average daily motion of the Moon, and which form the 28 lunar mansions.

These degrees are termed the sex or 'critical' degrees, and the position of the Moon and Ascendant in relation to these degrees is important. It is unusual for either the Moon or Ascendant to occupy the exact degree and minute of these critical degrees, but if they are placed within a certain distance of the exact point, they are considered within orb of the particular sex degrees. The orb allowed for the Moon is $6\frac{3}{7}°$, or one-half of each mansion, and for the Ascendant the orb is $4\frac{2}{7}$, or one-third of each mansion.

Quadrants

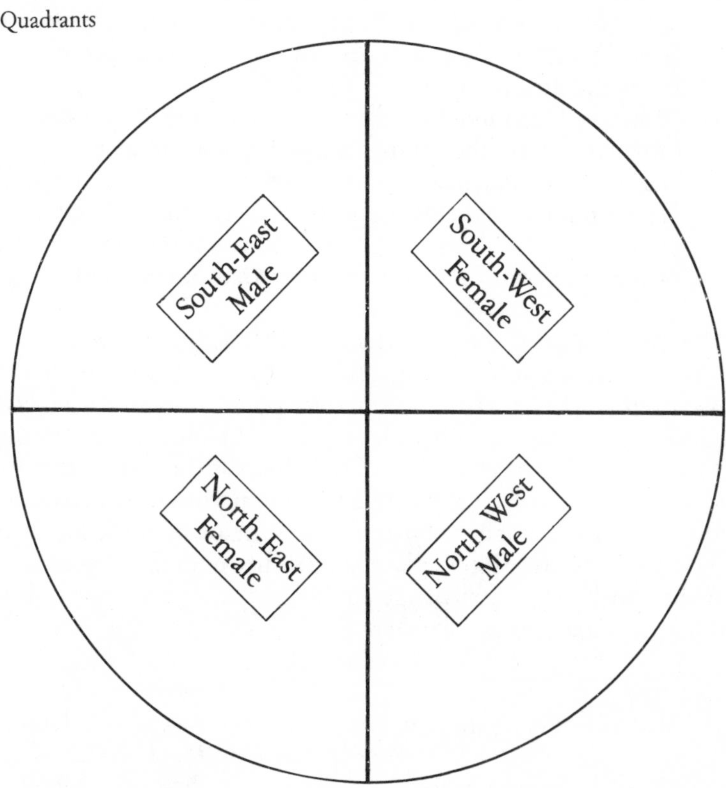

Figure 54 Epoch Figure.

The position of the Moon will be either one sex or another. The Ascendant, when within $4\frac{2}{7}$ of an exact sex point, can be either sex, but when outside that limit, it is negative. The Moon will determine a space equal to $12\frac{6}{7}$°, in equal parts of $6\frac{3}{7}$° on each side of an exact point. The Ascendant will determine only $8\frac{4}{7}$° or equal parts of $4\frac{2}{7}$° on each side of the exact degree. It is the position of the Moon and Ascendant relative to the sex degrees in the epoch figure which determines the sex, and not those positions in the birth chart. In determining the sex of the child from the epoch chart, the following rules apply:

1. When the Ascendant is negative, the sex of the area occupied by the Moon will be the sex of the child.
2. When both the Moon and Ascendant are within their respective orbs of a degree of the same sex, the sex of the child is the same sex as the area occupied.
3. When the Moon and Ascendant are placed within their respective orbs of degrees of the opposite sex — the Moon in a female area, and the Ascendant in a male, or vice-versa — the sex of the child is determined by the quadrant held by the Moon (see Figure 54 on page 279). This will give two points of one sex, and one of the other; the predominant sex is that of the child.

The interchange of the Ascendant at birth with the Moon at the epoch, or its opposite point, and the Moon at birth with the Ascendant at the epoch or its opposite point, is termed a *regular epoch.* In a regular epoch with an increasing Moon at birth, the Ascendant at birth is the place of the Moon at the epoch, and the Moon's place at birth is the Ascendant at the epoch. With a decreasing Moon, the Descendant at birth becomes the place of the Moon at the epoch and the Moon's place at birth becomes the Descendant at the epoch. This interchange applies to the regular epochs, but there are variations as follows:

Variation	*Birth*		*Epoch*
1. Moon increasing in light	Asc.	=	Moon
	Moon	=	Desc.
Moon decreasing in light	Desc.	=	Moon
	Moon	=	Asc.
2. Moon increasing in light	Desc.	=	Moon
	Moon	=	Asc.
Moon decreasing in light	Asc.	=	Moon
	Moon	=	Desc.

3. Moon increasing in light	Desc.	=	Moon
	Moon	=	Desc.
Moon decreasing in light	Asc.	=	Moon
	Moon	=	Asc.

All epochs are subject to well-defined laws, and if calculations for a regular epoch do not yield an epoch in agreement with the birth time or closely thereto, then the procedure for irregular epochs should be considered. A correct epoch will have:

1. The Moon in or near a 'critical' degree.
2. The Ascendant in or near a 'critical' degree.
3. Both the Moon and Ascendant will be in or near 'critical' degrees.
4. Neither the Moon nor the Ascendant will be in such degrees.
5. The Moon will be in a male or female quadrant.

The pre-natal epoch laws are closely related to the Law of Sex, and a correct epoch should observe the following rules:

1. The epoch Ascendant denotes the sex of the child (i.e. the Ascendant in a male degree or vice-versa).
2. The Moon in a critical degree and the Ascendant not in a critical degree, then the Moon's position denotes the sex in accordance with its longitude either male or female.
3. When both the Moon and Ascendant are in critical degrees of the same sex, then the birth will be of that sex.
4. If neither the Moon nor the Ascendant is in a critical degree, the quadrant occupied by the Moon will determine the sex.
5. If the Moon and Ascendant are in critical degrees of opposite sexes, the quadrant occupied by the Moon will determine the sex.

Calculation of the Epoch

1. Calculate the longitude of the Ascendant and Moon for the given time of birth.
2. Note whether the Moon is above or below the horizon, and whether it is increasing or decreasing. This will show whether the norm (273 days) is increased or decreased.
3. Calculate the *Index Date* by counting backwards from the birthdate ten lunar months = nine calendar months. This date will be the same date as that of the birth, or within three days,

in the ninth month preceding that of the birth. The easiest method is to add three months to the date of birth and to refer to the corresponding date in the year preceding. On this date or within three days of it, the Moon will be in the same longitude as at birth. This is the *Index Date.*

4. Having found the Moon's place on the Index Date, count forward or backward as required and note the day when the Moon is in the sign rising or descending at birth, according to the laws. The day that the Moon transits the exact degree on the horizon at birth is the *Day of Epoch.*
5. To find the time of day when the epoch occurred, the place of residence of the mother has to be known, particularly in these days of high-speed travel when conception and birth can occur in widely separated places.
6. From Tables of Houses for the latitude of the place on the day of epoch, bring the Moon's longitude at birth to the Ascendant or Descendant as required, and note the sidereal time. This will be the sidereal time at the epoch. From the sidereal time at noon on the day of epoch, note the difference between this sidereal time and the sidereal time at the epoch. This gives the time before or after noon at which the epoch occurred.
7. Find the Moon's longitude for this time on the day of epoch, and this will give the Ascendant or Descendant at birth according to the general laws of the epoch.

Although the foregoing is a broad outline of the pre-natal epoch as formulated and propounded by Bailey and others, its rules and laws have not been universally accepted by many modern researchers. Various objections, either technical or medical, have been raised from time to time. Research using well-attested data has not always confirmed its validity, but this, of course, in no way proves that the theory is totally wrong, because many of the arguments and investigations were unsound and lacked the clarity and scientific approach necessary in investigations of this kind.

An amateurish attempt concerning rectification using the pre-natal epoch was conducted in the early 1950s (*Astrology*, Vol. 27, No. 2), but the experiment was a failure, principally because all the necessary factors such as dates and places of conception, the dates of the menstrual period and the places where the parents were residing at those times, were not considered. This experiment was roundly condemned for the unscientific manner in which it had been conducted (*Astrology,* Vol. 27, No. 3, 1953, Letter to the Editor). George Bailey of Bath, one of the foremost 'technical' astrologers of his generation, severely criticized the experiment, and showed in two articles printed in *Astrology*, how investigations into pre-natal epochs should be approached (*Astrology,* Vol. 28, No. 4; Vol. 29, No. 1, 1954/55).

The theory of the epoch is extremely intriguing, and although the calculations associated with it can be tedious, the use of computers should reduce the labour and enable investigations to be made, provided that all the essential factors concerning dates, times and places are known.

Rectification

Any error in the recorded time of birth will cause the angles of the chart to be incorrect, with the result that progressions and directions involving the Midheaven or Ascendant will be 'off-mark', that is, they will not operate at the expected time. The discrepancy in timing is related to the amount of the error in the recorded time; four minutes difference in time will throw out the Midheaven by one degree, which is equivalent to one year of life.

Several methods of rectification are available using techniques such as the pre-natal epoch, events of life or various returns of one kind or another. By combining several techniques, the actual birth time may be estimated and subsequently confirmed by future progressions or directions actingly closely in time.

The important events of life and those which have a decisive effect on the individual normally coincide with progressions which involve the angles. This is true, not only with secondary progressions, but also with returns and other systems used in assessing future trends.

The rectification of a chart, using the events of life, is probably the easiest method and often produces results with which further investigations can be made. The pre-natal epoch, with its complexities and variations of laws, is not always a suitable method, although it may prove useful in confirming a time found by other means. The 'guessing game' of deciding the Rising sign from an individual's appearance or mannerisms has little to commend it. It is true that certain signs may display the characteristics associated with them, and this may be helpful in deciding the Rising sign, but it is not an infallible guide.

Planets close to the angles often 'act' prominently, affecting either the appearance or the personality or both. In any case, even knowing the sign rising is not enough, as some signs rise more slowly than others. However, when the birth time is known within reasonable limits, an estimated time can be taken and used as a base for calculations.

The major events of life will always be reflected by appropriate angular contacts, and the individual's response to them will be governed in some measure on how they affect him personally. In attempting to rectify by events, a table or schedule listing all the main events of the life has to be prepared. This table will contain the year, month and day of the event and, if possible, also the time of the event. Using this data, a 'backward' survey can be made to see whether a given event coincided both in *time* and *nature* with any planetary progressions, particularly those aspecting the angles. One event taken singly, even if it does correlate with an appropriate contact, is seldom sufficient to confirm an uncertain time. However, when several events taken over a period of time, say many years, coincide with the various systems of forecasting, the indications are that the rectification is fairly correct. With the 'rectified' chart, the subsequent progressions and directions can be noted to see whether, in fact, they confirm the rectified time.

Prior to detailed work on rectification, a chart calculated for an estimated time can be studied to see whether there are planets close to the angles. For example, if a planet is twenty degrees from the Midheaven, we should expect that at about twenty years of age, using the one-degree method of progression, an event or condition of the nature of the planet will occur. This is a preliminary starting point, but it is often useful in narrowing the limits of an uncertain birth time.

All rectification work is time-consuming in that, whichever method is used, the initial findings need to be related to more than one system of forecasting. As the operation of directions and progressions are often accelerated or retarded by other phenomena such as transits or eclipses, it is essential that the rectified time is confirmed by other sources or systems. The rectified time of birth should produce a natal chart applicable to the person and his life and should indicate a close harmony concerning his progressions and events/conditions. Return charts — such as the solar and lunar returns — should also confirm the rectified time, particularly the solar return, where any uncertainty in time will result in a fictitious return chart.

The Tropical and Sidereal Zodiacs

When considering the relative merits of one system as compared with another, it is essential to understand what each represents. The term 'zodiacs' is misleading and confusing, for there is only one circle of the zodiac, and whether we call it 'Tropical' or 'Sidereal', will depend solely on the point from which it is measured.

The *tropical cycle* is the cycle of the seasons, corresponding to the Sun's yearly return each March to the Vernal Equinox — the intersection of the Celestial Equator with the Ecliptic — which we call the First Point of Aries; and the solar monthly progress is measured through the signs along the Ecliptic in degrees of longitude. The *sidereal cycle* is that of the retrogression of the Vernal Point through the twelve zodiacal constellations (at present from Pisces to Aquarius) during an era of some 25,800 years. It is measured from a fixed reference point on the same ecliptic circle which locates the fixed star Spica (Alpha Virginis) permanently in 29 degrees of Virgo.

Critics of astrology argue that it is a pseudo-science, because its advocates (or at least those who use the tropical zodiac) fail to take into account the phenomenon of precession. The argument is that 'astrology is not based on fact because the Vernal Equinox no longer corresponds with the constellation Aries, but has moved in relation to the stars.'

Consequently, the division of the zodiac no longer coincides with the constellations, and although the Sun 'enters' Aries at the Vernal Equinox, it is in fact in the constellation Pisces. Whether this criticism has validity or not, depends on which cycle is considered the more important. If the yearly solar cycle, which is seasonal, is considered to have greater significance, then the *tropical* or *moving* zodiac is more important. Likewise, the *sidereal* (starry) or *fixed* zodiac merits consideration, if the precession of the Equinoctial Points is regarded as being significant.

The Vernal Point is important astronomically as well as astrologically, for it is from this that astronomers check movements and determine positions on the celestial sphere. They measure in right ascension along the Celestial Equator eastward from the Vernal Equinox to the Hour Circle of a heavenly body (a great circle passing through the celestial poles and the heavenly body). Right ascension corresponds to terrestrial longitude; and declination, which is measured north or south of the Celestial Equator, corresponds to terrestrial latitude. The basis of this system is that the planes of the Earth's Equator and the parallels of latitude are projected onto the celestial sphere to form the Celestial Equator and the parallels of declination. Likewise, the Earth's meridians of longitude are projected to form the celestial meridians. As the Greenwich meridian is the zero point for measuring distances along the Earth's Equator, so the Vernal Point or First Point of Aries is the zero point for measuring distances along the Celestial Equator.

In contrast to the tropical zodiac, the sidereal or fixed zodiac of the constellations is non-moving and non-precessional, being permanently aligned to the fixed stars. According to modern researchers, notably Cyril Fagan and Donald Bradley (Garth Allen), the 'zodiac of antiquity' was the zodiac of the constellations, and was used particularly by the Babylonian astronomers-astrologers. As a result of the extensive researches into the history of astronomy, and into the archaeology of the Tigris and Euphrates valley civilizations, it was concluded that this was the zodiac used. Furthermore, these researches tended to confirm that the Babylonians and the Egyptians measured their longitudes from 'markers' in the heavens. These fiducials were the Pleiades in 5° Taurus, Aldebaran in 15° Taurus, Regulus in 5 ° Leo, Spica in 29° Virgo, and Antares in 15° Scorpio. As 'watchers of the heavens', the Babylonians were observational astronomers, and in the course of time, were able to adapt and refine their knowledge of celestial motions and phenomena. The Babylonian astronomical knowledge and the associated traditions formed the basis upon which early Greek astronomy was founded. Hipparchus, who established astronomy on a sound geometrical basis, confirmed from his observations that the position of the Equinox was the initial point for measurements both in right ascension and longitude.

The year 221 AD was, according to Fagan, the 'zero' year when 'both zodiacs' coincided, i.e. the Vernal Point had retrogressed to the exact conjunction with its sidereal counterpart. However, owing to the continual shift of the Vernal Point in relation to the fixed stars, the difference between 0° Aries tropical and 0° Aries sidereal is now approximately 24°. This difference, termed the *ayanamsa* by the sidereal advocates, has to be subtracted from all tropical longitudes in order to convert to sidereal longitudes. In subtracting this difference, the precession which has accrued since 221 AD is expunged from the tropical longitudes. The 'ayanamsa' for a given date is found by subtracting the sidereal longitude of the Vernal Point for the same date from 360°. Tables to facilitate the conversion from the tropical longitudes are given in publications dealing with sidereal astrology.

Many of the techniques utilized in sidereal astrology may, at first sight, appear rather involved and complicated. Basically, the computations needed to set up the various charts are not difficult, but the sidereal system has a wide terminology, and the multiplicity of charts which can be used may, initially, appear confusing. Not only are the solar and lunar returns employed, which will differ considerably from the tropical counterpart owing to precession being eliminated, but also various systems of progressions are used in conjunction with the different types of returns. The sidereal ingress charts, both solar and lunar, form a main basis for mundane prediction, and these charts are calculated in the same manner as the usual returns. The sidereal ingress chart for the Sun's entry in Capricorn is considered to be of the utmost importance, and is regarded as the 'master chart of the year'. Certainly the evidence produced concerning this chart in relation to disasters and natural catastrophes, i.e. earthquakes, etc., substantiates the claim for this particular chart, especially when it is progressed for the date and time of an event at a definite locality. The Tropical Capricorn ingress is also highly significant, and warrants more attention than is normally assigned to it. In addition to the solar/lunar/ingress returns, sidereal astrologers also refer to the solar and lunar quotidian charts which are dependent on the increase of Right Ascension of the Mean Sun. This *R.A.M.S.* is the sidereal time at noon, as tabulated in a Greenwich-based ephemeris such as *Raphael's.*

The increase of the R.A.M.S. between the date of the return and the date and time of an event is added to the sidereal time of the return, and the sum is the sidereal time of the quotidian chart. Other techniques such as converse returns are used, but probably one of the most effective returns is the 'Kinetic Lunar Return' introduced by Cyril Fagan in the 1960s (see page 259).

The sidereal approach regarding interpretation of charts differs from the traditional tropical view, particularly in relation to natal charts. The effect of an aspect is considered according to the intrinsic nature of the planets involved, and not on the aspect. Venus-Jupiter for example, irrespective of the aspect, is considered beneficial, whilst Mars-Saturn, regardless of the aspect formed, would be judged unfortunate. Planets in the remote background, i.e., in the cadent houses, or in the middle of the succedent houses are enfeebled; but planets in close proximity to the angles (foreground) are strong, and the closer a planet is to the angles, the greater is its importance. A planet in exact aspect to the Midheaven or Ascendant is strong, and planets which are in exact aspect acquire prominence wherever they are situated.

Many of the methods associated with the sidereal techniques are, of course, applicable to the tropical system, and are not necessarily unique to the sidereal system. Nevertheless, the sidereal approach deserves impartial investigation and research.

APPENDIX 1
CALCULATION TABLES

Table 1: Conversion of Mean Solar into Mean Sidereal Time (9.86 seconds per hour)

Mean Time Hours	*Amount* ′	″	*Mean Time* ′	*Amount* ″	*Mean Time* ′	*Amount* ″
1	0	9.86	1	0.16	31	5.09
2	0	19.71	2	0.33	32	5.26
3	0	29.57	3	0.49	33	5.42
4	0	39.43	4	0.66	34	5.59
5	0	49.28	5	0.82	35	5.75
6	0	59.14	6	0.99	36	5.92
7	1	09.00	7	1.15	37	6.08
8	1	18.85	8	1.31	38	6.24
9	1	28.71	9	1.48	39	6.41
10	1	38.56	10	1.64	40	6.57
11	1	48.42	11	1.81	41	6.74
12	1	58.28	12	1.97	42	6.90
13	2	08.13	13	2.14	43	7.07
14	2	17.99	14	2.30	44	7.23
15	2	27.85	15	2.46	45	7.39
16	2	37.70	16	2.63	46	7.56
17	2	47.56	17	2.79	47	7.72
18	2	57.42	18	2.96	48	7.89
19	3	07.27	19	3.12	49	8.05
20	3	17.13	20	3.29	50	8.22
21	3	26.99	21	3.45	51	8.38
22	3	36.84	22	3.61	52	8.54
23	3	46.70	23	3.78	53	8.71
24	3	56.56	24	3.94	54	8.87
			25	4.11	55	9.04
			26	4.27	56	9.20
			27	4.44	57	9.37
			28	4.60	58	9.53
			29	4.76	59	9.69
			30	4.93		

Table 2: Minutes as a decimal of a Degree or Hour; Seconds as a decimal of a Minute

′ ″	Decimal	′ ″	Decimal
1	0.0166	31	0.5166
2	.0333	32	.5333
3	.0500	33	.5500
4	.0666	34	.5666
5	.0833	35	.5833
6	.1000	36	.6000
7	.1166	37	.6166
8	.1333	38	.6333
9	.1500	39	.6500
10	.1666	40	.6666
11	.1833	41	.6833
12	.2000	42	.7000
13	.2166	43	.7166
14	.2333	44	.7333
15	.2500	45	.7500
16	.2666	46	.7666
17	.2833	47	.7833
18	.3000	48	.8000
19	.3166	49	.8166
20	.3333	50	.8333
21	.3500	51	.8500
22	.3666	52	.8666
23	.3833	53	.8833
24	.4000	54	.9000
25	.4166	55	.9166
26	.4333	56	.9333
27	.4500	57	.9500
28	.4666	58	.9666
29	.4833	59	.9833
30	.5000		

Table 3: Longitude Equivalent in Time

Long °	*Equiv.* *Hours*	*Mins*
1	0	04
2	0	08
3	0	12
4	0	16
5	0	20
6	0	24
7	0	28
8	0	32
9	0	36
10	0	40
11	0	44
12	0	48
13	0	52
14	0	56
15	1	00
16	1	04
17	1	08
18	1	12
19	1	16
20	1	20
21	1	24
22	1	28
23	1	32
24	1	36
25	1	40
26	1	44
27	1	48
28	1	52
29	1	56
30	2	00
31	2	04
32	2	08
33	2	12
34	2	16
35	2	20
36	2	24
37	2	28
38	2	32

Long °	*Equiv.* *Hours*	*Mins*
39	2	36
40	2	40
41	2	44
42	2	48
43	2	52
44	2	56
45	3	00
46	3	04
47	3	08
48	3	12
49	3	16
50	3	20
51	3	24
52	3	28
53	3	32
54	3	36
55	3	40
56	3	44
57	3	48
58	3	52
59	3	56
60	4	00
61	4	04
62	4	08
63	4	12
64	4	16
65	4	20
66	4	24
67	4	28
68	4	32
69	4	36
70	4	40
71	4	44
72	4	48
73	4	52
74	4	56
75	5	00
76	5	04

Long °	*Equiv.* *Hours*	*Mins*
77	5	08
78	5	12
79	5	16
80	5	20
81	5	24
82	5	28
83	5	32
84	5	36
85	5	40
86	5	44
87	5	48
88	5	52
89	5	56
90	6	00
91	6	04
92	6	08
93	6	12
94	6	16
95	6	20
96	6	24
97	6	28
98	6	32
99	6	36
100	6	40
101	6	44
102	6	48
103	6	52
104	6	56
105	7	00
106	7	04
107	7	08
108	7	12
109	7	16
110	7	20
111	7	24
112	7	28
113	7	32
114	7	36

Long °	*Equiv.* *Hours*	*Mins*
115	7	40
116	7	44
117	7	48
118	7	52
119	7	56
120	8	00
121	8	04
122	8	08
123	8	12
124	8	16
125	8	20
126	8	24
127	8	28
128	8	32
129	8	36
130	8	40
131	8	44
132	8	48
133	8	52
134	8	56
135	9	00
136	9	04
137	9	08
138	9	12
139	9	16
140	9	20
141	9	24
142	9	28
143	9	32
144	9	36
145	9	40
146	9	44
147	9	48
148	9	52
149	9	56
150	10	00

Long °	*Equiv.* *Hours*	*Mins*
151	10	04
152	10	08
153	10	12
154	10	16
155	10	20
156	10	24
157	10	28
158	10	32
159	10	36
160	10	40
161	10	44
162	10	48
163	10	52
164	10	56
165	11	00

Long °	*Equiv.* *Hours*	*Mins*
166	11	04
167	11	08
168	11	12
169	11	16
170	11	20
171	11	24
172	11	28
173	11	32
174	11	36
175	11	40
176	11	44
177	11	48
178	11	52
179	11	56
180	12	00

Long ′	*Equiv.* ′	″
1	0	04
2	0	08
3	0	12
4	0	16
5	0	20
6	0	24
7	0	28
8	0	32
9	0	36
10	0	40
11	0	44
12	0	48
13	0	52
14	0	56
15	1	00

Long ′	*Equiv.* ′	″
16	1	04
17	1	08
18	1	12
19	1	16
20	1	20
21	1	24
22	1	28
23	1	32
24	1	36
25	1	40
26	1	44
27	1	48
28	1	52
29	1	56
30	2	00

Long °	*Equiv.* ′	″
31	2	04
32	2	08
33	2	12
34	2	16
35	2	20
36	2	24
37	2	28
38	2	32
39	2	36
40	2	40
41	2	44
42	2	48
43	2	52
44	2	56
45	3	00

Long °	*Equiv.* ′	″
46	3	04
47	3	08
48	3	12
49	3	16
50	3	20
51	3	24
52	3	28
53	3	32
54	3	36
55	3	40
56	3	44
57	3	48
58	3	52
59	3	56

Example:
What is the longitude equivalent in time of 145° 18′?

		H.	*M.*	*S.*	
From Tables: 145°	=	9	40	00	
18′	=	0	01	12	+
		9	41	12	

Or using calculator:

$$145°\ 18' = \frac{145.3}{15} = 9.6866 \qquad = 9 \quad 41 \quad 12$$

Table 4: British Summer Time: All changes 2 a.m. G.M.T.**

	Commenced					Ended					
	Jan	Feb	Mar	April	May	Jul	Aug	Sep	Oct	Nov	Dec
1916					21				1		
1917				8				17			
1918			24					30			
1919			30					29			
1920			28						25		
1921				3					3		
1922			26						8		
1923				22				16			
1924				13				21			
1925				19					4		
1926				18					3		
1927				10					2		
1928				22					7		
1929				21					6		
1930				13					5		
1931				19					4		
1932				17					2		
1933				9					8		
1934				22					7		
1935				14					6		
1936				19					4		
1937				18					3		
1938				10					2		
1939				16						19	
1940		25									31
*1941	1				*		*				31
*1942	1			*			*				31
*1943	1			*			*				31
*1944	1			*				*			31
*1945	1			*		*			7		
1946				14					6		
*1947			16	*			*			2	
1948			14						31		
1949				3					30		
* Denotes *Double* Summer Time in operation as listed below.											

**1 a.m. G.M.T. from 1981.

		April	May	Jul	Aug	Sep	
1941			4		10		
1942		5			9		
1943		4			15		
1944		2				17	
1945		2		15			
1946	Not observed						
1947		13			10		

* From 1941-1947 except 1946 *Double Summer Time* (+ 2 hours ahead of G.M.T.) from dates shown. Remainder of year 1 hour ahead from dates shown.

Example:
1941 from 1 January to 31 December 1 hour in advance of G.M.T. except for the period 4 May to 10 August + 2 (*Double Summer Time*).

	Commenced			Ended	
	Mar	April		Oct	
1950		16		22	
1951		15		21	
1952		20		26	
1953		19		4	
1954		11		3	
1955		17		2	
1956		22		7	
1957		14		6	
1958		20		5	
1959		19		4	
1960		10		2	
1961	26			29	
1962	25			28	
1963	31			27	
1964	22			25	
1965	21			24	
1966	20			23	

Commenced			Ended		
	Mar	April		Oct	
1967	19			29	
1972	19			29	
1973	18			28	
1974	17			27	
1975	16			26	
1976	21			24	
1977	20			23	
1978	19			29	
1979	18			28	
1980	16			26	
1981	29			25	
1982	28			24	
1983	27			23	
1984	25			28	
1985	31			27	

1968 from 18 February to 31 October 1971 British Standard Time in operation, 1 hour in advance of G.M.T.

Table 5: (i) Trigonometrical Formulae

1. *To convert longitude into right ascension (R.A.) without latitude.*
   Log. cosine of Obliquity of Ecliptic (O/E) 23°27′
 \+ Log. tangent longitude from Aries or Libra, (or log. cotangent longitude from Cancer or Capricorn).
 = Log. tangent R.A. from Aries or Libra, (or log cotangent R.A. from Cancer or Capricorn).

In Aries, Taurus, Gemini the result will be the R.A. required.
For Cancer, Leo, Virgo — Add 90°
For Libra, Scorpio, Sagittarius — Add 180°
For Capricorn, Aquarius, Pisces — Add 270°

2. *To convert right ascension into longitude, without latitude.*
   Log. cosine of Ecliptic (23°27′)
 \+ Log. cotangent R.A. from Aries or Libra, (or log. tangent R.A. from Cancer or Capricorn).
 = Log. cotangent longitude from Aries or Libra, (or log. tangent longitude from Cancer or Capricorn).

3. *To find declination, without latitude (longitude being given).*
Log. sine Obliquity of Ecliptic (23°27′)
\+ Log. sine longitude from Aries or Libra (or log. cosine from Cancer or Capricorn).
= Log. sine declination.

4. *To find ascensional difference.*
Log. tangent declination.
\+ Log. tangent latitude of locality.
= Log. sine ascensional difference.

5. *To find oblique ascension (places in northern latitudes):*
With north declination: right ascension *less* ascensional difference = oblique ascension.
With south declination: right ascension *plus* Ascensional difference = oblique ascension

(For places in southern latitudes, reverse the above rules, for *less* read plus, and for *plus* read less.)

6. *To find the oblique ascension (O.A.) of the cusp of a house.*
Right ascension of the Midheaven (R.A.M.C.)
\+ 30° = O.A. of 11th
\+ 60° = O.A. of 12th
\+ 90° = O.A. of 1st
\+ 120° = O.A. of 2nd
\+ 150° = O.A. of 3rd

7. *To find semi-arc (northern latitudes):*
Diurnal semi-arc with north declination: 90° + Asc. diff.
Diurnal semi-arc with south declination: 90° − Asc. diff.
Nocturnal semi-arc with north declination: 90° − Asc. diff.
Nocturnal semi-arc with south declination: 90° + Asc. diff.

(Reverse rules for places in southern latitudes, for *plus* read minus, and for *minus* read plus.)

Table 6: Right Ascension of the Apparent Sun

(For Libra to Pisces ADD 12 hours)

Deg.	Aries			Taurus			Gemini			Cancer			Leo			Virgo		
	H	M	S	H	M	S	H	M	S	H	M	S	H	M	S	H	M	S
0	0	00	00	1	51	37	3	51	15	6	00	00	8	08	45	10	08	23
1	0	03	40	1	55	27	3	55	25	6	04	22	8	12	54	10	12	12
2	0	07	20	1	59	17	3	59	36	6	08	43	8	17	03	10	16	00
3	0	11	00	2	03	08	4	03	48	6	13	05	8	21	11	10	19	48
4	0	14	41	2	06	59	4	08	00	6	17	26	8	25	19	10	23	35
5	0	18	21	2	10	51	4	12	13	6	21	48	8	29	26	10	27	22
6	0	22	02	2	14	44	4	16	26	6	26	09	8	33	31	10	31	08
7	0	25	42	2	18	37	4	20	40	6	30	30	8	37	37	10	34	54
8	0	29	23	2	22	31	4	24	55	6	34	51	8	41	41	10	38	40
9	0	33	04	2	26	25	4	29	10	6	39	11	8	45	45	10	42	25
10	0	36	45	2	30	20	4	33	26	6	43	31	8	49	48	10	46	09
11	0	40	26	2	34	16	4	37	42	6	47	51	8	53	51	10	49	53
12	0	44	08	2	38	13	4	41	59	6	52	11	8	57	52	10	53	37
13	0	47	50	2	42	10	4	46	16	6	56	31	9	01	53	10	57	20
14	0	51	32	2	46	08	4	50	34	7	00	50	9	05	53	11	01	03
15	0	55	14	2	50	07	4	54	52	7	05	08	9	09	53	11	04	46
16	0	58	57	2	54	07	4	59	10	7	09	26	9	13	52	11	08	28
17	1	02	40	2	58	07	5	03	29	7	13	44	9	17	50	11	12	10
18	1	06	23	3	02	08	5	07	49	7	18	01	9	21	47	11	15	52
19	1	10	07	3	06	09	5	12	09	7	22	18	9	25	44	11	19	34
20	1	13	51	3	10	12	5	16	29	7	26	34	9	29	40	11	23	15
21	1	17	35	3	14	15	5	20	49	7	30	50	9	33	35	11	26	56
22	1	21	20	3	18	19	5	25	09	7	35	05	9	37	29	11	30	37
23	1	25	06	3	22	23	5	29	30	7	39	20	9	41	23	11	34	18
24	1	28	52	3	26	29	5	33	51	7	43	34	9	45	16	11	37	58
25	1	32	38	3	30	35	5	38	12	7	47	47	9	49	09	11	41	39
26	1	36	25	3	34	41	5	42	34	7	52	00	9	53	01	11	45	19
27	1	40	12	3	38	49	5	46	55	7	56	12	9	56	52	11	49	00
28	1	44	00	3	42	57	5	51	17	8	00	24	10	00	43	11	52	40
29	1	47	48	3	47	06	5	55	38	8	04	35	10	04	33	11	56	20
	Libra			Scorpio			Sagitt.			Capricorn			Aqua.			Pisces		

Intermediate values found by interpolation:
Example Sun's longitude 16°54′ Scorpio = from tables

		H M S	
17° Scorpio		14 58 07	(Taurus table + 12 hours)
16 Scorpio	–	14 54 07	
1 (60′)		0 04 00	Difference.

Therefore if 60 mins. = 4 mins. difference
Therefore if 54 mins. = $\frac{54 \times 4}{60}$ = 3 mins. 36 secs. which added to 14.54.07 = 14.57.43 = Right Ascension of the Apparent Sun as required.

Trigonometrical formulae:
tan A = cos E, tan L. where A is the required R.A., E the obliquity of the Ecliptic and L the Sun's tropical longitude.

16°54′ Scorpio = 46°54′ from Libra:
46°54′ Tan. 1.06862 × 23°27′ (E) Cos. 0.9174 = Tan. 44.4318 plus 180° = 224.43 (224°26′) divided by 15 = 14.57.43 as required.

APPENDIX 2
ASTRONOMICAL DATA

Table 1: Conjunctions of Major Planets (First contact)

Date	*U.T.*	*Planet*	*Long.*
1900 Oct. 20	08.17	Jupiter/Uranus	10° Sagittarius
1901 Nov. 28	16.32	Jupiter/Saturn	14° Capricorn
1906 June 26	18.05	Jupiter/Pluto	22° Gemini
1907 May 22	11.47	Jupiter/Neptune	10° Cancer
1914 Mar. 4	03.26	Jupiter/Uranus	9° Aquarius
1914 Oct. 4	18.21	Saturn/Pluto	2° Cancer
1917 Aug. 1	05.18	Saturn/Neptune	4° Leo
1918 Aug. 10	20.04	Jupiter/Pluto	6° Cancer
1919 Sept. 24	02.01	Jupiter/Neptune	11° Leo
1921 Sept. 10	04.17	Jupiter/Saturn	26° Virgo
1927 July 15	21.26	Jupiter/Uranus	3° Aries
1931 May 27	03.18	Jupiter/Pluto	19° Cancer
1932 Sept. 19	04.41	Jupiter/Neptune	8° Virgo
1940 Aug. 8	01.21	Jupiter/Saturn	14° Taurus
1941 May 8	00.20	Jupiter/Uranus	25° Taurus
1942 May 3	13.16	Saturn/Uranus	29° Taurus
1943 Aug. 1	08.08	Jupiter/Pluto	6° Leo
1945 Sept. 22	09.02	Jupiter/Neptune	6° Libra
1947 Aug. 11	01.15	Saturn/Pluto	13° Leo
1952 Nov. 21	13.22	Saturn/Neptune	22° Libra
1954 Oct. 7	09.58	Jupiter/Uranus	27° Cancer
1955 Nov. 2	23.02	Jupiter/Pluto	28° Leo
1958 Sept. 24	16.15	Jupiter/Neptune	3° Scorpio
1961 Feb. 19	00.00	Jupiter/Saturn	25° Capricorn
1965 Oct. 9	18.07	Uranus/Pluto	17° Virgo
1968 Oct. 13	04.56	Jupiter/Pluto	23° Virgo
1968 Dec. 11	15.02	Jupiter/Uranus	3° Libra
1971 Feb. 1	07.01	Jupiter/Neptune	2° Sagittarius
1980 Dec. 31	21.19	Jupiter/Saturn	9° Libra
1981 Nov. 2	08.48	Jupiter/Pluto	25° Libra
1982 Nov. 8	01.51	Saturn/Pluto	27° Libra
1983 Feb. 18	22.35	Jupiter/Uranus	8° Sagittarius

Date	*U.T.*	*Planet*	*Long.*
1984 Jan. 19	17.41	Jupiter/Neptune	0° Capricorn
1988 Feb. 13	00.49	Saturn/Uranus	29° Sagittarius
1989 Mar. 3	12.03	Saturn/Neptune	12° Capricorn
1993 Feb. 2	13.01	Uranus/Neptune	19° Capricorn
1994 Dec. 2	09.23	Jupiter/Pluto	28° Scorpio
1997 Jan. 9	12.06	Jupiter/Neptune	27° Capricorn
1997 Feb. 16	02.13	Jupiter/Uranus	6° Aquarius
2000 May 28	15.58	Jupiter/Saturn	22° Taurus

Table 2: Sun's Entry into Capricorn (December Solstice)

Tropical

Year	*Dec.*	*Time*
1900	22	06.42
1901	22	12.37
1902	22	18.36
1903	23	00.20
1904	22	06.14
1905	22	12.03
1906	22	17.54
1907	22	23.51
1908	22	05.33
1909	22	11.20
1910	22	17.12
1911	22	22.53
1912	22	04.45
1913	22	10.35
1914	22	16.23
1915	22	22.16
1916	22	03.58
1917	22	09.46
1918	22	15.42
1919	22	21.27

Year	*Dec.*	*Time*
1920	22	03.17
1921	22	09.07
1922	22	14.57
1923	22	20.53
1924	22	02.45
1925	22	08.37
1926	22	14.34
1927	22	20.18
1928	22	02.04
1929	22	07.53
1930	22	13.39
1931	22	19.30
1932	22	01.15
1933	22	06.58
1934	22	12.49
1935	22	18.37
1936	22	00.27
1937	22	06.21
1938	22	12.14
1939	22	18.06

Year	Dec.	Time
1940	21	23.54
1941	22	05.44
1942	22	11.39
1943	22	17.29
1944	21	23.15
1945	22	05.03
1946	22	10.54
1947	22	16.43
1948	21	22.33
1949	22	04.24
1950	22	10.14
1951	22	16.00
1952	21	21.43
1953	22	03.32
1954	22	09.25
1955	22	15.11
1956	21	20.59
1957	22	02.49
1958	22	08.40
1959	22	14.35
1960	21	20.26
1961	22	02.19
1962	22	08.16
1963	22	14.02
1964	21	19.50
1965	22	01.40
1966	22	07.28
1967	22	13.17
1968	21	19.00
1969	22	00.44

Year	Dec.	Time
1970	22	06.36
1971	22	12.24
1972	21	18.13
1973	22	00.08
1974	22	05.57
1975	22	11.46
1976	21	17.36
1977	21	23.24
1978	22	05.21
1979	22	11.10
1980	21	16.57
1981	21	22.51
1982	22	04.39
1983	22	10.30
1984	21	16.23
1985	21	22.08
1986	22	04.02
1987	22	09.46
1988	21	15.28
1989	21	21.22
1990	22	03.07
1991	22	08.54
1992	21	14.43
1993	21	20.26
1994	22	02.23
1995	22	08.17
1996	21	14.06
1997	21	20.07
1998	22	01.57
1999	22	07.44
2000	21	13.38

Table 3: Solar Eclipses 1900-2000

Date	*U.T.*	*Long.*
1900 May 28	14.50	7° Gemini
Nov. 22	07.17	29° Scorpio
1901 May 18	05.38	26° Taurus
Nov. 11	07.34	18° Scorpio
1902 Apr. 8	13.50	18° Aries
May 7	22.45	16° Taurus
Oct. 31	08.13	7° Scorpio
1903 Mar. 29	01.26	7° Aries
Sept. 21	04.31	27° Virgo
1904 Mar. 17	05.39	26° Pisces
Sept. 9	20.43	17° Virgo
1905 Mar. 6	05.19	15° Pisces
Aug. 30	13.13	6° Virgo
1906 Feb. 23	07.57	4° Pisces
July 21	12.59	28° Cancer
Aug. 20	01.27	26° Leo
1907 Jan. 14	05.57	23° Capricorn
July 10	15.17	17° Cancer
1908 Jan. 3	21.43	12° Capricorn
June 28	16.31	6° Cancer
Dec. 23	11.50	1° Capricorn
1909 June 17	23.28	26° Gemini
·Dec. 12	19.58	20° Sagittarius
1910 May 9	05.33	18° Taurus
Nov. 2	01.56	9° Scorpio
1911 Apr. 28	22.25	7° Taurus
Oct. 22	04.09	27° Libra
1912 Apr. 17	11.40	27° Aries
Oct. 10	13.40	17° Libra
1913 Apr. 6	17.48	16° Aries
Aug. 31	20.38	8° Virgo
Sept. 30	04.56	6° Libra
1914 Feb. 25	00.02	5° Pisces
Aug. 21	12.26	27° Leo
1915 Feb. 14	04.31	24° Aquarius
Aug. 10	22.52	17° Leo

Date	U.T.	Long.
1916 Feb. 3	16.05	13° Aquarius
July 30	02.15	6° Leo
Dec. 24	20.31	3° Capricorn
1917 Jan. 23	07.40	3° Aquarius
June 19	13.02	27° Gemini
July 19	03.00	26° Cancer
Dec. 14	09.17	22° Sagittarius
1918 June 8	22.02	17° Gemini
Dec. 3	15.19	11° Sagittarius
1919 May 29	13.12	7° Gemini
Nov. 22	15.19	29° Scorpio
1920 May 18	06.25	27° Taurus
Nov. 10	16.05	18° Scorpio
1921 Apr. 8	09.05	18° Aries
Oct. 1	12.26	8° Libra
1922 Mar. 28	13.03	7° Aries
Sept. 21	04.38	27° Virgo
1923 Mar. 17	12.51	26° Pisces
Sept. 10	20.52	17° Virgo
1924 Mar. 5	15.58	15° Pisces
July 31	19.42	8° Leo
Aug. 30	08.37	7° Virgo
1925 Jan. 24	14.45	4° Aquarius
July 20	21.40	27° Cancer
1926 Jan. 14	06.34	23° Capricorn
July 9	23.06	17° Cancer
1927 Jan. 3	20.28	12° Capricorn
June 29	06.32	6° Cancer
Dec. 24	04.13	1° Capricorn
1928 May 19	13.14	28° Taurus
June 17	20.42	26° Gemini
Nov. 12	09.35	20° Scorpio
1929 May 9	06.07	18° Taurus
Nov. 1	12.01	8° Scorpio
1930 Apr. 28	19.08	8° Taurus
Oct. 21	21.47	28° Libra
1931 Apr. 18	01.00	27° Aries
Sept. 12	04.26	18° Virgo
Oct. 11	13.06	17° Libra

Date	*U.T.*	*Long.*
1932 Mar. 7	07.44	16° Pisces
Aug. 31	19.54	8° Virgo
1933 Feb. 24	12.44	5° Pisces
Aug. 21	05.48	28° Leo
1934 Feb. 14	00.43	24° Aquarius
Aug. 10	08.45	17° Leo
1935 Jan. 5	05.20	14° Capricorn
Feb. 3	16.27	14° Aquarius
June 30	19.44	8° Cancer
July 30	09.32	6° Leo
Dec. 25	17.49	3° Capricorn
1936 June 19	05.14	28° Gemini
Dec. 13	23.25	22° Sagittarius
1937 June 8	20.43	17° Gemini
Dec. 2	23.11	10° Sagittarius
1938 May 29	13.59	7° Gemini
Nov. 22	00.05	29° Scorpio
1939 Apr. 19	16.35	29° Aries
Oct. 12	20.30	18° Libra
1940 Apr. 7	20.18	18° Aries
Oct. 1	12.41	8° Libra
1941 Mar. 27	20.14	7° Aries
Sept. 21	04.38	28° Virgo
1942 Mar. 16	23.50	26° Pisces
Aug. 12	02.28	19° Leo
Sept. 10	15.33	17° Virgo
1943 Feb. 4	23.29	15° Aquarius
Aug. 1	04.06	8° Leo
1944 Jan. 25	15.24	4° Aquarius
July 20	05.42	27° Cancer
1945 Jan. 14	05.06	24° Capricorn
July 9	13.35	17° Cancer
1946 Jan. 3	12.30	12° Capricorn
May 30	20.49	9° Gemini
June 29	04.06	7° Cancer
Nov. 23	17.24	1° Sagittarius
1947 May 20	13.44	29° Taurus
Nov. 12	20.01	19° Scorpio
1948 May 9	02.30	18° Taurus
Nov. 1	06.03	9° Scorpio

Date	*U.T.*	*Long.*
1949 Apr. 28	08.02	8° Taurus
Oct. 21	21.23	28° Libra
1950 Mar. 18	15.20	27° Pisces
Sept. 12	03.29	19° Virgo
1951 Mar. 7	20.51	16° Pisces
Sept. 1	12.50	8° Virgo
1952 Feb. 25	09.16	6° Pisces
Aug. 20	15.20	27° Leo
1953 Feb. 14	01.10	25° Aquarius
July 11	02.28	18° Cancer
Aug. 9	16.10	17° Leo
1954 Jan. 5	02.21	14° Capricorn
June 30	12.26	8° Cancer
Dec. 25	07.33	3° Capricorn
1955 June 20	04.12	28° Gemini
Dec. 14	07.07	21° Sagittarius
1956 June 8	21.29	18° Gemini
Dec. 2	08.13	10° Sagittarius
1957 Apr. 29	23.54	9° Taurus
Oct. 23	04.43	29° Libra
1958 Apr. 19	03.23	28° Aries
Oct. 12	20.52	19° Libra
1959 Apr. 8	03.29	17° Aries
Oct. 2	12.31	8° Libra
1960 Mar. 27	07.37	6° Aries
Sept. 20	23.12	28° Virgo
1961 Feb. 15	08.10	26° Aquarius
Aug. 11	10.36	18° Leo
1962 Feb. 5	00.10	16° Aquarius
July 31	12.24	8° Leo
1963 Jan. 25	13.42	5° Aquarius
July 20	20.43	27° Cancer
1964 Jan. 14	20.43	24° Capricorn
June 10	04.22	19° Gemini
July 9	11.31	17° Cancer
Dec. 4	01.18	12° Sagittarius
1965 May 30	21.13	9° Gemini
Nov. 23	04.10	1° Sagittarius
1966 May 20	09.42	29° Taurus
Nov. 12	14.26	20° Scorpio

Date	*U.T.*	*Long.*
1967 May 9	14.55	18° Taurus
Nov. 2	05.48	9° Scorpio
1968 Mar. 28	22.48	8° Aries
Sept. 22	11.08	29° Virgo
1969 Mar. 18	04.51	27° Pisces
Sept. 11	19.56	19° Virgo
1970 Mar. 7	17.42	17° Pisces
Aug. 31	22.01	8° Virgo
1971 Feb. 25	09.48	6° Pisces
July 22	09.15	29° Cancer
Aug. 20	22.53	27° Leo
1972 Jan. 16	10.52	25° Capricorn
July 10	19.39	18° Cancer
1973 Jan. 4	15.42	14° Capricorn
June 30	11.39	8° Cancer
Dec. 24	15.07	3° Capricorn
1974 June 20	04.56	28° Gemini
Dec. 13	16.25	21° Sagittarius
1975 May 11	07.05	20° Taurus
Nov. 3	13.05	10° Scorpio
1976 Apr. 29	10.19	9° Taurus
Oct. 23	05.10	29° Libra
1977 Apr. 18	10.35	28° Aries
Oct. 12	20.31	19° Libra
1978 Apr. 7	15.15	17° Aries
Oct. 2	06.41	9° Libra
1979 Feb. 26	16.45	7° Pisces
Aug. 22	17.10	29° Leo
1980 Feb. 16	08.51	27° Aquarius
Aug. 10	19.09	18° Leo
1981 Feb. 4	22.14	16° Aquarius
July 31	03.52	8° Leo
1982 Jan. 25	04.56	5° Aquarius
June 21	11.52	29° Gemini
July 20	18.57	28° Cancer
Dec. 15	09.18	23° Sagittarius
1983 June 11	04.37	20° Gemini
Dec. 4	12.26	12° Sagittarius

Date	*U.T.*	*Long.*
1984 May 30	16.48	9° Gemini
Nov. 22	22.57	1° Sagittarius
1985 May 19	21.41	29° Taurus
Nov. 12	14.20	20° Scorpio
1986 Apr. 9	06.08	19° Aries
Oct. 3	18.55	10° Libra
1987 Mar. 29	12.46	8° Aries
Sept. 23	03.08	29° Virgo
1988 Mar. 18	02.02	28° Pisces
Sept. 11	04.49	19° Virgo
1989 Mar. 7	18.19	17° Pisces
Aug. 31	05.45	8° Virgo
1990 Jan. 26	19.20	6° Aquarius
July 22	02.54	29° Cancer
1991 Jan. 15	23.50	25° Capricorn
July 11	19.06	19° Cancer
1992 Jan. 4	23.10	14° Capricorn
Jun. 30	12.18	9° Cancer
Dec. 24	00.43	2° Capricorn
1993 May 21	14.07	0° Gemini
Nov. 13	21.34	21° Scorpio
1994 May 10	17.07	20° Taurus
Nov. 3	13.35	11° Scorpio
1995 Apr. 29	17.36	9° Taurus
Oct. 24	04.36	0° Scorpio
1996 Apr. 17	22.49	28° Aries
Oct. 12	14.14	19° Libra
1997 Mar. 9	01.15	18° Pisces
Sept. 1	23.52	9° Virgo
1998 Feb. 26	17.26	8° Pisces
Aug. 22	02.03	29° Leo
1999 Feb. 16	06.39	27° Aquarius
Aug. 11	11.09	18° Leo
2000 Feb. 5	13.03	16° Aquarius
July 1	19.20	10° Cancer
July 31	02.25	8° Leo
Dec. 25	17.22	4° Capricorn

APPENDIX 3.
ASTROLOGICAL DATA

Abbreviations: General

A.A.	*American Astrology*
ABC	*American Book of Charts,* L.M. Rodden.
A.J.	*Astrological Journal*
A.Q.	*Astrologer's Quarterly*
D.T. Comm. Supp.	*Daily Telegraph, 125 years Commemorative Supplement*
Ency. Brit.	*Encyclopaedia Britannica*
M.A.	*Modern Astrology* (An Alan Leo publication now defunct)
O.S.	Old Style

Abbreviations: Time

		Hrs slow/fast on G.M.T
B.S.T.	British Summer Time	1 fast
C.D.S.T.	Central Daylight Saving Time	5 slow
C.E.T.	Central European Time	1 fast
C.S.T.	Central Standard Time	6 slow
C.W.T.	Central War Time	5 slow
D.B.S.T.	Double British Summer Time	2 fast
E.D.S.T.	Eastern Daylight Saving Time	4 slow
E.S.T.	Eastern Standard Time	5 slow
E.W.T.	Eastern War Time	4 slow
G.M.T.	Greenwich Mean Time	
J.S.T.	Japanese Standard Time	9 fast
L.T.	Local Time (normally the clock time of of a particular locality)	
M.D.S.T.	Mountain Daylight Saving Time	6 slow
M.S.T.	Mountain Standard Time	7 slow
M.W.T.	Mountain War Time	6 slow
P.D.S.T.	Pacific Daylight Saving Time	7 slow
P.S.T.	Pacific Standard Time	8 slow
P.W.T.	Pacific War Time	7 slow
U.T.	Universal Time (G.M.T. reckoned from 0 hours)	

Charting Information

Astrology		
Event	*Data*	*Source*
Astrological Lodge founded	7.15 p.m. G.M.T., 13.7.1915, Finchley, London	A.Q. Winter 1969
C. Carter (President) born	10.55 p.m. G.M.T., 31.1.1887, Parkstone, Dorset	A.Q. Winter 1968
Faculty of Astrological Studies founded	6.50 p.m. G.M.T., 7.6.1948, Queen Square, West London	A.Q. Autumn 1948
Astrological Association founded	7.22 p.m. G.M.T., 21.6.1958, West London	A.Q. Autumn 1958
Astrologer's Quarterly (Editor C. Carter), Vol 1, No. 1	Noon G.M.T., 1.12.1926, London	A.Q. Summer 1976
Astronomy		
Copernicus born	4.48 p.m. L.T., 28.2.1473 N.S., Torun, Poland	ABC
Galileo born	3.00 p.m. Sundial 25.2.1564 N.S., Pisa, Italy	ABC, from A.A. June 1970
Kepler born	2.30 p.m. L.T., 7.1.1572 N.S., Weil, Germany 47°36′ N; 7°39′ E	ABC from *Kepler*, Max Caspar, 1959

Natal Positions

	(A) *Copernicus*	(B) *Galileo*	(C) *Kepler*
Sun	*10* ♓	6 ♓	16 ♑
Moon	5 ♐	20 ♈	16 ♊
Mercury	26 ♓	13 ♓	7 ♑
Venus	7 ♈	20 ♓	20 ♑
Mars	21 ♒	29 ♉	8 ♎
Jupiter	4 ♐	29 ♋	19 ♓
Saturn	18 ♊	27 ♋	13 ♏
Uranus	5 ♏	9 ♐	10 ♑
Neptune	17 ♏	4 ♊	23 ♊
Pluto	17 ♍	12 ♓	21 ♓
Asc.	3 ♍	6 ♌	22 ♊
M.C.	23 ♉	21 ♈	21 ♒

	♈-♎	♉-♏	♊-♐	♋-♑	♌-♒	♍-♓
(A)	♀ 7 ♈	♅ 5 ♏ ♆ 17 ♏ MC 23 ♉	♃ 4 ♐ ☽ 5 ♐ ♄ 18 ♊		♂ 21 ♒	☉ 10 ♓ ♇ 17 ♍ ☿ 26 ♓ Asc 3 ♍
(B)	☽ 20 ♈ MC 21 ♈	♂ 29 ♉	♆ 4 ♊ ♅ 9 ♐	♄ 27 ♋ ♃ 29 ♋	Asc 6 ♌	☉ 6 ♓ ♇ 12 ♓ ☿ 13 ♓ ♀ 20 ♓
(C)	♂ 8 ♎	♄ 13 ♏	☽ 16 ♊ ♆ 23 ♊ Asc 22 ♊	☿ 7 ♑ ♅ 10 ♑ ☉ 16 ♑ ♀ 20 ♑	MC 21 ♒	♃ 19 ♓ ♇ 21 ♓

Astronomy

Greenwich Observatory founded by Flamsteed	3.14 p.m. L.T., 10.8.1675, O.S., Greenwich	*Textbook of Astrology*, A.J. Pearce, 1911

Flamsteed's chart quoted by Pearce (Pluto added)

Planetary positions to the nearest degree:

Sun	27° Leo	Jupiter	10° Sagittarius
Moon	21° Leo	Saturn	12° Taurus
Mercury	3° Virgo	Uranus	29° Pisces
Venus	4° Leo	Neptune	13° Aquarius
Mars	19° Virgo	Pluto	8° Cancer
Ascendant	18° Sagittarius	M.C.	20° Libra

Psychology

A. Adler born	2.00 p.m. L.T., 7.2.1870, Vienna	A.Q. Spring 1967
C. Jung born	7.32 p.m. L.T., 26.7.1875, Kesswil, Switzerland	A.Q. Autumn 1954
S. Freud born	6.30 p.m. L.T., 6.5.1856, Freiburg, Moravia	A.J. Summer 1981

British History

Crowning of William 1	True noon, 25.12.1066, Westminster	A.Q. Summer 1940
Union of Scotland and England	00.00 L.T., 1.5.1707 O.S., Westminster	A.Q. Summer 1940
The United Kingdom (Union of Great Britain and Ireland)	00.00 L.T., 1.1.1801, Westminster	A.Q. Summer 1940 (see Fig. 27)*

*See also *Mundane Astrology* by M. Baigent, N. Campion and C. Harvey: Aquarian Press 1984, for charts and comments.

Statute of Westminster (Dominion Status)	9.30 a.m. G.M.T., 12.12.1931, Westminster	A.Q. Autumn 1959
British Monarchy	3.15 p.m. L.T., 1.1.1801, Wesminster	N. Campion, *Transit,* Nov. 1984 quoted from *The Times,* 2.1.1801

Irish History

Easter Rising	12.00 Local noon, 24.4.1916, Dublin	Sheila Lindsay *Transit,* February 1985
Irish Treaty signed	2.15 a.m. G.M.T., 6.12.1921, Downing St, London	D.T. Comm. Supp.
Irish Free State founded	8.45 p.m. G.M.T., 7.1.1922, Dublin	A.Q. Summer 1973 (letter from L. Black)
Northern Ireland	3.28 p.m. G.M.T., 7.12.1922, Belfast	A.Q. Spring 1962
Republic of Ireland (Eire)	11.00 p.m. G.M.T., 17.4.1949, Dublin	*Mundane Astrology* Aquarian Press 1984

German History

Proclamation of Wilhelm 1 as Emperor	1.00 p.m. L.T., 18.1.1871, Versailles	*Mundane Astrology,* Aquarian Press, 1984
Hitler born	6.30 p.m. L.T., 20.4.1889, Braunau, 48°15′ N; 13°03′ E	*Mundane Astrology* Aquarian Press, 1984

Nazi Party founded	7.29 p.m. C.E.T., 6.29 p.m. G.M.T., 24.2.1920, Munich	A.Q. Summer 1940
The Third Reich (inauguration of Hitler as Chancellor)	11.15 a.m. C.E.T.,* 10.15 a.m. G.M.T., 30.1.1933, Berlin	A.Q. Winter 1938/39 (10 a.m.).

*A.J. Winter 1984/85, letter from R. Leggett quotes shortly after 11.15 a.m. C.E.T.

Munich Pact signed	12.30 a.m. C.E.T., 30.9.1938	A.Q. Spring 1939, quoted from *The Times,* 30.9.38

War and Peace

Archduke Franz Ferdinand assassinated (shot)	11.15 a.m. C.E.T.,* 10.15 a.m. G.M.T., 28.6.1914, Sarajevo 43°37′ N; 18°27′E.	Catastrophe and Crisis. Aldous Books, 1979. D.T. Comm. Supp. report 29.6.14.

*First attempt (bomb) at 10.10 a.m. C.E.T. failed. Time of fatal shot quoted as 11.30 a.m. by BBC radio documentary 10.5.85, 'Murder at Sarajevo'.

First World War: declaration by Britain — expiry of ultimatum	11.00 p.m. G.M.T., 4.8.1914, London. (Midnight C.E.T. Berlin)	*The Home Fronts,* John Williams, Constable, 1972
Armistice signed	5.00 a.m. G.M.T., 11.11.1918, Compiegne, 49°25′N; 2°29′E	Ency. Brit.
Hostilities ceased	11.00 a.m. G.M.T., 11.11.1918	Ency. Brit.
Treaty of Versailles	2.00 p.m. G.M.T.,* 28.6.1919, Versailles	*The End of Order (Versailles),* C. L. Mee Jr., Secker & Warburg, 1980

*Delegates assembled at about 2.45 p.m. local time (French Summer Time = G.M.T. + 1); 2 p.m. an approximation.

Second World War: declaration by Britain	11.00 a.m. B.S.T., 10.00 a.m. G.M.T., 3.9.1939	Contemporary reports
Surrender of the German Armies of the north	6.25 p.m. L.T.,* 4.25 p.m. G.M.T., 4.5.1945, Luneburg Heath	D.T. Comm. Supp. report 5.5.45

*Assumed that the time quoted is in German Summer Time.

Unconditional German surrender signed	2.41 a.m. French time 0.41 a.m. G.M.T., 7.5.1945, Rheims	*Manchester Guardian,* Tuesday 8 May 1945
Victory in Europe (VE Day); end of European war	Midnight* 8/9 May 1945; 10.00 p.m. G.M.T. 8.5.1945	*The Struggle for Europe,* C. Wilmot Fontana/Collins 1974

*Double Summer Time operated in Britain: C.E.T. + 1 = G.M.T. + 2 in Germany.

Japanese Surrender ceremony aboard the U.S. battleship *Missouri*	10.30 a.m. J.S.T., 1.30 a.m. G.M.T., 2.9.1945 Tokyo Bay	A.Q. Winter 1945/46

Disasters

Lake View School Collinwood, Ohio (fire)	8.30 a.m. C.S.T., 2.30 p.m. G.M.T., 4.3.1908, 41°30′N; 81°43′W	From data supplied to author by Garth Allen
Football stand fire (heavy loss of life)	3.43 p.m. B.S.T.,* 2.43 p.m. G.M.T., 11.5.1985 Bradford, Yorks., 53°48′N; 1°45′W	*Guardian* 13.5.1985

*Other press reports stated 'about ten minutes before half-time.

Bismarck battleship: Launched	11.15 a.m. C.E.T., 10.15 a.m. G.M.T., 14.2.1939, Hamburg, 53°33′N; 10°00′E	A.Q. Spring 1955
Sunk	8.40 a.m. G.M.T., 27.5.1941, 49°N; 9′W.	
Brighton Bomb Tory Party Conference hotel.	02.54.01 B.S.T.,* 01.54.01 G.M.T., 12.10.1984, Brighton, 50°50′N; 0°08′W	*Guardian* 13.10.84

*Time as recorded by a time-lapse security camera.

Gas explosion Bhopal, India.	Approx. 01.00 a.m. I.S.T., 3.12.1984, Bhopal, 23°16′N; 77°24′E	*Sunday Times* 9.12.84
Explosion of oil tanker *Betelgeuse*	00.55 a.m. G.M.T., 8.1.1979, Bantry Bay, Ireland, 51°37′N; 9°38′W	*Mundane Astrology* C. Harvey
Titanic: Keel laid	22.3.1909	*Daily Express* 23.3.1909
Launched	12.15 p.m. L.T., 12.39 p.m. G.M.T., 31.5.1911, Belfast, 54°36′n; 5°55′W	1.6.1911
Maiden voyage	Noon G.M.T., 10.4.1912, Southampton, 50°54′N; 1°23′W	11.4.1912 as quoted in *Modern Astrology* June 1912, Vol. 9, No. 6
Struck iceberg and sank about three hours later	11.40 p.m. 'ship's time',* 14.4.1912; 02.37 a.m. G.M.T., 15.4.1912, 41°46′N; 50°14′W	

*The following is an extract from a correspondent to *Modern Astrology* July 1912:

'. . . according to evidence the ship struck the berg at 11.40 p.m., "ship's time". The vessel had made 260 knots or 5°50′ since the previous noon, therefore the ship's time was local mean time for 50.14 — 5.50 or 44°24′W, making G.M.T. 2.37½ a.m. 15.4.12. The vessel sank three hours later. Watches on corpses had stopped at 2.20 to 2.30 a.m. equivalent to G.M.T. 5.22½ a.m.' It is interesting to note as this correspondent stated, that at the time of the collision, Uranus was exactly on the Ascendant at London, and at the time of the final catastrophe, exactly on the Ascendant at the place of the disaster.

Titanic
Planetary correspondences

	♈-♎	♉-♏	♊-♐	♋-♑	♌-♒	♍-♓
1. Keel laid	☉ 1 ♈ ☽ 10 ♈ ♄ 11 ♈		♇ 24 ♊	♆ 14 ♋ ⛢ 17 ♑ ♅ 20 ♑		☿ 7 ♓ ♃ 7 ♍ ♀ 21 ♓
2. Launched		♄ 13 ♉ ☿ 15 ♉	☉ 9 ♊ MC13 ♊ ♇ 27 ♊	♆ 19 ♋ ♀ 21 ♋ ☽ 25 ♋ ♅ 29 ♑		♃ 6 ♍ Asc 18 ♍ ⛢ 28 ♓
3. Maiden voyage	☉ 20 ♈ ☿ 28 ♈ MC18 ♈	♄ 19 ♉	♃ 15 ♐ ♇ 27 ♊	⛢ 3 ♋ ♆ 21 ♋ ☽ 29 ♑	♅ 3 ♒ Asc 9 ♌	♀ 27 ♓
4. Struck iceberg	♀ 3 ♈ ☉ 25 ♈ ☿ 25 ♈ MC13 ♎	♄ 20 ♉	♃ 15 ♐ Asc20 ♐ ♇ 27 ♊	⛢ 5 ♋ ♆ 21 ♋	♅ 3 ♒	☽ 26 ♓
5. Sank		MC26 ♏			Asc 2 ♒	☽ 27 ♓

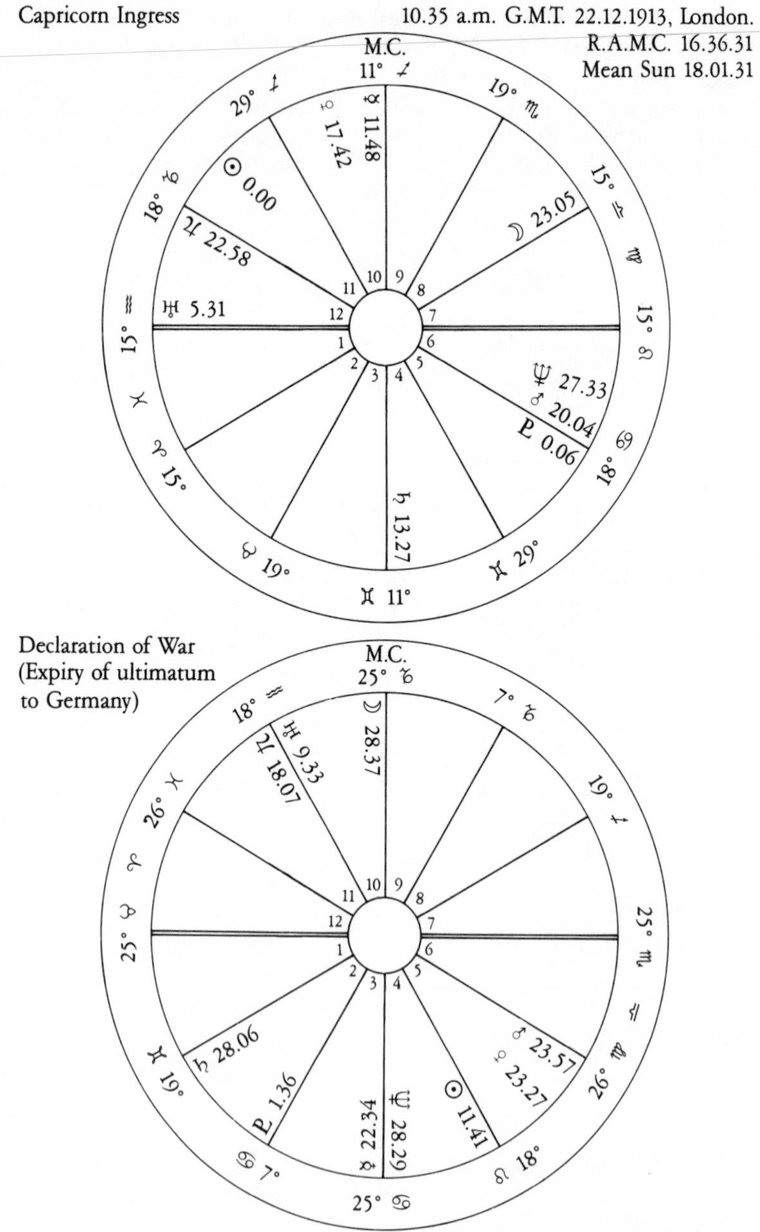

11.00 p.m. G.M.T. 4.8.1914, London.
R.A.M.C. 19.50.38
Mean Sun 8.50.38

Figure 55

Capricorn Ingress — 12.14 p.m. G.M.T., 22.12.1938, London.
R.A.M.C. 18.14.34
Mean Sun 18.01.34

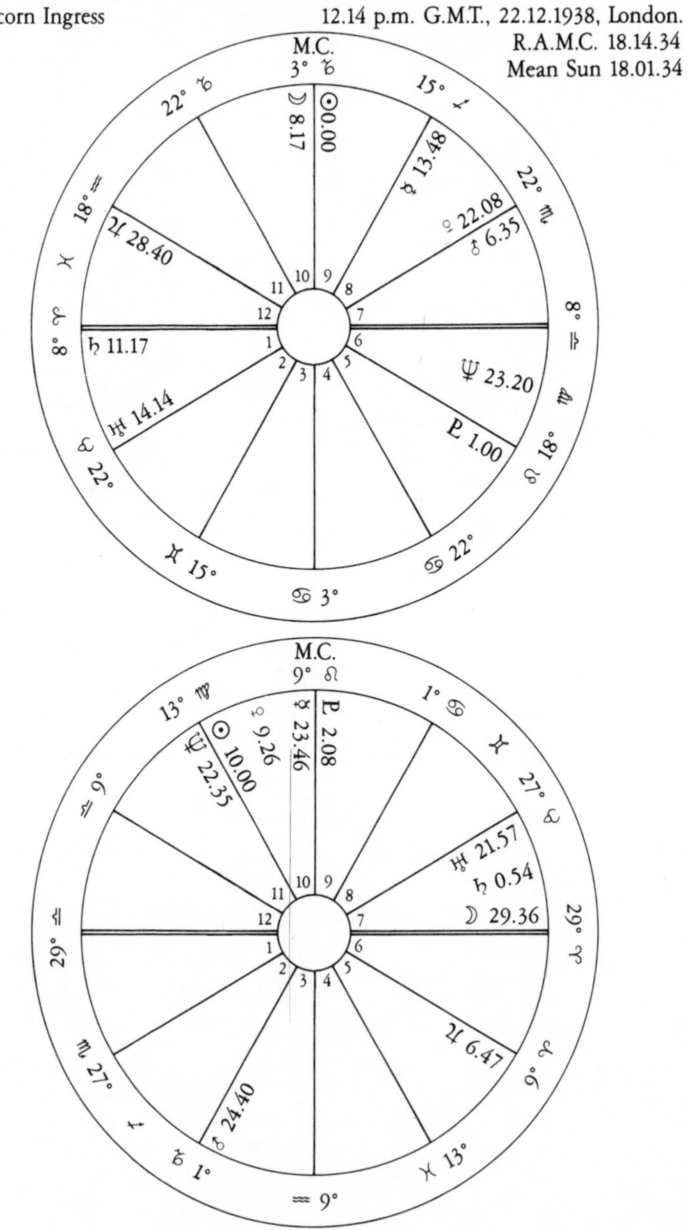

Declaration of War 10.00 a.m. G.M.T., 3.9.1939, London.
R.A.M.C. 8.46.34
Mean Sun 10.46.34

Figure 56

APPENDIX 4.
ADDRESSES

The Astrological Association
c/o Membership Secretary,
Bay Villa,
Plymouth Road,
Totnes, Devon TQ9 5PQ.

(Please enclose s.a.e.)

The Astrological Lodge
The Secretary,
The Astrological Lodge,
c/o Art Worker's Guild,
6 Queen Square,
London WC1 3AR.

(Please enclose s.a.e.)

Faculty of Astrological Studies
c/o The Registrar,
Hook Cottage,
Vines Cross,
Heathfield,
Sussex TN21 9EN.

(Teaching and examining body. Please enclose s.a.e.)

BIBLIOGRAPHY
SUGGESTED READING AND REFERENCE MATERIALS

General Interest

Addey, J., *Astrology Reborn*, J. Addey/Faculty of Astrological Studies (1971).

Gauquelin, M., *Astrology and Science*, Mayflower (1972).

____, *The Cosmic Clocks*, Paladin (1973).

____, *Cosmic Influences on Human Behaviour*, Garnstone Press (1974).

____, *Spheres of Destiny*, Dent (1980).

____, *The Truth about Astrology*, Hutchinson (1984).

Parker, D., *The Question of Astrology*, Eyre & Spottiswoode (1970).

Technical

Filbey, J.M. *Natal Charting*, Aquarian Press (1981).

Filbey, J.M. and P.M., *Astronomy for Astrologers*, Aquarian Press (1984).

Holden, R., *The Elements of House Division*, Fowler (1977).

Jayne, C., *Progressions and Directions*, Astrological Bureau (American).

Kemp. C., *Progressions* (booklet), Astrological Association (1972).

Leo, A., *The Progressed Horoscope*, Fowler, 5th Edition (1936). (For explanation and examples of Primary Directions.)

Lorenz, Dona Marie, *Tools of Astrology: Houses*, Eomega Press, Topanga, Calif. (1973).

Powell, R. and Treadgold, P., *The Sidereal Zodiac*. Anthroposophical Publications (1979).

Astrological Analysis and Interpretation

Arroyo, S., *Relationships and Life Cycles*, CRCS Publications (1979).

____, *Astrology, Psychology and the Four Elements*, CRCS Publications (1975).

____, *Astrology, Karma and Transformation,* CRCS Publications (1978).

Carter, C., *Astrological Aspects,* Fowler (1969).

Davison, R., *Synastry*, Aurora Press (1983).

Dobyns, Z. and Roof, N., *The Astrologer's Casebook,* T.I.A. Publications (1973).

Freeman, M., *How to Interpret a Birth Chart,* Aquarian Press (1981).

Geddes, S., *The Art of Astrology,* Aquarian Press (1980).

____, *Astrology and Health,* Aquarian Press (1981).

Greene, L., *Saturn,* Weiser (1976).

____, *Relating,* Coventure (1977).

Parker, D. and J., *The New Compleat Astrologer,* Mitchell Beazley (1984).

Rose, C., *Astrological Counselling,* Aquarian Press (1982).

Thornton, P., *Synastry*, Aquarian Press (1982).

Evaluating Future Trends

Carter, C., *Symbolic Directions in Modern Astrology,* Macoy Publishing (1947).

Davison, R., *The Technique of Prediction,* Fowler (1955).

De Luce, R., *Complete Method of Prediction,* ASI Publishers (1978).

Freeman, M., *Forecasting by Astrology,* Aquarian Press (1982).

Ruperti, A., *Cycles of Becoming,* CRCS Publications (1978).

Other Techniques

Addey, J., *Harmonics,* Fowler (1976).

Baigent, M., Campion, N. and Harvey, C., *Mundane Astrology,* Aquarian Press (1984).

Bailey, E.H., *The Prenatal Epoch,* Foulsham (1916).

Bradley, D., *Solar and Lunar Returns* (Sidereal), The Llewellyn Foundation of Astrological Research (1950).

Carter, C., *Introduction to Political Astrology,* Fowler (1951).

Dean, G., *Recent Advances in Natal Astrology,* (A critical review 1900-1976), Astrological Association (1977).

Fagan, C. and Firebrace, R., *A Primer of the Sidereal Zodiac,* Moray Series No. 1 (1961).

Hamblin, D., *Harmonic Charts,* Aquarian Press (1983).

Astronomy (General Interest)

Asimov, I., *The Universe,* Pelican Books (1971).

Hill, D., *The Comet,* New English Library (1973).

Hoyle, F., *Nicolaus Copernicus,* Heinemann (1973).
Klepesta, J. and Rukl, A., *Constellations — Concise Guide,* Hamlyn Artia (1972).
Kuhn, T., *The Copernican Revolution,* Harvard University Press (1971).
Moore, P., *Astronomy for 'O' Level,* Duckworth (1970).
Ronan, C., *Their Majesties' Astronomers,* Bodley Head (1967).
Worvill, R., *Night Skies of the Year,* Stanmore Press (1968).
Yeomans, D.K., *The Comet Halley Handbook,* NASA/JPL (1981).

Astronomy (Technical and Reference)

McNally, D., *Positional Astronomy,* Muller (1974).
Mitton, S., *The Cambridge Encyclopaedia of Astronomy,* Trewin Copplestone Publishing (1979).
Moore, P., *Concise Atlas of the Universe,* Mitchell Beazley (1974).
Rudaux, L. and de Vaucoleurs, G., *Larousse Encyclopaedia of Astronomy*, Hamlyn (1968).
Schroeder, W., *Practical Astronomy,* Werner Laurie (1961).
Smart, W. M., *Textbook of Spherical Astronomy,* 5th edition, Cambridge University Press (1971).
Wallenquist, A., *The Penguin Dictionary of Astronomy,* Penguin Reference Books (1968).

Reference Materials

Raphael's Ephemerides, Foulsham.
Raphael's Tables of Houses for Northern Latitudes, Foulsham.
Raphael's Tables of Houses for Great Britain, Foulsham.
The American Ephemeris for the Twentieth Century (1900-2000) (includes Pluto), Neil Michelson (Astro Computing Services).
Longitudes and Latitudes Throughout the World (excluding U.S.A.), E. Dernay (American Federation of Astrologers).
Longitudes and Latitudes in the U.S.A. E. Dernay.
Time Changes in the U.S.A., Time Changes in Canada and Mexico, Doris Chase Doane (American Federation of Astrologers).
Time Changes in the World (excluding U.S.A., Canada and Mexico), Doane (AFA).
The Schneider — Gauquelin Research Journal (formerly Astro-Psychological Problems), Marie Schneider and Françoise Gauquelin, Paris. Vol. 1 1982/3 to date contains valuable European time data.

Journals (Astrological)

'Astrology', The Astrologer's Quarterly, The Astrological Lodge of London.

The Astrological Journal, The Astrological Association.

Correlation (Research journal), The Astrological Association.

Transit (issued to members), The Astrological Association.

INDEX

Of further interest . . .

ASTRONOMY FOR ASTROLOGERS

An Introduction to the Astronomical Basis of Modern Astrology

John Filbey, D.F. Astrol.S., Peter Filbey, B.Sc. An invaluable reference guide for all students and professional astrologers. This much-needed book provides a guide to the fundamentals of astronomy as they relate to modern astrological practice. John and Peter Filbey explain the technical framework of astronomy and its historical development. They deal with lines of latitude and longitude, the calendar, time changes, the mechanics of the solar system, cosmic crystals, asteroids, comets — and even black holes. The result is a fascinating and informative manual that no serious astrologer should be without.

THE TWELVE HOUSES

"I recommend this book not only for the clarity and depth of content, but also because I am well aware that the interpretations it offers are built upon many years of direct experience." Liz Greene

This book by **Howard Sasportas, D.F. Astrol.S.**, explores in detail the field of experience associated with each of the twelve houses, elucidating not only the concrete and tangible, but also the more subtle meanings of the spheres of life. Guidelines are given for the interpretation of the planets and signs through the houses, including the Moon's Nodes and the newly discovered planetoid Chiron. Example charts illustrate and highlight techniques and principles.